D1553757

Kornei Chukovsky's
A HIGH ART

THE ART OF TRANSLATION

KORNEI CHUKOVSKY'S
A HIGH ART

Translated and Edited by

LAUREN G. LEIGHTON

The University of Tennessee Press / Knoxville

PUBLICATION OF THIS BOOK has been aided by a grant from the Research Board of the Graduate College of the University of Illinois at Chicago.

The paper in this book meets the guidelines for permanence and durability of the Committee on Production Guidelines for Book Longevity of the Council on Library Resources. Binding materials have been chosen for durability.

Library of Congress Cataloging in Publication Data
Chukovskii, Kornei, 1882-1969.
    The art of translation.

    Translation of: A high art.
    Includes bibliographical references and index.
    1. Translating and interpreting. I. Leighton,
Lauren G. II. Title. III. Title: Kornei Chukovsky's
A high art.

PN241.C5313   1983   418'.02   83–6457
ISBN 0–87049–405–8

THIS TRANSLATION OF *A HIGH ART* IS DEDICATED

TO LIDYA KORNEYEVNA CHUKOVSKAYA

AND TO HERA, DENY, AND JAMIE

Contents

Translator's Introduction:
Kornei Chukovsky and *A High Art*

THE Anglo-American world of letters, as also
the European world, does not have a fully
worked out, singly authored, full-length study of the principles,
theory, and criticism of the art of translation. Indeed, translation
is not generally considered an art in the Anglo-American world,
and English-language publishers still tend to treat translation as a
skill (inferior) to be hired (and poorly paid) under commercial
conditions (by the word and inevitably with a rushed deadline).
In Soviet letters, on the other hand, translation is not only considered an art, but a high art indeed. The major Russian writers
—Pushkin, Dostoyevsky, Turgenev, Bunin, Blok, Pasternak,
Akhmatova—have always been translators, and did not consider
themselves writers unless they translated. Russian scholars and
critics have always considered translation to be an indispensable
part of their work. Those literary Russians who have devoted
their careers exclusively to the art of translation have not viewed
themselves as inferior to original writers, and translations quite
regularly are honored over original poetry and novels in the
competition for national awards. The author of this first major
study in world literature of the art of translation, Kornei
Ivanovich Chukovsky (1882–1969), has some very unkind words
to say about the state of the art in Western letters. He has some

kind words to say too, and he does not neglect to turn his cutting
sarcasm against Soviet translators of Western literature who
failed to meet his exacting demands, but his well-considered and
incontestably proved opinion of the state of the art is that its
practice in Soviet culture is far superior to that in the West.

True, in some instances Chukovsky is decidedly unfair in his
assessments of some Anglo-American translators of Russian literature. He could also be accused of being too lenient on some
Soviet translators to whom he has partisan attachments. But both
generally and particularly his indignation over the quality of the
Western translations of Russian literature he has examined is all
too well founded. He understood very well that Western publishers place profit and marketability over literary quality. His
angry criticisms of Anglo-American and French translations of
Pushkin, Gogol, Turgenev, Tolstoy, Dostoyevsky, Leskov,
Chekhov, Pasternak, Solzhenitsyn, and other Russian classics
cannot be dismissed because they are supported by devastatingly
detailed and expert analyses that speak an undeniable and shame-
ful truth about the way Russian literature is treated under Western conditions of translation. What he says about the shoddiness
of American translations of Solzhenitsyn's *One Day in the Life of
Ivan Denisovich*—which were rushed into print in a disgraceful
quest for political sensationalism—is true. His sarcasm over the
ignorance of Chekhov's first translator in America is also too
clearly justified—the Russian artist Ghe was indeed confused
with Goya, and the Russian critic Dobrolyubov really was turned
into St. Francis of Assisi because his name sounds like the Russian
word for a doer of good deeds (*dobroliubets*). He is understandably
disappointed that Sir Bernard Pares turned the fables of Ivan
Krylov, the most ineffably Russian of all Russian writers, into
the homeland of English squires, Irish elves, and all kinds of
neighbor Soggs, Johnsons, Cousin Bills, and (one he missed)
John Moneybags. Chukovsky's admiration for Mrs. Constance
Garnett and Babette Deutsch is real, but he was aware that Mrs.
Garnett's great work was deprived of the authoritative criticism
that could have made her translations better and he did not at all
appreciate what Miss Deutsch did to his own children's poem *The*

Crocodile. Following his assessment of Russian translators of Hemingway, Fitzgerald, Graham Greene, Cheever, Updike, Steinbeck, and Harper Lee, Chukovsky turns to their counterparts in the West with great despair: "You read, you delight in every line, and you think sadly—why is it that neither in the United States, nor in England, nor in France, has a single translator been found who with such art and with such intense love would translate our Gogol, Lermontov, Griboyedov, Krylov, Mayakovsky, Pasternak, Mandelstam, and Blok?"

Indeed, Western publishers, critics, scholars, and translators had better look carefully to Chukovsky's criticisms, for they leave no doubt why his authority—growing out of seven decades' experience as both a critic of translation and a supreme master of the art of translation himself—is still absolute in his country. And though we might be chagrined by his judgments, and even wince at his occasional unfairness, *A High Art* leaves no doubt that its author was the most expert theorist and critic of the art of translation who ever lived in any country or time of this world. Chukovsky knew only too well that translations of major works of world literature are reviewed by American and British critics who, if they have ever been so vulgar as to study a foreign language, seldom if ever reveal it in their reviews. Even little magazines and scholarly journals in the field of foreign languages usually review the content of works in translation, without paying attention to the sort of detailed, linguistically expert, analyses of translations based on exhaustive comparisons of texts which Chukovsky pioneered and made an everyday phenomenon even in the popular press of his country. Our critical vocabulary is still limited to "it sounds authentic" and "it reads smoothly in translation." Or "the translator seems to have done justice to his subject." Where Chukovsky and his contemporary translators have often turned some translations into questions of national debate—read here in *A High Art* his account of the polemic over "scientific" translations of Shakespeare in the 1930s—the only time in recent memory that a translation was debated on a wide basis was in 1964 when Vladimir Nabokov's literalist translation of *Eugene Onegin* outraged so many critics. Chukovsky is right, too, that American and British writers do not take enough pride in their work to oversee their translations abroad. Such matters are usually left to agents or publishers. What American writer in the history of our literature, other than Vladimir Nabokov, personally selected and supervised his translators, or did his own translations into the languages he knew? We all remember the legend that the still unestablished William Faulkner once withdrew a novel from publication because a few commas had been rearranged, but what evidence do we have that Faulkner—or Vidal, Capote, Mailer, Updike, Cheever—has taken a responsible personal interest in who translates his works and how they are translated? Where translators frequently enjoy the prestige of writers and poets in the Soviet Union, and Soviet poets are esteemed as highly for their translations as for their original poetry, American translators are still sneered at as hacks and drudges. It is not likely, for example, that any American writer would take seriously the comment by one Leningrad poet-translator that "anyone could have written *Crime and Punishment*, but only a literary genius could ever translate it." But that comment was taken very seriously in literary Leningrad, and Chukovsky would have taken it seriously too. All the more so in that he, more than any other single man of letters in Russian culture, raised the respect and prestige of the art of translation to a level that could not be comprehended in the West.

Chukovsky is right again that Western cultures do not have a school of translation comparable to the school he founded together with Maxim Gorky, Boris Pasternak, Samuil Marshak, and other contemporaries. For there *is* a school of translation in Soviet letters—not only in Russia but in all the republics and nationalities of the Union—and that school has established beyond doubt that translation is a high art. Only in the Soviet Union have the principles of the art of translation been so fully worked out and exhaustively tested that Chukovsky and his colleagues can sneer at the state of the art in the West as "unprincipled amateurishness." We have not tested our principles in American literature; we have not rejected the methods of translation that Chukovsky so clearly proves are false in *A High Art*; our translators are not held to commonly accepted (because absolutely proved) standards; our critics are not expected to have an expert knowledge of one, if not several, foreign languages before they can be considered professionals; our literary publications do not seek the expertise of foreign-language teachers; our translations are not subjected to strict scrutiny by experts who use carefully tested linguistic methodologies. More than a few British and American eyebrows will be raised by Chukovsky's furious criticism of Robert Graves's defense of his translation of *The Iliad*. But those who read *A High Art* will come to understand why its author is so scornful of any translator who would practice the outmoded method of "correcting" an original masterpiece to accommodate the tastes of a current reading public. They will come to understand, too, why Chukovsky despises literal translations which "sound like a translation," or "protocol-translations" which explain what is going on in the original, or those translations by poets who believe that "only a poet can appreciate a poet" and inevitably turn another's poetry into their own. Kornei Chukovsky *knows* that these and other methods of translation are outmoded, while others are better, and others still better yet. And he *proves* his contentions throughout this book.

Above all, he does so with wit and point. *A High Art* is not a "dull book about foreign languages." Throughout his long life as a critic of translation Chukovsky developed marvelous devices for making the nuances of language and style not simply interesting, but absolutely fascinating to the lay reader. One hardly knows whether to turn first for praise to the many problems and questions he raises, or to his polemical expertise, his keen sense of professionalism, his contagious enthusiasm for his beloved art, or his fine humor. *A High Art* is not a specialized study; it is a literate and very literary work of a critic who delights in his subject and makes us take delight too. Even expert literary scholars will learn a great deal that is new to them about their subjects, for *A High Art* treats the works of the literary greats in ways that cannot be appreciated without the particular "Russian language" view that Chukovsky applies to styles in other languages. Homer, Ovid, Dante, Shakespeare, Burns, Byron, Shelley, Dickens,

Thackeray, Kipling, Goethe, Schiller, Kafka, Mann, Poe, Whitman, Twain, Longfellow, Hemingway, Faulkner, Steinbeck, Balzac, Hugo, Flaubert, Maupassant, Verlaine, Baudelaire, Verhaeren, Mallarmé, Rolland—the materials on these and many, many other world authors are certain to be new to both scholars and general readers.

As for Kornei Ivanovich Chukovsky himself, he was more than a translator and critic of translation. His long life—almost nine decades—seems rather too short for all he achieved in so many intellectual areas. He was a Renaissance man in an age of sometimes medieval obscurantism, and it seems as if there is almost no area of the verbal craft in which he did not actively participate and forcefully dominate. He began his career in 1901 as a journalist and editor of satirical magazines, and in the following decades he made his reputation as an editor and critic, linguist, translator and popularizer of the art of translation, writer of verses for children and international authority on the "wonderful world of children." He was a literary and political polemicist such as one would not want to meet in a dark alley of a literary and political night. He was a biographer, memoirist, and literary historian, and an author of satirical sketches, short stories, and literary studies. He was Russia's Dr. Seuss and Lewis Carroll in one; he was the "Russian Whitman" and the translator of Shakespeare, Twain, Oscar Wilde, Taras Shevchenko, and scores of other classics besides.

He was, to begin with, Russia's "singer to children," the "Uncle Chukosha" to generations of Russian children and their children, grandchildren, and great-grandchildren. His dacha in the writers village of Peredelkino near Moscow (where he was a neighbor of Stalin, Khrushchev, and Pasternak at once) was a mecca to children and parents who journeyed there to hear the poet recite his verses and see the "wizard" do his feats of nonsensical magic. His library, one of the finest existing collections of children's literature, his school for children and teachers, his stage in the woods behind his home—all these became a one-man institution. He was the "Pied Piper of Peredelkino."[1] There is an anecdote about a Moscow journalist who used to bring his son every weekend to Peredelkino and, when the son grew too old for such childish things, continued to show up each weekend, seated huge among the flock of children entranced by the marvelous wizard. His daughter Lidya has told of the time when he received a distinguished honor in the august company of Nikita Khrushchev. When he seated himself next to the Soviet leader he was startled to be embraced and greeted with the loud exclamation, "Kornei Ivanovich! My eternal persecutor!" It seems that when Khrushchev came home in the evening he was inevitably greeted by his grandchildren with the plea, "Grampa, read Chukovsky! Read Chukovsky!"

Chukovsky's tales for children—*The Crocodile, The Clicky-Fly, Doctor Aybolit* ("Ouch–It–Hurts"), *The Cockroach, The Magic-Tree, The Stolen Sun, Wash–'em–Clean, The Telephone*—have been translated into many languages and appeal to adults and children alike. He wrote nonsense verse, lyrics and songs, ballads, tales, riddles, and "heroic epics." He was an admirer of Lewis Carroll, Mark Twain, Rudyard Kipling, and Edward Lear, and a friend of Ogden Nash, Dr. Seuss, and Charlie Brown. He crusaded against Soviet educationists who demand "edifying" prose, and he seldom visited a city without stopping at local elementary schools to scold teachers who fail to realize that children's literature must be *good* literature. He insisted that verse for children is the most demanding of all literary genres and believed that while poor standards in adult literature might be tolerable, the slightest lapse in artistic taste in a work for children causes irreparable damage. In his view, the attraction of children to fantasy corresponds in direct ratio to attempts to come to grips with reality— in this he would undoubtedly approve of Maurice Sendak—and in his study of the language of children, *From Two to Five*, he put forth twelve commandments which are known to writers for children today.[2]

The genesis of *From Two to Five* reveals how easily Chukovsky was attracted to the world of children. In the 1920s he happened to live near a beach for children, and—of course—spent his days playing in the sand with them. He quickly became aware of the merciless logic with which children master language, and he began taking notes. His study, first published in 1925, has seen thirteen revised editions to 1960. It has been translated and is available in English.[3] Since children master almost the entire structure and concept of language in the years from two to five, Chukovsky believed that every child is a "linguistic genius" and has a natural taste for good literature. In his opinion, poetry for children must be brief, fast-moving, clear, and variegated. It should have heightened musicality, frequent shifts in tone, meter, and rhythm, lots of rhymes which must bear the burden of semantic content, swift action, and subtle feeling. Children demand clear and simple imagery—they are bored by metaphors. Verse for children ought to abound in nouns and verbs, but should avoid adjectives. Imaginative and nonsensical in content, poetry for children calls for vivid illustrations.

Chukovsky was taken with Tolstoy's notion of "infectiousness" in art, and he insisted that if children's verse does not bring spontaneous laughter, clapping, dancing, and shouting, it is bad verse. He considered it quite easy to delude adults with insincerity, fraudulence, and poor taste—in fact, he once remarked that they sometimes seem to thrive on it—but children quickly detect dishonesty and shoddy quality. In his last published essay, an uncompleted account of his writing for children, Chukovsky added two more commandments to writers of works for children.[4] Because he considered children's literature the most demanding of all literary efforts, he pointed out that it takes preparation. It was not until he had familiarized himself with his own national literature and several foreign literatures, knew intimately the vast store of international literature for children, and could look back on almost two decades' experience as a professional man of letters that he considered himself competent to write his first verse work for nonadults. Even more important than experience and knowledge, he believed, is the natural ability to think like a child. And so the most important of all his commandments is this: for those who lack the ability to "return to childhood," it is not possible to be a writer for children.

He also translated children's literature: *The Adventures of Tom Sawyer, Gulliver's Travels, Robinson Crusoe*, Kipling, Burns, Lear.

After he had written the first version of *Doctor Aybolit* he discovered Hugh Lofting's "Dr. Dolittle" series and translated from it with supplements from discarded episodes of *Doctor Aybolit*. He first became entranced with children's literature in England, where he discovered nursery rhymes. He translated many samples, but acknowledged that the true master of this genre was his friend Samuil Marshak. Together with Marshak and others he formed a pleiad of modern Soviet writers for children.

As a writer for children he was the most severe critic of his own work and he rejected lines, stanzas, and entire works with great cruelty. In his last essay he mentioned that the total number of printed lines of his verses represent a minute percentage of the thousands of lines he actually wrote—and preserved—in his notebooks. He terms this process of selection a "struggle for the survival of the fittest," and illustrates it with samples of his rejected work. He was not modest about his work and he does not disguise his pride in the lines that survived. He points out that their "dynamism" is attained from vowel and consonant repetitions and patterns. He sought to shift pace, action, tone, and rhythm. Children's verses must be "uninterrupted whirlwinds of motions and actions." Humans, beasts, and even objects must be animated—they must "run pell-mell from page to page through adventures, battles, feats." His tales are filled with journeys, parades, pursuits, contests, dances, parties. Adventure follows adventure in a constant shift of subject and pace. Children's verses must not only be dynamic, but their dynamism must be geared to their subject. Rhythm, sound patterns, and intonations must convey both subject and action to the eyes and ears of a child. The hero of *The Clicky-Fly* is cast into the deadly clutches of a villainous spider, and his impending doom is conveyed by "mournful anapests." And when destruction seems inescapable, there is a swift transition to a stanza structured rhythmically on anapests and trochees and alliteratively on the stressed sound "i," conveying the fly's wail of despair.

But of course, the ill-fated fly escapes. For of all the things Chukovsky learned from children, he valued most his knowledge that a child will not accept unhappiness or misery in this world.

And so, though his kind Doctor Aybolit, and his clicky-fly, and his cockroach, and his stolen sun fall into one mishap after another, they always miraculously survive, or are rescued by some self-sacrificing hero, and live happily ever after.

He was a prolific memoirist. As a polemicist and critic he was a gadfly, but in his life he was a star-struck chaser after literary greats. Mayakovsky once sketched him as a shabbily dressed young student, his suit stuffed with books and papers, his body stretched in a long serpentine curl through the door of a literary salon and up around the ceiling, with a winning smile on his long homely face, outrightly adoring the room filled with literary Brahmins—Blok, Bely, Bryusov, Balmont, Mayakovsky himself. The last letter Tolstoy wrote before leaving Yasnaya Polyana was to the young Chukovsky. He was a close associate of Gorky (whom he credits for initiating *A High Art*); he admired Chekhov above all other writers; he knew and wrote about Kuprin, Korolenko, Andreyev, Artsybashev, Bunin, Mandelstam, Khlebnikov, Esenin, Zamyatin, Ehrenburg, Sholokhov, Pasternak, Panova, Berggolts. He was presented to the King of England with his fellow Anglophile Vladimir Nabokov. He wrote major studies of Walt Whitman and Oscar Wilde. His collections of memoirs—*From Chekhov to Our Days, A Book about Contemporary Writers, Faces and Masks, Contemporaries: Portraits and Sketches, My Recollections*—are regularly used by scholars and critics. During the 1920s and 1930s he was able to persuade such émigrés as Gorky, Kuprin, and D.S. Mirsky to return to the Soviet Union—an act of personal friendship and service to the new state that later developments gave him cause to regret. (How he himself survived the Stalinist years is a mystery.) During his lifetime he kept a notebook of autographs, photographs, and sketches as a record of his associations with literary and art figures. Titled *Chukokkala* by its first contributor, the artist Ilya Repin, who joined its keeper's name with the Finnish village where he kept a dacha, it has recently been published in the Soviet Union.[5] In his later years he defended such literary figures as Joseph Brodsky and Alexander Solzhenitsyn, and his work as a defender of dissidents is carried on today by his daughter, the dissident novelist and scholar Lidya Korneyevna Chukovskaya.

As *A High Art* shows, Chukovsky was a sharp polemicist. E.G. Etkind, whose book *Poetry and Translation* is indebted to Chukovsky's manual for translators and is in its turn a source for many materials of the later editions, has told an anecdote which indicates Chukovsky's love of polemics. Etkind once fell asleep in an armchair in the Chukovsky apartment on Gorky Street in Moscow, and was awakened by the sight of the eighty–seven–year–old man dancing about the room and giggling with a high-pitched "gi–gi–gi–gi" over a telling point he had just made in a polemical article.[6] As a young man, barely in his twenties, Chukovsky launched a campaign against the Symbolist poet and translator of Whitman, Konstantin Balmont, decimating Balmont's reputation as a translator of poetry. Chukovsky, of course, soon became Russia's Whitman, the Soviet Union's best-known and most influential translator and scholar on Whitman. He continually opposed the view of Gorky and A.V. Lunacharsky of Whitman as a revolutionary poet, and firmly established his own view of the American poet as a liberal democrat. The reader of *A High Art* will note that even after Chukovsky has finished off a bad translator, he returns to his subject with cutting, deliberately irrelevant, and gratuitously snide remarks to the side. He disliked the nineteenth-century journalist and novelist Joseph Senkovsky, for example, and he never misses a chance in *A High Art* to mention Senkovsky's bad taste. In the 1930s Chukovsky took out after the ruling method of translation in Soviet letters —the method of the so-called *bukvalisty,* or "literalists"— and he set off a major debate in Moscow over the "scientific" translators who almost ruined Shakespeare with their translations. Chukovsky's interpretations of scores of foreign authors have become generally accepted by Russian intellectuals today—Twain, Whitman, Balzac, Burns, Shakespeare, Byron, Goethe, Rustaveli, Shevchenko, Dickens. At the time of his death he was working with the translator Rita Rayt-Kovalyova on a major critique of Nabokov's four-volume translation-study of Pushkin's *Eugene Onegin.*

If he did not care to be known as an exacting scholar, Chukovsky was an exacting editor. He was an authority on the nineteenth-century poet N.A. Nekrasov and spent some ten years restoring over 10,000 lines of Nekrasov's poetry which had been mangled by the censorship or by editorial or financial exigencies. He published several hundred articles and essays, and took both socio-biographical and thematic-stylistic approaches to his work. His studies are not confined to Russian literature, but also deal with Ukrainian, English, American, French, German, and Caucasian and Central Asian literatures. Among his major studies are *Nekrasov as an Artist, The Craft of Nekrasov, Pushkin and Nekrasov, Men and Books of the 1860s, Alexander Blok as a Man and Poet, Chekhov the Man, On Chekhov, Walt Whitman and His "Leaves of Grass," Walt Whitman: The Poet of Dawning Democracy,* and *Repin, Gorky, Mayakovsky, Bryusov.* He contributed to scholarly collections on Whitman, Shakespeare, Kipling, Burns, Hemingway, Twain, Dickens, and Shevchenko, and he actively influenced the writing of the several studies of the art of translation he cites as his sources for *A High Art* in his introduction.

By chance, Chukovsky's name is similar to that of the greatest Russian translator of the nineteenth century, so that Soviet translators speak readily of "Zhukovsky and Chukovsky." Etkind credits Chukovsky with almost single-handedly raising the art of translation to the high level of prestige it enjoys today in Russian letters. His principles and standards—as he points out in his introduction, he began his manual for translators at a time when virtually nothing had ever been written about the art of translation—are the basis of translation seminars and *kollektivy* in the Soviet Union today. Beginning in 1907 Chukovsky became the acknowledged expert on Whitman, whom he celebrated as the "singer of democracy" and the "poet of the cosmos." His collected works of Whitman have appeared in numerous editions from 1907 to 1955, with introductions by men as diverse as A.V. Lunacharsky and D.S. Mirsky. His book *My Whitman*, which appeared twice in the 1960s and is still reprinted from time to time, is both a collection of his favorite translations from *Leaves of Grass* and a personal appreciation of the poet whom he unabashedly calls in the very first sentence of the book "the idol of my youth." It is due to his encouragement that Soviet translators prepared the academic edition of Whitman's complete collected works. Chukovsky translated from Ukrainian, French, and English. In 1962 he was invited to Oxford University, where he delivered a series of lectures and received an honorary degree for his contributions to English literature, especially his translations of Shakespeare's sonnets. In addition to Whitman, Twain, Swift, and Defoe, he translated Oscar Wilde, G.K. Chesterton, Burns, Kipling, Romain Rolland, Taras Shevchenko, and O. Henry. He helped found and was for many years editor-in-chief of the State Foreign Language Publishing House. He helped organize the *kollektivy* which have produced complete collections of Dickens, Whitman, Burns, and Hemingway.

As he points out in his introduction, Chukovsky first began work on the translator's manual which became *A High Art* in 1918 at the urging of Gorky. In the years since, as he also points out, the art of translation has become the subject of many highly scholarly methodological studies which have carried his essentially popularizing work to refinements far ahead of anything known in Western cultures. Translation is indeed a high art in the Soviet Union, and it is thanks to Chukovsky's pioneering work that Soviet standards of translation are so high. The criteria he established are as simple today as ABC. A translator must know his subject language to perfection, and he must be an original master of his own language. A translator must know everything about the writer he presumes to translate—his style, his themes, tones, devices, narrative techniques, intonations, his life and outlook, his time and place, his national culture. A translator must be an exacting scholar, and there can be no excuse for a failure to understand every detail, every nuance, every fact relevant to the task of translation. A translator must be both an artist and a scientist. Every semantic and stylistic nuance of the original should be conveyed to the reader in the new language, and the translator must resist temptations to "improve" his subject. A translator must not be a literalist—literal precision leads directly to imprecision. Some styles are impossible to translate, especially colloquial styles, but this cannot be an excuse for a poor translation and colloquial style must not be turned into "blandscript."

If the translator searches long enough and carefully enough, he will find the "key" to conveying any style. For Kipling, Chukovsky found the key in swiftly shifting cadences and an emphasis on "jingoistic" masculine line endings. For Burns he used (as did Samuil Marshak) a "signal" device—the adroit and sparing use of Church Slavonicisms and eighteenth-century morphology to "signal" the reader that this poetry is rustic, quaint, and vexedly colloquial. In the case of Whitman, Chukovsky found two keys to the conveyance: a realization that the basic element of Whitman's poetry is the syntax—the casting out of lines in syntactic strands; and a similar recognition that the rhetorical and declamatory effects of the "singer of freedom" are based on intonational devices. By concentrating first on the syntactical and rhythmic configurations of the lines and then on the musicality and tonality as derived from lexical choice and positioning, he went a long way toward the ideal of achieving both semantic and dynamic fidelity to the original. Translators must be principled, and they must have standards which are uniformly observed throughout a national culture. Yet, in the final analysis he concluded that everything depends on the translator's own originality—his honesty, his tact, his sensitivity and sense of proportion, his common sense, and his knowledge of both his subject and his subject's language.

Chukovsky was, like Whitman, a natural democrat and a liberal. He was also an activist, both politically and literarily. In his last work he speaks of a certain dark period when he almost fell by the wayside—clearly the 1930s when so many of his contemporaries did in fact fall—but he was an activist to the end. His last article ends with an apology for not elaborating on a point—"because I must hurry to draw a conclusion from what I have just said." He worked almost every day of his life—there was a law in his family that he was not to be interrupted from late morning to late afternoon when he was in his study, no matter how important a visitor or a family problem—and on the day he died he completed the day's work.

As for this translation of *A High Art*, it presented particular problems which required untypical methods. And these methods require explanation. Over the course of seven decades Kornei Chukovsky developed myriads of devices for making the details of language and style not only interesting to the lay reader, but downright fascinating. The reader of *A High Art* will find that it does not have a single boring moment in it—Chukovsky's enthusiasm for his subject is overwhelming. But *A High Art* is a study of the art of translation aimed at Russian, not English readers, and its explications of problems of foreign language are intended for people whose native language is Russian. This translation therefore required more than a simple conveyance of materials from one language to another, for its author's explanations must be transposed for its new English-language audience— they must be redirected away from the Russian reader and toward the reader of English.

It would be silly, for example, to translate for English readers the synonyms provided by the author for the benefit of his original readers. That is, it would be redundant to inform English readers that the English word "wee" means "wee," or that the English word "bus" means "bus." Conversely, where Chukovsky had no need to explain or gloss Russian words for his Russian readers, it would seem advisable to add an explanation, or at least insert a synonym, in order to make his discussion of a particular semantic problem comprehensible to English readers. English readers are not likely to know, for example, that the Russian word *pravda* means not only "truth" but "justice," and that the word can signify both meanings at once or separately. And where in his discussion of John Steinbeck's *Travels with Charley* Chukovsky presents a quote from the Russian translation involving the word *psikh*, 'psycho,' he can let the quote stand on its own, speak for itself, because the Russian reader knows that this current Russian slang word is not as strong as it is in English and does not necessarily refer to a seriously deranged person. The English reader, however, requires an additional explanation of the word *psikh*—he has to be told, where the Russian reader does not, that the word is a common slang equivalent to something like the American slang words "nut" or "character." Were this explanation not worked somehow into Chukovsky's text, the reader of English would be left to wonder why the word "psycho" is used so casually in the Russian translation of *Travels with Charley*. If explanations of such fine points were not provided, Chukovsky's intent would be as mystifying to English readers as it is obvious to Russian readers of the original.

And then there is the problem of Chukovsky's quotations—sometimes long quotations—from the Russian translations of foreign literature he criticizes in *A High Art*. Obviously, they cannot be left in Russian, for to do so would be to make them stand as useless referents for the English readers of Chukovsky's subsequent discussions of them. It would be simply impossible for English readers to understand, from a long quotation from Dickens's *Oliver Twist* in Russian translation, precisely why and how the translation is awkward, overly literal, and ungrammatical. Just as obviously, it would be impossible to substitute, without some sort of modification, the original foreign-language text of a quotation, for this would cause the English reader to wonder why Chukovsky berates the translator for such marvelous writing. English readers would be dumbfounded, for example, by Chukovsky's criticism of a translator for misunderstanding and improperly conveying Shakespeare's epithet "vaulting ambition" if, right there in the original text provided for them, stood the epithet "vaulting ambition."

What is to be done here? In many cases it seemed reasonable to replace the quotation from the Russian translation with the original foreign-language text—and then modify Chukovsky's discussion of the quotation to suit. That is, where Chukovsky quotes a list of examples of bad translations of lines from Shakespeare's *Othello* and then explains to his Russian readers how the translations are bad by describing the original lines and elucidating their semantic-stylistic nuances, the translator has been obliged to quote the original lines and explain to English readers how the translations are bad by describing the lines in Russian translation and eludicating their semantic-stylistic failings. Clearly, any attempt to translate Chukovsky this way is on dangerous ground. Care has had to be taken not to add to or change Chukovsky's critical judgments, but only to reverse the audience-direction without changing the points under discussion or distorting the judgments.

For example, in his criticisms of V. D. Merkureva's translation of Shelley's "Similes for Two Political Characters of 1819" Chukovsky explains and partly paraphrases lines of the original poem for the benefit of his Russian readers and then proceeds to discuss the Russian translation, for which he provides selected excerpts. Were his discussion to be offered without reversing the audience-direction, it would turn out like this:

> And here is what remains of this entire system of images:
>
> > Kak by (?) *parochka* (!) akul,
> > Ne smeniaias' s *zorkikh vakht*,
> > Gde pod okeanskii gul
> > Brig nevol'nichii *mel'knul*
> > Obsuzhdaiut vkusnyi *frakht* . . .
>
> Gone are the Atlantic isle, the dogfish, the red gill—everything that makes these lines concrete has been banished, and in their place we are given some sort of *gul* and some sort of *zorkii vakht*, in addition to which it is impossible to imagine that the most musical of all English poets could resort to such cacophonic rhymes as *vakht–frakht*.

The result of this literal translation being meaningless to English readers, it seemed more advisable to translate the discussion by using the original English lines as a referent and modifying the discussion to suit:

> In 1819 Shelley dedicated to Lord Castlereagh and Prince George (the future King George IV) a cruel satire titled "Similes for Two Political Characters of 1819." The satire contains these lines:

> As a shark and dogfish wait
> Under an Atlantic isle
> For the Negro-ship whose freight
> Is the theme of their debate,
> Wrinkling their red gill the while—

Gone from Merkureva's translation are the Atlantic isle, the dogfish, the red gill—everything that makes these lines concrete has been banished, and in their place we are given a pair of sharks, a vigilant watch, a booming ocean, and a tasty freight! The translation leaves us wondering how one of the most musical of all English poets could resort to such cacophonic rhymes as *vakht–frakht*.

Here the substitution of the English original for the text of the Russian translation has required the addition of explanation and elucidation, in this instance by inserting into the text the images which Chukovsky drew attention to in his quotation of the translation with parenthetical queries and exclamations. The reversal of the discussion for English readers required, as can be seen, only a slight modification (not simply "gone are," but "gone from Merkureva's translation are").

Happily, in many instances where Chukovsky quotes and criticizes a bad translation, it has been found to be quite easy to translate it back into English "as badly and in just the same way as badly" (to use Chukovsky's own formulation). That is, in cases of bad translations (but not good translations) it has been found to be possible to give English readers a precise idea of the poor quality of a translation and at the same time render Chukovsky's discussion meaningful without having to modify it. Thus, it is a simple task to translate back into English this quotation from a Russian translation of Dickens's novel *Martin Chuzzlewit* which Chukovsky criticizes for blandscript—the rendering of colloquial speech into standard literary language:

> "Ah, lord, Missis Chuzzlewit! Who would have ever thought that I would see in this blessed house, Miss Pecksniff, my dear mistress, after all I know perfectly well that such homes are few, more's the

pity, and one would wish there were a few more, then this, Mister Chuffey, would not be a vale of tears, but a garden of Eden."

It is then possible to translate Chukovsky's discussion of the translation directly: there is not a single departure from correct speech, the translation gives the standard literary form "house" instead of "ouse," "were" instead of "ware," "garden" instead of "guardian," and so on. It is even possible to make the import of Chukovsky's criticism of the translation more significant to English readers by adding a quotation from the original text of *Martin Chuzzlewit*:

> "Why goodness me! . . . Missis Chuzzlewit! to think as I should see beneath this blessed ouse, which ware I know it, Miss Pecksniff, my sweet young lady, to be a ouse as there is not many like, worse luck, and wishin' it were not so, which then this tearful walley would be changed into a flowerin' guardian, Mr. Chuffey."

Such incorporations are perfectly in keeping with Chukovsky's own practice throughout *A High Art* of providing his own translations to be compared against a bad one, or of quoting an existing good translation as a comparison.

It was quickly discovered that good translations cannot always be translated effectively back into English. Either the original foreign text has to be provided, as demonstrated, or the quotation of the Russian translation has to be replaced with a paraphrase, in accordance with Chukovsky's own established practice, or some sort of graphic model has to be provided to enable English readers to appreciate, and even to visually realize, the points being made in discussion. This latter method seems to be especially appropriate in those instances where Chukovsky criticizes Russian translations of such exotic poetry as Kirghiz, Kazakh, Kabardinian, or Georgian. Thus, where Chukovsky discusses what he considers to be almost miraculously precise Russian reproductions of the intricate form of the Kabardinian national epic *The Legend of Narta Sosruko*—the intricacy evolving from a complex arrangement of anaphoras and "echoing" internal and end rhymes—it is possible to replace his lines from the Russian translation with this graphic model:

```
. . . . . . . . . . . rechi
0 . . . . . seche . . . . . .
0 putiakh . . . . . . . imykh
0 koniakh . . . . . . . imykh
0 . . . . . . . . . . . itykh
```

English readers do not need to understand the Russian words and word segments here for the discussion to be meaningful. The point Chukovsky makes has to do not with semantics, but with the easy to visualize sound patterns provided by the model here: the anaphoric sounds "O" and the echoing of internal with end rhymes—*rechi–seche, imykh–imykh–itykh*. English readers can detect the intricate sound patterns as readily from the model as Russian readers can detect them from the full text of the lines of the translation provided by Chukovsky, and neither English nor Russian readers need to be provided with the original Kabardinian text in order to appreciate what a difficult task it was for the Russian translator to reproduce the form of the original with such amazing fidelity through many, many lines of a long epic poem. And just as Chukovsky's Russian readers can appreciate the difficulty of reproducing nine end rhymes from a reading of the complete text of a Russian translation of lines from the Kazakh epic *Kozy-Korpesh and Bayan-Slu*, so can English readers appreciate the translator's artistry from a simple model of the rhymes in Russian: *bagréts–prishléts–obrazéts–ovéts–tvoréts–otéts–ptenéts–mudréts–serdéts.* Nine consecutive rhymes!

Of course, in many instances, it is simply impossible to convey the sense of some complicated problem of translation without retaining the Russian original. In some of these instances it seemed permissible, as already stated, to gloss a Russian word or phrase in the same way that Chukovsky glosses English, French, German, Italian, and other foreign words elsewhere. In other instances it seemed advisable to work explanations into the discussion. Thus, where Chukovsky complains about the glaring imprecision of English translations of a line from Solzhenitsyn's *One Day in the Life of Ivan Denisovich*—"Oy, liut' tam segodnia budet: dvadtsat' sem' s veterkom i ni ukryva, ni greva!"—an explanation has to be worked into the discussion in Chukovsky's own style: "After all, the style of the Russian original is folk, peasant. Here are *liut'* [a peasant colloquialism for a fierce frost], and *ukryv* [another peasant colloquialism for a place of concealment, often of stolen goods], and *grev* [a colloquial word meaning to warm up or thaw out], words which are next to kin to words Pushkin treated with sympathy in his time." Here, three words of a quotation are explained with the addition of clauses, and the whole sentence—"Oy, it'd be fierce out there today: minus twenty-seven with a bit of a breeze and no coverin' up, no thawin' out"—can be explained to English readers with incorporations into subsequent discussion.

In a few instances, no attempt has been made to explain or apologize for words in Russian which will be incomprehensible to English readers. After all, if Chukovsky saw fit to let his Russian readers struggle with the meaning of such impossible lines from Burns as "Wee sleekit, little beastie" and "For auld lang syne," it would seem not unfair to let the English readers deal with Russian words clearly identified as "Russian folk words and turns of speech": *nekhrist', kaby, plutiaga, vedro.*

Of course, this process of transposing and redirecting Chukovsky's text for readers of a different language is a process of editing. But although the translator has worked here as an editor, the task is seen as essentially that of a translator, as the seeking of a translator's solutions to particular problems presented by an unusual text. After all, as the reader will discover, Chukovsky himself believed that every translation presents its own problems and it is the task of a translator to deal with these problems *as a task of language and translation.* Chukovsky despised formalistic literalism, and it was he who first devised the axiom that literal precision frequently leads directly to the worst possible imprecision—artistic imprecision. Translation is an art, and like all arts it requires tact, judgment, and imagination. This

English-language version of *A High Art* is not, therefore, an editing job in the accepted sense of that word, but rather a hopefully common-sense transposition which, however many liberties this may require, remains semantically and stylistically faithful to the original.

As Chukovsky states in his introduction, "About This Book," he did not consider himself a scholar. This is reflected in *A High Art*. In some instances Chukovsky carefully cites text and page number; in others, he provides no citations at all. His page numbers and other data are often incorrect, and sometimes his quotations are not exact. *A High Art* is not a scholarly study—it is the work of a critic and man of letters. It is not even a completed work, but rather a lifelong work in progress which he attempted to bring to a reasonably complete condition shortly before his death. For this reason, this translation of his work has not eliminated all scholarly errata and inconsistencies. It seemed reasonable, however, to provide correct page numbers. It also seemed reasonable, all the more so in that the translation required a great deal of scrambling around through numerous texts for the exact original English and other foreign-language quotations used throughout Chukovsky's book, to provide correct citations where they are wrong. The standard method of American citation, not the more general Soviet method, has been used. Citations of works in Russian have been given in English translation incorporated into discussion in the text wherever possible, and cited in Russian in the notes. Wherever English titles could not be incorporated in the text without making the style cumbersome, the Russian citations in the notes have been provided with English translations in brackets. The system of transliteration of Russian used by American publishers has been used in the text (Chukovsky), and the more precise modified version of the Library of Congress system has been used for Russian words as Russian words in the text and for the notes (Chukovskii). Translations are not provided for easily recognizable cognates (*russkaia literatura*) or for the following common titles always given with English translations on Library of Congress cards:

Izbrannye proizvedeniia	*Selected Works*
Polnoe sobranie sochinenii	*Complete Collected Works*
Polnoe sobranie stikhotvorenii	*Complete Collected Poetry*
Sobranie sochinenii	*Collected Works*
Sochineniia	*Works*

In his introduction Chukovsky mentions several major Russian studies of the art of translation used as primary sources. As explained in the notes to the introduction, these primary sources are not cited in subsequent notes, but are instead cited in the text in accordance with current standard American usage. Only one chapter has been omitted from this translation—the last chapter devoted to Russian translations of the poetry of Taras Shevchenko. It has been omitted because it depends in its entirety on long quotations of verse in both Ukrainian and Russian translation which require a knowledge of both languages. Most of the many Soviet translators Chukovsky praises and damns are well known in his country, but they are likely to be new to Anglo-American readers. This is also true of the many minor poets and writers mentioned throughout *A High Art*. The index to this translation is therefore selectively definitive: it provides biographical and other data only for those persons not likely to be included in Western encyclopedias; well-known Russian and Western writers are not so identified.

In an Addendum to *A High Art*, Chukovsky augments his prefatory remarks on the origin and development of his work-in-progress. The first version of *Principles of Artistic Translation* appeared in 1919 as a small in-house brochure for Gorky's World Literature Publishing House, and a revised brochure was printed, again without being offered for sale, in 1920. In 1930 a considerably enlarged version was published under the title *The Art of Translation*, and in 1936 a revised version was again published under the same title. In 1941 the same book, "amended and extensively supplemented," was published as *A High Art*, but its appearance was "devoured by the war." A quarter of a century later Chukovsky read his book again, and he completely modernized it for publication in 1964 under its now established title *A High Art*. A still larger and more up-to-date version was included in Chukovsky's *Collected Works*, published in 1965–67, and in 1968 *A High Art* was published under separate cover. The 1968 text excluded Chukovsky's remarks on translations of Alexander Solzhenitsyn's *One Day in the Life of Ivan Denisovich*, and he therefore considered the version of his *Collected Works* to be the final, canonical text. The canonical text was used for this translation. The various titles and editions of *A High Art*, including the names of Chukovsky's collaborators on the early versions, are:

K. Chukovskii and N. Gumilev, *Printsipy khudozhestvennogo perevoda* (Petrograd: Vsemirnaia literatura, 1919; F.D. Batiushkov, K. Chukovskii, and N. Gumilev, *Printsipy khudozhestvennogo perevoda*, 2d ed. rev. (Petrograd: Vsemirnaia literatura, 1920).

Kornei Chukovskii and Andrei Fedorov, *Iskusstvo perevoda* (Leningrad: Academia, 1930).

Kornei Chukovskii, *Iskusstvo perevoda* (Leningrad: Academia, 1936).

Kornei Chukovskii, *Vysokoe iskusstvo* (Leningrad: Gosudarstvennaia literatura, 1941).

Kornei Chukovskii, *Vysokoe iskusstvo* (Moscow: Iskusstvo, 1964).

Kornei Chukovskii, *Vysokoe iskusstvo* (Moscow: Iskusstvo, 1968).

Kornei Chukovskii, *Vysokoe iskusstvo; Sobranie sochinenii* (6 vols.; Moscow: Khudozhestvennaia literatura, 1965–67), III, 237–628.

I would like to thank Albert J. Wehrle, Ray Parrott, Jr., Gerald Janacek, Alexander Nakhimovsky, Slava Paperno, and H. W. Tjalsma for checking individual chapters and for suggesting better equivalents and stylistic formulations. I would also like to thank: *Russian Review* for permission to use a previously published article, "A Homage to Kornei Chukovsky," as it was revised for this introduction; and *Soviet Studies in Literature* for permission to use a previously published excerpt from *A High Art* under the title "On Colloquial Translation."

Kornei Chukovsky's
A HIGH ART

About This Book

NEVER before in our country has the art of translation flourished so richly as right now. In the entire history of Russian literature there has never been another period in which such a large pleiad of gifted writers has devoted its talents to translation. There have been geniuses of translation before—Pushkin, Zhukovsky—but these were giants among Lilliputians: they towered alone above a crowd of clumsy and feeble contemporaries, solitary, peerless figures. But now the very number of brilliant men of letters engaged in this difficult labor testifies that something heretofore unknown has occurred. Indeed and in truth, never before have such great men of talent labored together, shoulder to shoulder, within the confines of a single decade, at the art of translation. Even the most original of our poets—with their own powerfully expressed styles and vivid creative personalities—are devoting their powers to the art of translation.

No small role in the development of this high art was played, as is well known, by A.M. Gorky, who in 1918 with the support of V.I. Lenin founded the World Literature Publishing House in Petrograd. This publishing venture, which recruited some hundred men of letters, set as its specific goal the raising of the level of the translator's art and the preparation of a generation of young translators who could give the new Soviet reader, first coming into contact with the cultural heritage of all times and all peoples, the finest books ever written. This goal was first enunciated by Gorky in 1919 in his preface to the *Catalogue of the World Literature Publishing House.*[1] The academicians, professors, and writers enlisted by Gorky for the realization of this task subjected to the most stringent possible scrutiny the old translations of the works of Dante, Cervantes, Goethe, Byron, Flaubert, Zola, Dickens, Balzac, and Thackeray, as well as the classics of the Chinese, Arabs, Persians, and Turks; and they came to the most sad conclusion that with a very few rare exceptions the vast majority of these translations was utterly useless and would have to be done over on the different basis of solid scholarship that would exclude the previous methods of unprincipled amateurishness.

In order to accomplish this, a theory of artistic translation was needed which would arm the translator with clear and simple principles, so that every translator—even the most ordinary—could become a better craftsman. Some of us had a vague sense of these principles, but they had not yet been formulated. Gorky therefore proposed that several members of the editorial board of World Literature (myself included) compile something like a manual for old and new masters of translation—we were to formulate the principles needed to help translators in their work. I remember how impossible this task seemed to me at the time. Once, at a meeting of the editorial board, Aleksey Maksimovich turned to me with a question intended for all present:

"What do you consider a good translation?"

I was nonplused and mumbled a reply. "That . . . which . . . is most artistic."

"And what do you consider most artistic?"

"That . . . which . . . faithfully conveys the poetic qualities of the original."

"And what do you mean by faithfully convey? And what do you mean by the poetic qualities of the original?"

Here I fell into utter confusion. I already had the literary instinct to distinguish a good translation from a bad one, but I was not yet prepared to articulate the theoretical basis for my judgments. At that time there was not a single book devoted to theory of translation in existence. When I undertook to write such a book, I felt like a lonely traveler wandering along an unexplored road.

This is all ancient history now, and it seems almost incredible to me that the writers of previous periods left us with nothing in the way of a methodology for artistic translation except a few isolated, occasionally perceptive statements. Now times have changed and methodological studies occupy a prominent place in our literary scholarship. There are many such studies, and every year there are more. Here is a list which is far from complete: M.P. Alekseyev's book *Problems of Artistic Translation* (1931); A.V. Fyodorov's book *On Artistic Translation* (1941); the same author's *Introduction to Theory of Translation* (1958); E. Etkind's book *Poetry and Translation* (1963); the four collections published by Soviet Writer and joined under the common title *The Craft of Translation* (1955, 1959, 1963, 1964—the first was titled *Problems of Artistic Translation*); the three editions of *Translator's Notebook* (1960, 1961—publications of the First Moscow Pedagogical Institute of Foreign Languages, 1963—publication of the Institute of International Relations); the collection *International Links of Russian Literature* (published under the editorship of M.P. Alekseyev, 1963); and the collection *Theory and Criticism of Translation* (1962).[2]

In those days we could only dream about such books. But in recent decades a large group of first-class theorists of the translator's art has arisen in our literature, including (in addition to those just mentioned) Givi Gachechiladze, I.A. Kashkin, A.L. Kundzich, A.V. Kunin, Yu.D. Levin, P.M. Toper, Ya.I. Retsker, V.M. Rossels, V.E. Shor, and others. I could have learned a great deal from these people in those days, of course—if their works had existed then, in the year 1918. But I was expected to come right out with a fully formed and strict theory covering all aspects of this enormous problem. The creation of such a theory was beyond me. But so far as working out a few pragmatic rules of thumb which would offer translators a dependable working system—this I could do. Now, almost a half century later, in leafing through the slender brochure that was the first variant of the present book—*Principles of Artistic Translation*—I have more than just once or twice been reminded of the intense effort it took me to "discover" the simple truths that are now as simple as ABC.[3] Right now, for example, I read in one of the articles in *Theory and Criticism of Translation*: " 'Literal precision' often results in a complete distortion of the meaning of the original" (45).

Nowadays this is axiomatic to any schoolboy, but I can clearly recall the day it dawned on me as a great discovery which brought home to me yet another priceless truth: a good translator deserves respect in our literary world because he is not a handyman, not a copyist, but an artist. Contrary to what was generally believed in those days, a translator does not photograph an original text, he re-creates it through art. The text of an original serves him as material for a complex and often inspired creative work. The translator is first of all a man of talent. In order to translate Balzac, he must, if only in part, impersonate Balzac by assimilating his temperament and emotional makeup, his poetic feeling for life.

Even a translator of average ability needs such rare aptitudes and knowledge, such a feeling for language, such a loving penetration into the text being translated, that only the most ignorant person could ever look down on him. Unfortunately, in those days the ignorant people in whose eyes any scribbler of ephemeral doggerel enjoyed far greater respect and weight than, say, a translator of Cervantes's sonnets, were not yet extinct. These people were incapable of understanding that the former not infrequently needed no more than a dozen or so hackneyed clichés, while tne latter had to be a learned person possessing all the qualities of a literary master.

A little later, at the very start of the twenties, still another highly significant fact gradually became clear to us, one which raised the value of the translator's work even higher in our eyes. We realized that under the new Soviet system an artistic translation is a matter of state import in which millions of people have a practical stake: Ukrainians, Belorussians, Georgians, Armenians,

Azerbaidzhans, Uzbeks, Tadzhiks, and the other peoples who had for the first time received the opportunity to share their literary treasures with others. The victory of Lenin's nationalities policy fundamentally transformed the entire literary life of our multinational, multilingual country. So that when the poet-translators N. Grebnev and Ya. Kozlovsky add the songs of the wise Avarian Rasul Gamzatov to the riches of Russian poetry, or when Leonid Pervomaysky uses his ingenious talent to translate into Ukrainian the ballads of Ossetia, Moldavia, Slovakia, Serbia, and Mordovia, they are inspired by an awareness that they are not only enriching their own native letters, but also serving the great cause of uniting peoples. This same goal is served by the feat of Nikolay Zabolotsky in adapting such giants of Georgian poetry as Rustaveli, Guramishvili, Orbeliani, Chavchavadze, and Vazha Pshavela into Russian letters. Soviet translators perceive their main mission precisely in serving this lofty goal. Each of them could say of himself, in the soaring words of Boris Slutsky in his book *Today and Yesterday*: "I work so ardently on my translations because to me translations are soldiers breaching the ramparts between peoples."[4]

It is of course a temptation to offer my readers a complete and detailed survey of *all* the achievements of Soviet masters of translation during the past fifteen or twenty years. But the task of this book is far more modest. It treats only those masters whose works furnish illustrations of the ideas and principles expounded in it. This is why many of the very best translators have been excluded from the purview of this book, and I will not have opportunity to express my admiration for their work. Those readers who would like to obtain more detailed and varied information about what is happening in the field are referred to the already mentioned book by E.G. Etkind, *Poetry and Translation*. It offers literary portraits of *all* the best contemporary masters of translation of poetry whose work is typical of the artistic tastes and demands of our time.

I am not a linguist or a scholar. This book is written by a man of letters and literary critic, and this makes a great difference. Where the scholar impartially establishes the general principles of phenomena under study, the critic expresses joy, dissatisfaction, sorrow. He hates bad art with his very soul and expressly admires those who are talented. The facts and judgments I offer do not require any specialized knowledge on the part of the reader. I have written my book so that it can be understood by those who do not know a foreign language. I would be happy if, thanks to this book, the study of the problems involved in the craft of translation proved useful not only to neophyte translators, but also the reading public at large.

ONE

Slips of the Vocabulary

THIS happened in the thirties. Over at the
Academy of Sciences they were preparing
a book for publication in honor of Gorky. One of the members of
the editorial board called and asked whether I had ever heard of
an English writer named Orchard.

"Orchard?"

"Yes. Jerry Orchard."

I laughed right into the telephone and explained that Jerry
Orchard was not an English writer, but Chekhov's play *Cherry
Orchard*. They had mixed up the English words. They told me I
must be wrong and sent me a stack of Moscow papers for 25
September 1932 containing reports about a telegram to Gorky
from George Bernard Shaw. So far as I could make out, Shaw
praised Gorky's plays because they did not have the weak-willed
and spiritless heroes typical of Chekhov's *Cherry Orchard*, but a
worker for TASS must have translated it so hastily that he transformed a play by Chekhov into some mythical citizen of the
British Empire, the bourgeois writer Jerry Orchard. And they
even took the poor fellow to task for not creating characters
worthy of Gorky![1]

Such transformations are commonplace in the practice of
translation. The gifted poet Mikhail Froman did something

9

similar in a translation of a poem in Kipling's *Selected Verses*. He speaks in it of a Goddess Tara passing through a hot red sunset over a mountain. Unhappily, Tara is not a goddess, and not even a woman, but the mountain Tara Devi, one of the Himalayan peaks. The original stanza speaks clearly and unmistakably about a mountain:

> I had seen, as dawn was breaking
> And I staggered to my rest,
> Tara Devi softly shaking
> From the Cart Road to the crest.[2]

A great many such slips could be mentioned. One incident is particularly striking. In his translation from German of a French novel by Charles-Louis Phillippe the very good translator Valentin Smetanich (Stenich) depicts a young girl sending money from Paris to her old grandfather in the country, and giving him the unlikely advice, "Spend this money on girls so you won't have to trouble grandma." This sentence decided the translator's subsequent attitude toward the heroine. He decided that life in Paris had corrupted her, and he therefore added a touch of cynicism to all her actions. Imagine his surprise when a few years later he became acquainted with the French original and discovered that the girl did not at all advise her grandfather to spend the money on debauchery, but simply to hire a servant to help her grandmother with the housework.

More dismaying is a mistake made by M.K. Lemke in editing the *Complete Collected Works* of Alexander Herzen. While leafing through this set one day I ran across a most strange item: it seems that Herzen loved Ogaryov so much that he sent him a piece of his own flesh. Lemke made this translation of a note from Herzen to Ogaryov: "Accept a filet of my loin à la Mazada. I am sending it in a few days."[3] Fortunately, this mutilation in token of friendship is a myth, because it turns out that the original states clearly: "Accept my *entrefilet* on Mazada." The French term for a newspaper piece is hardly equivalent to the Russian anatomical term *mezhduFILEInaia chast'*.

Of course, we have to be severe in our attitude toward slips of the vocabulary; the calamities that can be visited upon an original author by an incorrect interpretation of a single solitary word of another language are countless. If there were any further need for a graphic example of how so little as a single slip of the vocabulary can ruin an entire text from the first line to the last, I would cite a poem by the Negro poet Langston Hughes in the Russian translation of the experienced translator Mikhail Zenkevich. The poem is titled "Black Maria," from the collection *After Hours*, and to judge from the translation it is about the passionate love of a black man for a black woman who has rejected him. I can imagine how vexed the translator was when it came out that "Black Maria" is not a woman, but a prison van for transporting arrested persons. In actual fact the man was not at all eager to rush into the embraces of the despicable "Maria." The lines read this way in the original:

> Must be the Black Maria
> That I see,
> The Black Maria that I see—
> But I hope it
> Ain't comin' for me.[4]

Lev Ginzburg spoke the truth when he remarked in an article in *The Craft of Translation* that "not only the fate of a translation, but the professional fate of the translator hangs on a single word" (1959, 291).

In a Russian translation of the Ukrainian writer Pavel Tychyna a landowner loses his temper at a servant and shouts, "Marry him off! Marry him off!" The word used in the Ukrainian original is the imperative verb form *zhenit'*. Unhappily, the Russian translator did not know the word is equivalent not to the Russian verb infinitive *zhenit'*, 'to marry,' but *gnat'*, 'to chase, to drive away.' The original text does not have it that the servant should be married off, but that he should be fired (see *Translator's Notebooks*, 1960, 2). In still another example offered by the same source, in translating a poem by the Ukrainian poet Volodymyr Sosyura,

Mikhail Svetlov ascribed a curious line to his subject: "The trolley clanged of roses." Anyone reading this line would be fully justified in taking Sosyura for a mystical Symbolist trying to link an everyday urban phenomenon with ethereal roses of some sort, perhaps the blue roses of the German Romantics, perhaps with the rose in Alexander Blok's tragedy *The Rose and the Cross*, perhaps with the Sacred Rose of medieval chivalry, *Lumen coelum, sancta rosa*! When we read this line in Svetlov's translation about a trolley ringing of roses, we have to rank Sosyura immediately with the epigones of the Bryusov or Blok school. And this because the translator did not know that the Ukrainian word *rozi*—the prepositional case of *rih*—is equivalent not to the Russian word *roza*, 'rose,' but to *ugol*, 'corner.' The original says simply, "The trolley rang at the corner." With this single slip of the vocabulary Svetlov gave Russian readers an inaccurate impression of Sosyura's talent.

But does this mean that Svetlov is a bad translator? Not in the least. He is an authentic poet, an excellent lyricist, and his error is an accident.

Still, it is to be preferred that such accidents never happen in our translation practice. What is even worse is that some errors are repeated over and over again, from generation to generation, from period to period. I once read, for example, a scene in the Russian translation of *The Forsyte Saga* where young Michael Mont is rowing a young girl across a river and is lost in a conversation with her. Suddenly, it says in the translation, "Mont caught a little crab, and instead of replying, said, 'What a nasty creature that was!' " This is most strange, to say the least. Why should a young man in love begin fishing for crabs in the middle of an ardent conversation with his sweetheart, especially since, incidentally, crabs are not found in such places? And even were he to happen to do such a thing, why would he call his catch a "nasty creature," and refer to it in the past tense—that *was* a nasty creature? The explanation to this strange situation is to be found in the original. To the English, "to catch a crab" signifies a clumsy motion whereby the oar is thrust too deeply into the water. This means that Mont was not thinking about such a thing as fishing at such a delicate moment; he simply made a clumsy movement with the oars, because he was agitated. The original reads: "Mont caught a little crab, and answered: 'That was a nasty one!' "[5]

I would not even have mentioned this error except that it has been repeated so often and passed from generation to generation. Friedrich Engels ran across it once too. It happened as follows. A certain English sportsman rowing across the English Channel with a team of oarsmen made the clumsy motion that the English call "to catch a crab." The English press reported this athletic ineptitude to its readers, and the London correspondent of a large German newspaper relayed it as, "A crab caught on the oar of one of the boatsmen." This amusing error caught Engels's eye in 1855, and he had great fun at the translator's expense.[6] But as we have seen, this did not make the translator of *The Forsyte Saga* any wiser. Fifty years later, as if it had never been, she revived the same fishing for crabs.

Crabs are likely to be of any sort. Some are petty, some are rather more important. Galsworthy's play *Game without Rules* was offered for many years by the Moscow Theater of Drama and Comedy. One of the original play's heroines is characterized by the words, "gray mare," which means in English slang a resolute, energetic woman. But the theater's translation had it literally as a gray mare, which of course means nothing more than exactly what it says in Russian. In her version of Dostoyevsky's *Notes from the Underground* the distinguished English translator Mrs. Constance Garnett took the Russian artist N.N. Ghe for the Spanish artist Francesco Goya, and this cute little crab has been retained in all subsequent editions of her translation.[7] And Mr. Gerard Shelley, the English translator of Russian poets, translated Mayakovsky's line in his poem "Order to the Army of Art," "Let the piano cut loose," as "Lift the piano lid," because he confused the verb *raskroit'*, 'to smash, to cut (to pieces),' with *raskryt'*, 'to uncover.'[8]

But even these translators were surpassed by Miss Marian Fell, who published Chekhov's works in her translation in the United States some ten years after the author's death. In her translation she repaid her Russian colleagues a hundredfold for their mistakes and blunders. The early-nineteenth-century poet Batyushkov, mentioned by Chekhov in *Ivanov* (II, iv), was turned into a Russian Orthodox priest because she confused his name with *batiushka*, 'father.'[9] The French general Jomini, in Chekhov's rendition of the Russian saying taken from a poem by the poet-hussar Denis Davydov, "Jomini, yes, Jomini, but not a word of vodka" (*Ivanov*, III, i), was turned into Germany: "Here we are talking of Germany, Germany, and never a word about vodka" (116). The nineteenth-century critic N.A. Dobrolyubov (*Ivanov*, II, iv) was turned into St. Francis of Assisi (104) because of the similarity between his name and the Russian word for a doer of good deeds (*dobroliubets*). Gogol is identified as a fabulist in her translation (140) and the little dog Kashtanka in Chekhov's story by that name was turned into "The Chestnut Tree" (11) because Kashtanka is a favorite name for a dog of that color. Because of the similarity between the Russian words *genii* and *gnoi*, 'pus, matter,' Miss Fell translated the latter word as "genius" (73). In *Ivanov*, Count Shabelsky says he wasted some twenty thousand rubles for medical treatment (I, iii). Miss Fell translated this as, "I have treated thousands of sick people in my life" (79). In this line the characterization of Count Shabelsky was instantly shattered to smithereens. The drunkard Lebedev, whose wife keeps him half starving, unexpectedly hides away—unknown to Chekhov—one hundred thousand rubles (123), and Miss Fell's English readers are left wondering why a man who has so much money suffers in shame because he cannot serve his guests refreshments. In the original, Lebedev hid away only 1,200 rubles (III, v). Miss Fell took a thousand rubles from Doctor Dorn in *The Sea Gull* (207)—in the original he claims not to have one but two thousand rubles (IV, 1)—while to the age of Sorin she added an extra five years. Her arithmetic for the latter feat is as follows: the man is sixty-five years old (178, 179), two years pass, and he becomes sixty-two (208). In the original, Sorin's age is actually given as sixty (II, i) and sixty-two (IV, i). According to Chekhov one character in *Ivanov* says: "You, my friend, are mired in your milieu" (II, v). Miss Fell's translation reads: "You got out of bed on the wrong side this morning" (125). She might just as well have confused the Russian word *sreda*, 'milieu,' with its homonym while she was at it and have Chekhov's character get out of the bed on the wrong side on Wednesday (*sreda*)!

Such slips literally swarm over the pages of Miss Fell's translations. They have more than amply ruined Chekhov. But just imagine for a moment that Miss Fell were to repent and remove every last one of her mistakes and blunders. Her *batiushka* would become Batyushkov again, as Chekhov has it, "The Chestnut Tree" would become "Kashtanka," St. Francis would become Dobrolyubov. In a word, her translation would become an irreproachable linear model. And yet it would still be worthless, because it would still not have the most important quality of the original, its chief essence—its style, without which Chekhov is not Chekhov. For the most important thing here is that no matter how harmful individual slips of the vocabulary are, at times they are far from inflicting the terrible damage inflicted on a translation by distortions of style. And who is in a position to say that the translators I have treated here—Mikhail Svetlov, and Stenich (Smetanich), and Froman—are bad translators and their works are hopelessly bad? This would be a grave error, because artistic translations cannot be measured by such chance blunders, and they are not in the least typical of these particular translators. Despite these and similar blunders, it is still possible to consider a translation excellent and praiseworthy so long as it conveys the most important thing—*the artistic individuality of the original author in all the distinctiveness of his style.*

Of course, I am not speaking here of business translations, which aim for pure information. The most important thing for business translations is precision of vocabulary.

But in an artistic translation individual lexical discrepancies, though they lead at times to monstrous distortions of the text, more often play a role at least three times removed, and those who try to discredit a translation in the eyes of uninitiated readers by pointing out accidental, petty, and easily remedied blunders are employing demagoguery solely for the purpose of disorienting reader tastes. Far be it for me to step forth in defense of crabs. I believe that one must wage unrelenting war on them. But the chief calamity is not crabs per se.

In order to make clear precisely what the chief calamity really is, let's take another look at Miss Fell's translations of Chekhov. Of course, it is deplorable that she mixes up dates, numbers, currency, names, turns people into governments. But it is far more deplorable that she imputes to Chekhov an insipid, colorless, stingy style by excising from his works—systematically, page after page—every vivid, colorful sentence, every vital intonation. She eradicates his full-blooded verbalisms in every possible way and replaces them with flat, anemic banalities. If, for example, one of Chekhov's characters in *Ivanov* says, "I sit and expect death at any moment" (II, iv), the same character drawls out in Miss Fell's translation, "I must sit here prepared at any moment to have death come knocking at my door" (104). Her ideal is an anemic, blandscript which has neither color, nor smell, nor the least trace of individual creativity. If, for example, Chekhov has a line like, "But Mamenka is such a tightwad" (*Ivanov*, II, iv), Miss Fell corrects it to read, "But mother is so stingy" (106). If someone says ironically, "These landowners, devil take them, are lords of the world" (*Ivanov*, I, i), she translates it in her own wretched instruction-manual style as, "Do you think because you own an estate you can command the whole world?" (77). In just the same way she simply refuses to let one of Chekhov's characters say, "Again I have the feeling I've stuffed myself with rat poison" (*Ivanov*, I, ii). Instead, she forces him to say in a most ordinary, drab way, "I feel as if I am going insane" (109).

As a result of this violent treatment of Chekhov's works, all the intonations, all the color, all the characters' speech distinctiveness have been obliterated, and thus Medvedenko has come to resemble Treplyov, Lvov—Shabelsky, Marfa Babakina—Nina Zarechnaya. Anyone must agree that this replacement of an energetic, expressive, multicolored style with such gray, monotonous, blandscript has inflicted heavier losses on

Chekhov's works than the innumerable slips of the vocabulary that fill Miss Fell's translations. For slips of the vocabulary are only so many scratches and cuts which are easily treated. But what Miss Fell has committed is villainous murder, a criminal act—the complete destruction of the artistic personality revealed to us by Chekhov in his complex, powerful, and dynamic style, a substitution of Chekhov the artist with some dullish, somniferous person mumbling tedious sentences in his sleep.

TWO

The Translation—
Self-Portrait of the Translator

> The translator differs from the author
> only in name. —Vasily Trediakovsky

1 When all is said and done, we must demand that an artistic translation reproduce not only the original author's ideas and images, not only his plot schemes, but also his literary manner, his creative personality, his style. If this objective is not achieved, the translation is useless. It is an act of slander which is all the more repugnant because the original author almost never has an opportunity to repudiate it.

The nature of this slander varies considerably. In most instances it consists of offering the reader a personality unlike the original author's real personality, one which is not only unlike him but downright hostile to him. When the distinguished Georgian poet Simon Chikovani saw one of his poems in Russian translation he issued a general appeal to translators: "I beg you not to translate me at all."[1] Which is to say: I do not wish to be represented to Russian readers in the preposterous form my translators have given me. If they are incapable of reproducing my true creative personality in their translations, then let them leave my works alone.

For the sad thing is not that some bad translator distorts a line or two of Chikovani's poetry, but that he distorts Chikovani himself, puts an entirely different face on him. "All my work has been directed against the sentimentalizing of Georgian literature," the poet has said. "It is against all those shashlyks and daggers." And yet the translations "are filled with shashlyks and wine and sheepskin wine flasks which have never figured in my poetry and will never figure in my poetry, because in the first place the subject matter does not call for them and in the second place shashlyks and sheepskin wineflasks are not what my poetry is about." It turns out that in place of the real Chikovani we have been presented with someone who not only bears no resemblance to him, but is profoundly repugnant to him—the figure of the dagger-bearing Caucasian who might just as well have been brought out on a stage to dance the lezghinka. And this when it is precisely the shashlyk interpretation of the Caucasus that Chikovani fought against in his poetry. So that in this instance the translator acted as the original author's enemy and forced him to personify tendencies, ideas, and images repugnant to him.

Here is the chief danger posed by bad translators: they pervert not just individual words and phrases, but the very essence of the original author. This happens far more often than one might think. The translator puts a mask of his own making on the author, so to speak, and he represents this mask as his real face.

So far as style is concerned, every work of an artist is essentially a self-portrait, for willingly or unwillingly an artist mirrors himself in his style. This was stated long ago in the eighteenth century by the poet and literary theorist Vasily Trediakovsky: "An author's mien (that is, his style) bears infinite resemblance to the color of his hair, to the movements of his eyes, to the turns of his tongue, to the beating of his heart." Walt Whitman said almost the same thing:

Understand that you can have in your writing no qualities which you do not honestly entertain in yourself. Understand that you cannot keep out of your writing the indication of the evil or shallowness you entertain in yourself. If you love to have a servant stand behind your chair at dinner, it will appear in your writing; if you possess a vile opinion of women, or if you grudge anything, or doubt immortality, these will appear by what you leave unsaid more than by what you say. There is no trick or cunning, no art or recipe by which you can have in your writing that which you do not possess in yourself—that which is not in you can not appear in your writing. No rival of life—no sham for generation—no painting friendship or love by one who is neither friend nor lover.[2]

The reflection of the author's personality in the language of his works is called his individual style, and is peculiar to him alone. This is why I say that when we distort his style we also distort his face. If in our translation we foist our own style on him, we turn his self-portrait into a self-portrait of a translator. It is therefore useless for reviewers to criticize a translation merely by noting its slips of vocabulary. It is far more important to catch the pernicious departures from the original which are linked organically to the personality of the translator and which by reflecting the personality of the translator in the aggregate, shunt the original author aside. It is far more important to find the dominant of the departures from the norm by which the translator foists his own literary "I" on the reader.

A fatal role played by translators is that the poets they translate often become their twins. Indicative here are the old translations of Homer into English. *The Iliad* has been translated in England by such great poets as Chapman, Pope, and Cowper, and when one reads their translations one finds that they are as much like their translators as they are like Homer. With Chapman, Homer is florid like Chapman; with Pope, high-flown like Pope; with Cowper, dry and laconic like Cowper.

This is just what happened to the poetry of the great English lyric poet Percy Bysshe Shelley in the translation of his *Complete Collected Works* by the Russian Symbolist poet Konstantin Balmont. The translator's personality is far too sharply etched in the text of Balmont's translation. One is struck not by the individual errors in the translation (which are abundant enough), but by a complete system of errors, a complete system of concoctions which in their aggregate transform Shelley's personality beyond recognition. All of Balmont's concoctions are united into a sort of harmonious unity, every last one of them is in the same boudoir style of cheap love songs, and this has inflicted a thousand times more harm on the author than any chance slips of the vocabulary.

Where Shelley has "lute," Balmont translates it as "the murmur of a dear charmer's lute."[3] Where Shelley has "sleep" (623), Balmont translates it as "voluptuous bliss" (194). Where Shelley has "woman" (500), Balmont translates it as "a woman pretty as a picture" (213). Where Shelley has "sound" (505), Balmont translates it as "a lively concordance of harmonies" (203). In this way Balmont transforms line after line of Shelley's poetry, imbuing them with the prettiness of cheap love songs. And as if this were not enough, he sticks a hackneyed epithet on almost every word. Where Shelley has "stars" (532), Balmont has "fiery stars" (153). Where Shelley has "eye" (532), Balmont has "shining eye" (153). Where Shelley has "breast" (505), Balmont has "ardent bosom" (13). Where Shelley has "sorrow" (504), Balmont has "oppressive torments" (191). Thanks to these systematic textual changes, Shelley develops a most peculiar resemblance to Balmont.

In his Balmontization of Shelley, Balmont imparts his own boldly sweeping gestures to the British poet. Where in "A Song" Shelley has no more than a single solitary "bare wintry bough" (507), Balmont has a vast landscape:

> 'Midst copses of pines and birch,
> Where'er the eye is cast,
> A frigid snow drifts o'er the fields.   (211)

Out of no more than a bare bough Balmont has grown whole copses of pines and birches, while from the single word "wintry" he has laid out boundless fields of snow (and good old-fashioned Russian fields at that). This lavishness with boldly sweeping gestures can be found on literally every page of Balmont's translation. Where Shelley has "morn's undoubted light" (440), Balmont has a whole sunrise: "The sunrise burns and gleams of amber" (7). Where Shelley says, "Thou indeed are kind" (627),

Balmont pours forth a veritable fountain of pleasantries: "Thou art as dear unto me as night unto the gleam of day, / As one's homeland at the moment of banishment" (3). When Shelley sings "A Bridal Song" (529), he provides Balmont with an opportunity to pile up a whole supply of cheap phrases calculated to convey the image of a bridal night in the minds of prurient Philistines: "self-oblivion," "the merging of passions," "pillow," "voluptuous bliss" (108). Shelley refers in one poem to a nightingale, and we read in Balmont: "As if composing hymns to the moon" (108). After all, what sort of nightingale would it be if it did not sing praises of the moon! Shelley has only to mention the word "lightning" (532), and Balmont has three lines ready to go:

> . . . and a searing flash of lightning
> Sliced depths in the sky,
> And its loud laughter gave birth to a wave
> in the sea.   (18)

Shelley is thus gradually transformed into a languid serenader singing love songs in a sensuous falsetto to the accompaniment of a guitar, and so we are no longer surprised when we encounter such pretty words in this translation of his poetry as "tender purple of the day," "the sigh of dreams," "sweet moment of joy," "inexpressible rapture of existence," "fog-wraithed path of life," "mystery of fleeting dreams," and similar love-song trash. Even in a poem Balmont translated more or less faithfully, there is a vulgar insertion: "Oh, why, my charming friend, / Do we not merge into one?" (86). Compare this cheap contrivance to the actual lines of Shelley's poem "Love's Philosophy":

> All things by a law divine
> In one another's being mingle—
> Why not I with thine?   (503)

See how heavily the translator can mark the original author's personality with his own. It is not only Shelley's poems Balmont has disfigured in his translations, he has disfigured Shelley's very face, he has marked Shelley's beautiful face with features of his own personality. The result is a new face, half Shelley, half Balmont—a face I would call Shellmont.

This happens very often to poets. Translators make far too much of their own "I" in their translations, and the more expressive the translator's personality, the more the original author is shunted aside. Precisely because Balmont expresses his own literary personality so acutely, he is incapable, despite all his talent, of mirroring the individuality of another poet in his translations. And since Balmont's talent leaned to the dandified, Shelley became dandified in his translations.

Even more instructive in this regard are the translations of the American poet Walt Whitman by the same Balmont. Even without knowing these translations, anyone can predict that Whitman's literary personality has been distorted in a most perfidious manner, because in the entire world there is no poet more remote from him than Balmont. After all, Whitman spent his entire life fighting what we call Balmontism, with its flowery rhetoric, its high-flown "music of words," its external prettiness, which is in fact worse than monstrously ugly. Long before the appearance of Balmont, Whitman declared himself an implacable foe of the qualities which are the very basis of Balmontism. It is this implacable foe that Balmont tried to make over into his fellow poet, and we can easily imagine how Whitman's face was disfigured by Balmontization. The translation became a battle, an unceasing polemic between the translator and the poet he presumed to translate. It could not be otherwise, for Balmont essentially hates the American bard, refuses to let him be what he really is, tries in every way to "correct" him, foists his Balmontism—his pretentiously Modernist style—on him.

Under no circumstances, for example, does Balmont permit Whitman to speak in an ordinary language, and he persistently replaces Whitman's simple words with "noble," archaic Church Slavonicisms. Whitman, for example, says "banner," and Balmont translates it with the Church Slavonic word *stiag*.[4] Whitman says "rais'd it" (242), and Balmont translates it with the archaic word *pod''emliu* (133). It is as if Balmont's conscience could not bear to let Whitman write plainly and vulgarly. He simply has to sweeten his poetry with Church Slavonicisms. In one place he even uses the archaic word for "milk" (*mleko*, 138) and in another he uses the Church Slavonic word *dshcheri* (143), a word so archaic that it cannot even be found in most dictionaries. Read "Song of the Banner at Daybreak," from which I have taken these examples. The translation of this poem contains dozens of such Balmontisms as "the music of kissing words" (138), "countlessness of plowlands" (135), and "innumerability of wagons" (135). Where Whitman shuns rhyme in lines like, "I am not the wind with girlish laughter, / Not the immense wind which strengthens, not the wind which lashes" (240), Balmont introduces a rhyme like, "With the winds we shall whirl, / With the immense wind we shall swirl" (133). And again, where Whitman has simply, "Put in all, aye all will I, sword-shaped pennant for war" (243), Balmont again strains for a rhyme: "All, all, yes all will I hoard, / Martial banner, shaped like a sword" (137).

Especially repugnant to Balmont is the realistic, businesslike concreteness which Whitman always strove for. This is understandable, of course, because Balmont cultivated diffuse, hazy images. In the original it is said, precisely and definitively, "my ever running Mississippi . . . And my Illinois fields, and my Kansas fields, and my fields of Missouri" (243). But Balmont smooths out this geographical distinctness, deliberately making it vague in his translation: "And rivers and meadows and dales" (136). Whitman pursues the same businesslike, journalistic precision with numbers in the poem: "Over the area spread below, the three or four millions of square miles, the capitals, / The forty millions of people . . ." (242). But Balmont steals these precise figures from the author and replaces them with a diffuse fog of words: "an expanse of many thousands of versts," "populous cities," "millions of people" (136).

These are the sorts of unobtrusive devices a translator uses to subjugate an original author to his own pet style. In foisting the aesthetics of the Russian Symbolists on the American bard, Balmont even translated the title of the book incorrectly and manneredly. The title of Whitman's book is not *Shoots of Grass*, but

Leaves of Grass! It is because his mind was nourished on a diet of Decadent metaphors that the translator was simply incapable of mastering Whitman's honest simplicity and invented the inappropriate word "shoots."

In a word, if Whitman had known Russian and could have acquainted himself with Balmont's translations, he would have appealed to the translator, "I beg you not to translate me at all," because he would have realized his poems had fallen into the hands of an enemy determined to distort his personality to his own liking with a complete system of his own concoctions. I have not even mentioned the chance errors and slips, which are considerable in Balmont's translations. Forgetting, for example, that the English word "figure" means not only "form" but "number," he obliges an astronomer to stand in front of his class and draw strange "rows of forms" (121). The original line, in "When I Heard the Learn'd Astronomer," reads: "When the proofs, the figures, were ranged in columns before me" (228). Where Whitman addresses himself "To the Man-of-War Bird" with the observation, "thou art all wings" (218), Balmont translates it as, "You are winds, all winds" (111) because he confused the English words "wings" and "winds." Whitman delights in lilacs, an image which plays no small role in his poetry. The translator, however, mistook "lilac" for "lily" and thereby invented the heretofore unknown natural phenomenon of lilies growing on bushes, in his translation of "When Lilacs Last in the Dooryard Bloom'd."

Chance errors should not be ignored, of course, but still it is not chance errors that determine the quality of a translation. What is important here, I repeat, is a whole system of departures from the original text. Not one mistake, and not even two, but a whole grouping of mistakes which have one and the same destructive effect on the mind of the reader—the distortion of the original author's literary personality. Chance errors are mere trivia in comparison with the imperceptible violations of the author's will—the author's style—which in their aggregate reflect the translator's literary personality. No matter how insignificant such violations of the author's will may seem when taken individually, in their totality they are a tremendously harmful force which can transform any writer with a markedly personal style into a miserable scribbler and distort his literary personality beyond recognition. These bacilli work unnoticed, but fiercely: in one line they extinguish a brightly burning epithet, in another they destroy the vital pulsation of the rhythm, in a third they cause all colors to fade—and before you know it, there is nothing left of the original, it has become something entirely different, from start to finish, as if it had been created by someone who has nothing in common with the original author. And meanwhile the average reader is enamored of reviews which expose only the individual slips of some translator or another. They are sure that these slips—which are more or less by chance—provide the measure of the quality of a translation, when in fact (I repeat again and again) it is not a matter of individual mistakes but of the total complex of concoctions which in their aggregate change the style of the original.

2 In most cases the translations of the greatest Russian translator V.A. Zhukovsky reproduce the original with amazing precision. His language is so rich and powerful that it would seem there could be no difficulties he could not contend with. Pushkin called Zhukovsky "a genius of translation." He said of Zhukovsky in a letter that he was "in his struggles with difficulty, a man of extraordinary prowess."[5]

And yet the system of departures from the original in which Zhukovsky indulged again results in the original author's personality sometimes being replaced by the personality of the translator. When, for example, in his translation of Schiller's tragedy *Die Jungfrau von Orleans* Zhukovsky turns "devil" into "temptress" and "devilish maiden" into "sly trickster," this could of course be the result of chance. But when we examine his translations from the first page to the last, we realize this is Zhukovsky's basic tendency. All of the poetry translated by Zhukovsky has become his own poetry because it reflects his own quiet, eloquent, splendid, sentimental-melancholic, puritan personality. His peculiar brand of puritanism is evident in his translations with unusual vividness. He banishes from *Die Jungfrau von Orleans* even a phrase like "love for a man," apparently because it is too risqué for him, and in place of "Do not tempt thy heart with love for a man," he writes with decorous indirectness: "Fear thy hopes, know not the love of this world."[6] The same puritanism prevents him from offering a precise translation of Schiller's ballad *Das Siegesfest* where it is said that the hero Menelaeus, "exulting anew in his conquered wife, winds his arms in exquisite bliss around the charms of her beautiful body." In his attempts to avoid reproducing such sinful behavior Zhukovsky obliges Menelaeus to stand sedately beside Helen without manifestations of conjugal bliss: "And standing beside Helen / Menelaeus said . . ." (159). The later Romantic poet Fyodor Tyutchev has a far more faithful translation of this stanza.[7]

This is not said in condemnation of Zhukovsky, of course. His craftmanship and inspired creativity make him one of the greatest translators ever known in the history of world literature. Zhukovsky will long remain an unattainable model and teacher for all poets who translate poetry. But precisely because his best translations are so exact, the by no means accidental departures from the original which comprise the dominant of his literary style are all the more obtrusive. Indicative of Zhukovsky's translations, it seems to me, is the circumstance, petty enough by itself, that in his magnificent version of Gottfried Bürger's ballad *Lenore*, where the force of his lines sometimes reaches Pushkin's power, he permitted not so much as a hint that the lovers racing on horseback through the night are hurrying to the bridal bed. Wherever Bürger mentions the word "bed"—*Brautbett, Hochzeitbett*—Zhukovsky chastely writes "lodging," "abode," "refuge" (II, 186–87). The Soviet translator V. Levik has reproduced the full reality of the original in his brilliant translation of *Lenore* in his collection *From the European Poets of the Sixteenth through Nineteenth Centuries.*[8] According to an article by O. Kholmskaya in *The Craft of Translation*, Zhukovsky can be predicted to omit the line, "Receive us now, bridal bed!" Needless to say, he also omitted the lines where Bürger disrespectfully calls a priest a parson and likens the singing of a group of clergymen to the croaking of frogs in a pond (1959, 307).

We all know how Zhukovsky loved to fill his poems with tombs and coffins. It is hardly an accident, therefore, that in certain of his translations he introduces images of the grave which are not found that often in the originals. For example, where Ludwig Uhland, in his ballad *Junker Rechberger*, says simply "chapel," we read in Zhukovsky's translation, under the title *The Knight Rolland*: "He enters; in the chapel he sees a standing tomb, / Above it a lamp shines dimly, quivering" (II, 213). There is no mention whatsoever of a tomb in the corresponding lines of the original. Zhukovsky also had a great passion for lamps (*lampada*). In his reading of Uhland's lines on the death of the young minstrel in the ballad *Durand* (retitled *Alonzo*), Zhukovsky once again departs from the original and compares the death with a dying lamp. Just as a sudden draft stifles a lamp, so the young minstrel perishes from a word (II, 182). The word *lampada* was especially dear to Zhukovsky because by that time it had become strongly identified with the Church and came to signify an altar or icon lamp. Zhukovsky's penchant for Christian symbolism can be detected even in his translation of Byron's *The Prisoner of Chillon*, where he twice refers to the hero's younger brother as "our angel" and "gentle angel" (II, 274–75), although the original says nothing whatsoever about heavenly beings.

Even in Homer's *The Odyssey* Zhukovsky introduced, as translator, a note of melancholy peculiarly his own, a fact he announced in the foreword to his translation. Even though the critics of the time were enraptured by the consummate merit of his translation, they nevertheless could not but note its extreme subjectivity: in this Russian variant of the epic poem, Homer becomes amazingly like Zhukovsky in many ways. According to one scholar-critic, "Zhukovsky introduced into *The Odyssey* much moralizing and sentimentality, and even several almost Christian conceptions which were hardly known to the author of this pagan epic. . . . In several places the translation displays a character of Romantic meditation completely inappropriate to *The Odyssey*."[9] In his well-known ballad *Queen Oracca and the Five Martyrs of Morocco*, Robert Southey says of the monks that they went across the sea to the land of the Moors, and Zhukovsky translates the line by adding that they went to Africa bearing "the heavenly gift of Christ's teachings" (II, 199).

I repeat: these systematic, by no means accidental departures from the original text are particularly noticeable in Zhukovsky because in all other respects his translations, with very few exceptions, miraculously convey the most minute tonalities of the original. And too, it must be noted that the great majority of Zhukovsky's changes are in the spirit of the original. Though Uhland might not have featured a tomb in the line given, he might very easily have done so. The addition is fully in keeping with his *Weltanschauung* and style.

3 It is important here to note that an original text is sometimes (but by no means always!) falsified under the influence of a translator's partisan political biases. In extreme cases the practice becomes a deliberate distortion of an original text. In 1934 Shakespeare's tragedy *Coriolanus* was staged at the Comedie Française in Paris in a new translation by the French nationalist René-Louis Piachaud. By dint of numerous departures from the English text the translator endowed Coriolanus with the features of the perfect reactionary dictator who perishes in unequal combat with democracy. Thanks to this translation the old English play became a battle flag of French reaction. The dreams of strong dictatorial power and the destruction of the revolutionary plebes which were cherished by the French *rentiers* alarmed by the "red menace" found perfect reflection in this modernized translation of Shakespeare. The audience decoded the play as a broadside against the contemporary political condition of France, and after its very first performance the theater was divided into two stormily hostile camps. While Coriolanus's curse of the rabble evoked ardent applause from the stalls, the galleries whistled it down in a frenzy.

I learned about this translation from an article by L. Borovoy published at the time in *Literary Gazette*. Borovoy accused the translator with full justification of distorting Shakespeare's play for specific political purposes. The distortion was done consciously, a fact which the translator not only did not disguise, but proclaimed openly by titling his version *"The Tragedy of Coriolanus*, translated *freely* from the English text of Shakespeare and *adapted to the conventions of the French stage."*[10]

But let's imagine for a moment that the same translator intended to translate the same play verbatim, without any departures from the original. Even then it sometimes happens that the translator's ideological position is reflected in his translation against his will. The translator did not have to devote himself to the implacable goal of falsifying the original for this to happen. The Russian translator of the same *Coriolanus*, A.V. Druzhinin, was a man of good conscience who strove for maximum precision in his translation. Under no circumstances would he have consciously mutilated Shakespeare's text by adapting it to suit his own views. And yet his translation comes very close to being exactly the type of translation that so delighted the foes of French democracy, because Druzhinin did exactly in his translation unconsciously what Piachaud did consciously. In spite of its precision, Druzhinin's translation played the same reactionary role as Piachaud's.

Druzhinin translated *Coriolanus* in 1858. This was the time of the struggle between the liberal aristocrats and the revolutionary plebeians, the "Nihilists" of the sixties. For this reason Coriolanus's strife with the rabble in revolt was understood by Russian readers of the time as being applicable to Russian events, and all the curses Coriolanus calls down on the Roman plebes were understood as a condemnation of youthful Russian democracy.

Shakespeare's tragedy enabled Druzhinin to settle partisan scores with Chernyshevsky and his adherents, and both Turgenev and Vasily Botkin hailed the translation as a *political* act. "Your idea of translating *Coriolanus* is marvelous," Turgenev wrote to Druzhinin in October 1856. "It matches your tastes perfectly, you dearest of conservatives."[11] Botkin, who was at just this time going over to the reactionary camp, expressed himself even more frankly. "Thanks for your choice of *Coriolanus*," he wrote. "The play has great contemporary relevance."[12]

Thus, what happened with the translation of *Coriolanus* in the French theater in the winter of 1934 was essentially a repeat of what happened in Russia to the Russian translation of the play in the 1860s. Both there and here translations of *Coriolanus* served as propaganda for reactionary ideas propagated by its translators which caused both of them to strengthen the play's antidemocratic leanings independently of whether they strove for the most precise reproduction of the original or consciously distorted it.

Here it would not be inappropriate to return to Zhukovsky. He used others, melodies, plots, and images to mark out his literary "I" so firmly within the boundaries of literature that not even Byron could evict him from them. It would seem that his translation of *The Odyssey*, which he undertook in his old age, would be totally removed from any political storms. In his introduction to the translation, Zhukovsky pointed out right from the start that for him *The Odyssey* was a quiet haven in which he found longed-for repose: "I wished to cheer my soul with primitive poetry, which is so bright and *calm*, so life-giving and *soothing*."[13] And yet, when the translation appeared in print the readers of the time perceived in it not simply a retreat from the present, but a war against the present. They understood what would seem to be an ordinary academic work as a somehow hostile act against the contemporary Russian reality, which by that time was hateful to Zhukovsky. To Zhukovsky—as to his entire circle—the Russian reality of that time could not but have been hateful. This was the very height of the plebeian forties when it first became obvious that the foundations of his beloved feudal-patriarchal Russia were being shaken. Science, literature, virtually every area of civic life were being penetrated by pushy new men, the petty bourgeoisie, the plebeians. The voice of Nekrasov had already sounded forth. Belinsky, whose influence became so immense at just this time, had already fostered the young Natural School, and Zhukovsky and the majority of his fellow believers felt that this was a catastrophic destruction of Russian culture. To him, as to P.A. Pletnyov, S.P. Shevyryov, and M.P. Pogodin, "the age of mercantilism, railroads, and steamships" was "a spiritually painful period of stagnation."

It was in defiance of this hostile epoch, as a counter to its "realism," its "materialism," its "mercantilism," that Zhukovsky published his translation of *The Odyssey*. This is exactly how the publication of the poem was understood in 1848–49—as an actual polemic against the new era. The year 1848 was the year of European revolutions. Reactionary journalists used *The Odyssey* to vilify the West's "pernicious discord." Iosif Senkovsky, who wrote under the name Baron Brambeus, said as much in his journal *Library for Reading*:

> Forsaking the West, which is covered by dark clouds of calamity, Zhukovsky, with his brilliant word, with his captivating Russian verses, a poet now more than ever before, a poet at a time when all others have ceased to be poets, Zhukovsky, *the last of the poets*, has taken the very first poet by the arm, the blind poet, the decrepit but at times "divine" Homer whom everyone *in this time of deplorable inanity* has forgotten, and he has brought him forth before our compatriots and calls us to a magnificent feast of the Beautiful.[14]

The critic contrasted Zhukovsky's *The Odyssey* with the revolutions taking place in the West, or, as he expressed it, with the West's "machinations of evil and misery," "material extravagances," "disorders of materialistic heresy," and "torrents of absurdity" (332).

Senkovsky here followed the example of his antagonist Gogol. Whenever Gogol, who had already become an outright obscurantist, wrote about Zhukovsky's new work he inevitably contrasted it with "the troubling and difficult phenomena of the

present era." For Gogol *The Odyssey* in Zhukovsky's translation was a weapon in a political struggle. He wrote to P.A. Pletnyov:

> Its appearance at the present time is of unusual significance. Its
> influence on the public is still to be. It is even quite possible that in
> these feverish times the majority of the reading public will not only
> not sniff it out, but will not even discern its tracks. But for all that,
> it is a veritable paradise and gift to those in whose souls the sacred
> fire has not been extinguished and who have not lost heart over *the
> troubling and difficult phenomena of the present era.* It would be impossi-
> ble to devise anything more comforting. We must view this phe-
> nomenon, which brings encouragement and renewal to our souls, as
> a sign of God's mercy on us.

Praising especially the "clarity," the "counterbalancing effect of
its tranquil character," and the "quietude" of Zhukovsky's translation, Gogol declared that it was the finest medicine for the
bitterness and spiritual "turmoil" of the time. He wrote to the
militantly reactionary poet N.M. Yazykov:

> It is especially at this time that the sickly babble of dissatisfaction
> has begun to be heard, the voice of human displeasure with every-
> thing on earth—with the order of things, with the time, with one's
> very self . . . when through the ridiculous shouting and heedless
> sermonizing of new and still vaguely audible ideas there can be
> heard a certain universal striving to come closer to a certain desired
> median, to find a true law of action both in the masses and in
> individual persons—in a word, it is precisely at this time that *The
> Odyssey* has smitten us with the magnificent patriarchal order of the
> ancient world, the simple lack of complexity in the workings of its
> society, its freshness of life, the unblunted, childlike clarity of man.

Gogol was even more explicit about expressing the political
tendencies of Zhukovsky's translation of *The Odyssey*, and in his
essay "On Zhukovsky's Translation of *The Odyssey*" he emphasized
as particularly valuable the features which were the foundation
stone of the autocratic Nicholaevian order:

It is a strict reverence for tradition, it is a reverential respect for authority and the leaders of the nation . . . it is a respect and almost reverence for man *in the image of God*, it is a faith that not one single good thought is born in our minds except by the lofty will of the Great Being above us . . . .[15]

These are the features of Zhukovsky's new translation that seemed to be the most attractive to the Gogol of that time, to the Gogol of *Selected Correspondence with Friends*.

At times a translator's social views are revealed in an unusual manner through the most trivial and seemingly chance details. When Druzhinin translated *King Lear* he was particularly successful with the scenes featuring Kent, the king's faithful servant. He exclaimed with great emotion that "never, not through thousands of generations as yet unborn, will the poetic image of Shakespeare's Kent, the bright shining image of the *loyal servant*, that great loyal servant, ever perish."[16] This emotion could not but be reflected in his translation. So perceptive a person as Turgenev quite accurately formulated the political significance of Druzhinin's bias for Kent. "I must confess," he wrote to Druzhinin, "that if you were not a conservative you would never have been able to appreciate Kent as 'that great loyal servant.' I shed tears . . . over him" (III, 84). Which is to say that Turgenev perceived Kent's servile devotion to his monarch, which was propagated so energetically in Druzhinin's translation of *Lear* and in his commentaries to the tragedy, specifically on the plane of social struggle.

It is curious to note here that the first stage performance of *King Lear* in Russia, a half century before Druzhinin's translation appeared, had as its entire goal, from start to finish, the strengthening and glorification of the feelings of a loyal servant toward the tsar-autocrat. The distinguished poet N.I. Gnedich even eliminated Lear's madness from his version in order to strengthen spectator sympathy for the struggle of the monarch for his "lawful throne." Shakespeare's Edmund delivers tirades like this in Gnedich's translation: "To die for one's compatriots is praiseworthy, but to die for a good king—ah! one should be able to live again in order doubly to enjoy the sweetness of such a death!" A modern scholar has noted:

> Gnedich's *Lear* conforms to events being experienced by Russia at the moment of the appearance of the tragedy, and it fully reflects the mood of the nobility at the time and is of undoubted significance as an agitational work in the interests of this class. The tragedy of the aged father persecuted by his ungrateful daughters, which Gnedich reduced in toto to a struggle for the throne, for the "lawful" rights of the "lawful" ruler, could not but have reminded the spectator at the moment of the first performance of *Lear* of another "unlawful" seizure of the throne which was of actual importance at the time. Did not the Duke of Cornwall symbolize to the spectator of that time the real-life "usurper" who was shaking the foundations of the European system of peace and welfare and had cast even Russia into the universal European chaos—Napoleon Bonaparte? Did not Lear's ungrateful daughters symbolize the Republic of France which overthrew its king? And did not Lear himself symbolize the "lawful" occupant of the French throne, the future Louis XVIII? Indeed, this real-life usurper—Napoleon Bonaparte—terrified the Russian nobility in another way too. Whether justified or not, he represented the onset of the period of the bourgeoisie which presaged the destruction of the feudal nobility of Europe. The struggle against Napoleon became a matter of life and death for the Russian nobility as a class and for the entire feudal-serf system. The task of *Lear* was to arouse feelings of patriotism which were indispensable to the struggle against this dread menace to restore order and legality in Europe and—in the final analysis—to preserve the entire feudal-serf system in Russia. Gnedich's *Lear* could not but have reflected the patriotic mood of an author determined to share and express the views of the Russian nobility. Thus, Shakespeare's tragedy was transformed into a tool of agitation in the interests of the ruling class.[17]

Even *Hamlet* was filled with the spirit of Russian patriotism in its first performance on the Petersburg stage. According to P. Viskovatov's version of the tragedy, Hamlet the King exclaims: "My fatherland! I sacrifice myself for thee!" The basic intent of this version of *Hamlet* was to serve "the goal of rallying Russian society around the throne and the tsar for the struggle against the advancing Napoleonic hordes" (78).

4 Of course, translators like this do not even try to get to the gist of Shakespeare. But it not infrequently happens that a translator concentrates exclusively on conveying a writer he loves (in his own way!) as accurately and truthfully as possible, but the abyss between their aesthetic, political, and moral views impels the translator, despite his subjective intentions, to depart fatally from the original text. This can be discerned quite easily in the pre-Soviet translation of the great Armenian poet Avetik Isaakyan done by I. Belousov and E. Nechayev. According to the critic Levon Mkrtchian in his study *Avetik Isaakyan and Russian Literature*, the majority of their departures from the original are to be explained by the fact that both translators were at that time under the influence of certain Populist notions, under the sway of Nadsonian verses about "the poet and the crowd." As Mkrtchian puts it, "they subjugated Isaakyan's system of imagery to the system of imagery of Russian Populist poetry in its Nadsonian variant." As for distortions of the original texts introduced into translations of Isaakyan's poetry by translators of a later period, the critic explains these distortions by the fact that the translators "tried to fit Isaakyan to the poetics of Russian Symbolism." He says that "the translations of Isaakyan done at that time were characterized by images and intonations typical of the Symbolists."[18]

And when the Populist poet P.F. Yakubovich, who wrote under the pseudonym P. Ya., took it upon himself to do a translation of *Les Fleurs du Mal* by Charles Baudelaire, he foisted a melancholy Nekrasovian rhythm and a hackneyed Nadsonian vocabulary on him, so that Baudelaire turned into something quite peculiar—Baudelaire in a Populist style. The author of *Les Fleurs du Mal* would undoubtedly have registered dismayed protest against the concoctions with which P. Ya. larded his poetry, even forcing him to exclaim such things as, "They bring freedom / And tidings of the Resurrection / To a weary people," and, "The soul struggles powerlessly, / Grieves and aches, / And yearns for freedom."[19] Baudelaire has a poem beginning, "Une nuit que j'étais près d'une affreuse Juive," in which he likens himself and the Jewish woman to corpses: "Two corpses side by side we seemed." P.Ya. changed this to his own liking by referring to the Jewish woman as "sculpted in marble." He simply could not let Baudelaire see himself and his mistress as corpses. To him, the translator, it would be much nicer if Baudelaire did not experience such monstrous feelings. The woman should not seem like a repulsive corpse to him but, on the contrary, like a beautiful statue "sculpted in marble," perhaps even a Venus de Milo. In his opinion something like this would be far more "beautiful." True, nothing was left of Baudelaire in this translation, and he even became an anti-Baudelaire, but the translator was not in the least bothered by this. He would rather replace the "Decadent" Baudelaire with himself, because he valued his own morality and aesthetics far above Baudelaire's. Maybe he was right, but in this case he had no reason to undertake his translations of Baudelaire. One can just imagine how the author of *Les Fleurs du Mal* would have despised his translator if by some miracle he could have become familiar with the translations.

In a letter written while he was still a young man, Valery Bryusov clearly formulated the basic reason for the translator's failure. "Yakubovich," he wrote, "is a man of views completely contrary to Baudelaire's, and this is why he so often intentionally distorts the original. This is the case with his translations of a poem like 'Le Guignon' ('Pour soulever un poids si lourd, Sisyphe . . .'), where Mr. Yakubovich preaches humility. . . . Baudelaire's original, on the other hand, is one of his most arrogant poems. Examples of this sort could be cited by the hundreds (literally)."[20]

In a word, woe to the translator who does not want or is unable to control at every step of the way the tastes, devices, and habits which are a vital reflection of the basic *Weltanschauung* stemming from his own personality. The French scholar Charles Corbiére put this very well in an analysis in *International Links of Russian Literature* of a recent French translation of Pushkin's *Ruslan and Lyudmila*: ". . . the translator diluted the vitality and naturalness of the original with a fog of elegant Neoclassical pomposity; Pushkin's effervescent scintillating wine was turned into insipid lemonade" (202). The translators who most often achieve precision are those who feel such sympathy for their authors that they seem to be their twins. They do not have to turn themselves into someone else: the object of their translation is almost adequate to the subject. This is the source—to a significant degree—of Zhukovsky's success (his translations of Uhland, Hebbel, Southey), and of the success of Vasily Kurochkin, who gave us consummate translations of the poetry of Béranger, who is so very like him. This is the source of Valery Bryusov's success (his translations of Verhaeren), of Bunin's success (his translation of Longfellow's *Hiawatha*), of Tvardovsky's success (his translations of Shevchenko), or Blaginina's success (her translations of L. Kvitko). This is the source of Stephen Mallarmé's success (his translations of Edgar Allan Poe), of Fitzgerald's success (his translations of Omar Khayyam), and so on, and so on, and so on.

5   All this is true. It is indisputable truth. But is it true that the history of literature knows no translations executed with brilliant talent and distinguished by proximity to the original even though the translator's spiritual cast is far from coinciding (and at times does not coincide at all) with the spiritual cast of the original author? Just think how many great writers there are in the world who delight us with their genius but are infinitely distant from our psychological makeup and our time! Are we to leave Xenophon, Thucydides, Petrarch, Apuleius, Chaucer, Boccaccio, Ben Jonson, and the so many others untranslated simply because their *Weltanschauung* is in many ways alien—and even hostile—to our own? Of course not. These translations are fully within our power, but they are unspeakably difficult and they demand not only talent from the translator, not only instinct, but also the renunciation of personal intellectual and psychological modes. One of the most convincing examples of this is the translations of the classics of Georgian poetry done by the remarkable master of the word Nikolay Zabolotsky.

It is scarcely likely that in the middle of the twentieth century Zabolotsky could be of like mind with the medieval Georgian poet Shota Rustaveli, who in the twelfth century created his immortal masterpiece *The Knight in Tiger's Skin*. And yet it is impossible to even imagine a better translation than Zabolotsky's. The translation, which is included in his monumental anthology *Georgian Classical Poetry*,[21] is marked by a striking clarity of diction enhanced by an almost magical power over syntax, a feeling of breathless freedom in every stanza, for which the three obligatory rhymes are not a burden, not an impediment, as is often the case with other translations of *Knight*, but rather, powerful and light wings which impart the original's powerful dynamics to each line of the translation. There are no less than seven hundred stanzas in the poem, perhaps even more, and they are all translated in virtuoso fashion!

Neither was Zabolotsky constrained to feel that he was a fellow believer of the inspired Georgian singer David Guramishvili, who lived two hundred and fifty years ago, during the reign of Peter the Great, in order to re-create his subject's devout refrains.[22] What great need there was for an artist's imagination in order for a translator who had long since renounced religion to convey the religious meditations of this ancient author with such perfection! But Nikolay Zabolotsky always made the severest possible demands on the translator's craft. "If a translation from a foreign language does not read like a good Russian work," he wrote in an article in *The Craft of Translation*, "the translation is either mediocre or a failure" (1959, 252). And he brilliantly realized his own precept by making Russian poetry out of the poetry of David Guramishvili, whose poem *Happy Spring*, also included in the anthology, is captivating for the delicacy of its verse sketches and the charming elegance of its form. Because they are subordinated to the music of the line, images that seem to be very vulgar, far from conventional decorum, are apprehended as a naive pastorale, an idyll imbued with a simple-hearted and shining smile. And the entire poem is translated with such a transparent, crystal pure line—hundreds and hundreds of stanzas, each characterized by a rhymed couplet in iambic hexameter alternating with couplets in tetrameter followed by an unrhymed trimeter clausula.

Zabolotsky has conveyed the stylistic distinctiveness of *Happy Spring* marvelously, with all its bright, naive tonality. He has brought Vazha Pshavela, and Akaky Tsereteli, and Ilya Chavchavadze into his native language with the same classically severe and sharply delineated line. It is difficult to imagine a poet he could not translate with the same perfection. Diversity of style never troubles him. Every style is equally close to him.

Art like this is accessible only to great masters of translation—the kind of translators who possess the priceless ability to overcome their own ego and transform themselves artistically into the author they translate. This demands not only talent, but also a special versatility, a plasticity, a "communality" of intellect. This communality of intellect was possessed to a great degree by Pushkin. When Dostoyevsky praised the poet in his "Pushkin Address" for his amazing ability to transform himself into "the geniuses of foreign nations," he referred not only to Pushkin's original creations, but also to his translations. "The greatest of the European poets," Dostoyevsky said, "could never incarnate with such power the genius of a foreign . . . people, its spirit, all the hidden depths of its spirit."[23] And Dostoyevsky cited, along with *The Miserly Knight* and "Egyptian Nights," such verse translations from English as the fourth scene from John Wilson's comedy *The City of the Plague* and the first pages of John Bunyan's devout treatise *Pilgrim's Progress*, which Pushkin translated under the title "The Pilgrim." I repeat: only mature masters, persons of high culture and finely refined taste, can take upon themselves the translation of foreign writers who are alien to them in style, and in convictions, and in temperament. These masters possess a very rare gift—they know how to curb their individual biases, sympathies, tastes for the sake of a most bold revelation of the creative personality they must recreate in translation.

In one of Kipling's stories a pompous and bombastic German says of his monkey that "there is too much Ego in its Cosmos." The same thing could be said about certain translators. For now-days the modern reader, a person of a profoundly scholarly culture, is more and more insistently demanding that translators suppress by all means their excessive Ego. For that matter, this demand has sounded forth over many years now. "In a translation of Goethe," said Belinsky, "we want to see Goethe, not his translator. If Pushkin himself were to undertake to translate Goethe, we would demand that he give us Goethe, not Pushkin."[24] The same demand was made on translators by Gogol. "The translator acted as if he were invisible," he wrote about one translation, "he turned himself into glass so transparent that it seems as if the glass were not there" (XIV, 170). This is by no means easy. It has to be learned. Hard training is needed here. The highest virtue here is the discipline to limit one's own sympathies and tastes. The distinguished translator of *The Iliad*, N. I. Gnedich, has pointed out that the greatest difficulty facing the translator of a poet of antiquity is "the incessant struggle with ones own spirit, with one's own internal powers, the freedom of which one must control constantly."[25] The "incessant struggle with one's own spirit," the overcoming of one's own personal aesthetics, is the duty of all translators, particularly those who translate great poets. In this case it is necessary to love the original author more than oneself and to serve the realization of his ideas and images selflessly, manifesting one's own ego only in this service and never foisting one's own tastes and sympathies on the original.

This would seem to be an easy matter—to translate a writer without beautifying him, without improving him—but in fact it is only through long struggle that a translator learns to suppress the temptation of his own personal creativity so as to become the original author's faithful and honorable friend rather than his presumptuous master. It has been a long time since I first translated Walt Whitman, and since that time I have repaired my translations for each new edition. Almost every repair job consists of a thorough casting out of the verbal ornaments and designs my lack of experience caused me to introduce into the first edition. Only by dint of long effort over a period of many years have I gradually neared the "vulgarity" which marks the original. And I fear that despite all my efforts I have not managed to this very day to convey the "unbridled slovenliness" of the original, for it is very easy to write better, more elegantly, than Whitman, but it is extremely difficult to write just as "badly" as he. Here I am mindful of Gnedich again:

> It is very easy to decorate, or better, to touch up Homer's lines with the colors of our own palette, and he becomes more foppish, more opulent, better for our tastes. But it is incomparably more difficult to preserve him as Homer, as he really is, no worse and no better. This is the translator's duty, and for he who has tried it, the task is not easy. Quintillian understood this perfectly: *facilius est plus facere, quam idem*, it is easier to do more than to do the same.   (316)

Consequently, Gnedich begged his readers "not to pass judgment if some trope or expression seems strange, unusual, but first check it against the original" (316). This ought to be every translator's plea to his readers.

Just as a good actor will manifest his individuality all the more brilliantly if he transforms himself, without leaving a trace, into the Falstaff, the Khlestakov, or the Chatsky he is portraying by implementing the sacred will of the playwright in his every gesture, so also a good translator manifests his personality in all its fullness when he completely subordinates himself to the will of the Balzac, Flaubert, Zola, Hemingway, Salinger, Joyce, or Kafka who is the subject of his translation.

Such self-restraint on the part of translators has by no means always been considered obligatory. In Pushkin's time, for example, journals constantly published statements to the effect that "to translate a poet into one's native language means either *to borrow a basic idea and adorn it with the riches of one's own vernacular* or to convey it faithfully into one's own language by divining the power of its poetic expression."[26] It was considered fully lawful to "adorn" a translated text "with the riches of one's own vernacular," because at that time the goals of translation were totally different. But now the time of adorned translations has passed. *Premeditated* departures from a translated text will never be permitted by our era because its attitude to the literature of all nations and peoples is above all cognitive.

And there is no reason to fear that such a translation will somehow depersonalize a translator or deprive him of the opportunity to display his artistic talent. This has never happened yet. If a translator is talented, the author's will will not fetter him, but, on the contrary, give him wings. The translator's art, like the actor's art, is totally dependent on *material*. Just as the highest achievement of the actor's art is not in departing from the dramatist's will, but in merging with it, in full subordination to it, so also the translator's art is, in its highest achievement, in a merging with the author's will. To many this seems debatable. The late Professor F.D. Batyushkov wrote in a polemic with me:

> The translator cannot be likened to an actor. . . . True, an actor is subordinate to an author's intention. But every artistic intention has a series of possibilities, and an artist creates one of these opportunities. Othello is Rossi, Othello is Salvini, Othello is Aldridge, Othello is Zacconi, and so on—these are all different Othellos on the canvas of Shakespeare's intention. And we know so many Hamlets, Lears, and so on, and so on, and so on. Duse created a Marguerite Gautier totally unlike Sarah Bernhardt's, and both are alive, each in her own way. A translator cannot take advantage of this freedom by "re-creating the text." He must reproduce what is there. The actor has opportunities to discover something new; the translator, like the philologist, cognizes what has been cognized.[27]

Professor Batyushkov's rebuttal crumbles at the very first contact with the facts. Could it be that *The Song of Igor's Campaign* has not been translated by forty-five translators in forty-five different ways? Could it be that each of these forty-five translations does not reflect the artistic personality of its translator with all his individual qualities in the same measure that an actor's artistic personality is reflected in each role? In the same way that there exists an Othello as Rossi, an Othello as Salvini, an Othello as Aldridge, an Othello as Dalsky, an Othello as Ostuzhev, an

Othello as Pastazyan, and so on, so also there exists a *Song of Igor's Campaign* as Georgy Shtorm, a *Song of Igor's Campaign* as Ivan Novikov, a *Song of Igor's Campaign* as Mark Tarlovsky, and so on, and so on. All these poets would seem to have "cognized what has been cognized" by other poets, but each "what has been cognized" is revealed anew, in other aspects. We know so many translations of Shota Rustaveli, and not a single one of them in any way resembles the others. And this variety is conditioned upon the same causes of the variety among different realizations of a given theatrical form—by temperament, by giftedness, by the cultural rigging of each poet-translator's mast.

So that Professor Batyushkov's rebuttal confirms even more strongly the truth he argues against. And of course, to the Soviet spectator the ideal actor is that gifted one who completely—in voice, gestures, and posture—transforms himself into Richard III, or Falstaff, or Khlestakov, or Krechinsky. And the actor's personality—be assured!—will be expressed in these plays in and of itself, regardless of their desires and efforts. Under no circumstances do they have to make a conscious effort to thrust forth their personal "I."

The same goes for translators. The modern reader values most only that translator who in his translations *makes an effort not to overshadow* Heine, or Ronsard, or Rilke with his own personality.

The poet Leonid Martynov does not want to agree with this. The very idea of curbing his own personal biases and tastes seems offensive to him. Turn himself into a transparent pane of glass? Never! Addressing himself to poets he translated with great care and diligence, Martynov has now told them proudly, in a poem included in an article on "The Problem of Translation," that "I've introduced *my* tunes into others texts," "I've added *my* sins onto theirs," "I've modernized their verses." Martynov is unable to follow the lead of his originals "like a fine lady in a dance, or in a dance macabre." He does not convey their finest nuances, "for this I cannot do, I have my *own* existence!" Martynov will not be a parrot imitating a cockatoo. Though your works are those of genius, Martynov tells his subjects, "I translate *my* way." We all have a right to add our sorrow to another's grief, Martynov now insists, "our *own* fire to another's smoldering embers."[28] (Emphases are mine. K.Ch.) This translator's declaration of independence rings forth proudly, even arrogantly. But we, the readers, presume, more modestly, that the translator's will is irrelevant here. After all, as we have just seen, every translator willy-nilly introduces some part of his personality into every translation he does. In all times and places translators have added their own sorrow to another's grief, their own fire to another's smoldering embers. And sometimes their own smoldering embers to another's fire.

In the *Hamlet* translated by Boris Pasternak we can hear Pasternak's voice, in the *Hamlet* translated by Mikhail Lozinsky we can hear Lozinsky's voice, in the *Hamlet* translated by Vlas Kozhevnikov we can hear Kozhevnikov's voice, and there's simply no help for it. It is a fait accompli. Artistic translations are artistic because they reflect, like any other work of art, the master who created them, whether or not he wishes it. We, the readers, greatly welcome the translations in which Martynov is in some way reflected, but we nevertheless make so bold as to note that we would be most grateful to him if, say, his translations of Sandor Petöfi reflected Martynov as little as possible and Petöfi as much as possible. And this, by the way, has been the case until now. Martynov, in response to his own conscience, has strived to reproduce each of Petöfi's images, feelings, and ideas as precisely as possible. But now another time has come, and Martynov suddenly and without warning notifies his readers that if he were to translate, say, *Hamlet*, his *Hamlet* would not be so much Shakespearian as Martynovian. Because he considers it demeaning to follow Shakespeare's lead "like a fine lady in a dance, or in a dance macabre."

I fear that, in reply to Martynov's declaration, his respectful readers will say that even though at some other time and under different circumstances they would read the translator's own poetry with great pleasure, now, when they happen to need a familiarity with Shakespeare's tragedy *Hamlet*, they believe they have a right to as little of Martynov and as much of Shakespeare in the translation as possible. Of course, no one would ever demand "parrot" translations from him. Everyone is perfectly content with his previous translations, in which he conveys the poetic enchantments of the originals so well. I still remember, for example, his translation of Petöfi's "National Song."[29] And I would like to believe that here, as in his other fine translations, despite his brash declaration, he applied all his efforts to conveying this proud Magyar song as precisely as possible. And this is undoubtedly what he did. We can confirm this quite easily by comparing identical lines in the talented translation by the Ukrainian poet Leonid Pervomaysky.[30] A comparison of the translations shows us that both translators strove exclusively to convey Petöfi's inspired poem as precisely, exactly, and faithfully as possible by using every available resource of their own language. Any other concern—as can be seen throughout—was nonexistent. The same striving inspired both translators when they translated another poem by Petöfi, his well-known "Fetters." It is just such translations—those which place documentary fidelity, precision, authenticity, and realism above all other values—that are demanded by our era. And should it be revealed in the future that despite all his striving the translator still reflects himself in his translations, he can be condoned, perhaps, only in the event it happens unconsciously. And since the basic nature of every human personality is expressed not only in its conscious, but also in its unconscious manifestations, the translator's will will be reflected sufficiently anyway. To strive to do this is superfluous. Let the translator strive only for an exact and objective reproduction of the original. By so doing he will not only not do anything detrimental to his own artistic personality, he will, on the contrary, manifest it with the greatest possible force. This is what Leonid Martynov has always done until now. Generally speaking, I somehow have the feeling that all this rebellion against "dances" is a momentary whimsy on the poet's part, a fleeting outburst, a caprice which, I hope, will not be reflected in his future translation work.

THREE

Imprecise Precision

> In his attempt to convey Milton *word for word*
> Chateaubriand was unable to sustain accuracy of
> thought and expression. A linear translation can
> never be accurate. —Pushkin
>
> What is very good in French can be impoverished by
> accuracy in Russian. —Sumarokov

1 Slips of the vocabulary are encountered very often in the work of even the greatest translators, and yet their translations are far more artistic (and this means more accurate) than the vast multitude of translations where every last word is conveyed with maximum precision. Lermontov once confused the English word "kindly" with the German word "das Kind" and translated Robert Burns's line, "Had we never loved so kindly," as, "If we'd not been children."[1] In translating Flaubert's *Hérodias*, Turgenev turned the word "daughter" into "son," thereby turning Salome into a man.[2] V.G. Belinsky translated the French word "vaisseaux" as "ships," where the original had to do with "arteries" (blood vessels). Valery Bryusov translated the name Cherubino as "cherubim"—which is to say that he turned a person into a little angel. And yet, these translations, as we know, have great literary merit.

Lexical discrepancies are very easily caught. If the original says "lion" and the translation has "dog," it is obvious the translator made a mistake. But if the translator misconstrues not individual words and phrases, but the basic coloration of an entire piece, if he offers safe and hackneyed verses instead of explosive, innovatively bold verses, sugary phrases in place of ardent ones, halting instead of flowing syntax—we are almost powerless to convince the ordinary reader a fraud has been foisted on him.

I remember an instance where lines from Pushkin's verse tale *Poltava* were translated into German and back into Russian. Just try, if you please, to prove that even though there are no concoctions or blunders in this translation, even though the translator scrupulously copied the original line for line, even though "horse" is conveyed as "horse" and "furs" as "furs" and "Kochubey" as "Kochubey," the translation is repugnant to anyone who is not completely indifferent to poetry.[3] It is as if Pushkin was taken over by Dostoyevsky's Captain Lebyadkin, the very same Lebyadkin in *The Possessed* who composed the famous masterpiece:

> There once was a bug,
> A bug from his childhood,
> Who fell in a mug
> All full of fly food.

If we were to make our first acquaintance with Pushkin's work in a translation as cheap as this doggerel, we would conclude he was a blockheaded cretin.

Here is the chief tragedy of the art of translation: it often slanders the original author. I can testify that at this very time foreign journals and books are being published containing multitudes of translations of Tyutchev, Koltsov, Mayakovsky, Blok, Anna Akhmatova, Pasternak, and Esenin which are no more like their originals than the lines mentioned above are like Pushkin. But there is nothing more difficult than exposing this kind of slander, because it is stated not in words or phrases but in elusive tonalities of speech for which no methods of definition have yet been worked out. A literal translation—or as the early-nineteenth-century keeper of the Academy Dictionary Admiral A.S. Shishkov put it, a "slavish" translation—can never be artistic. A precise, literal copy of a poetic work is the most imprecise and false of all translations. The same can be said of translations of artistic prose.

As if just to prove this truth, a translation of Charles Dickens's novel *Oliver Twist* appeared in the thirties which was dictated in its entirety by a desire to give the Russian reader the most precise possible copy of the phraseology of the original. The desire is most considerate, but the result is deplorable. The "most precise possible copy" became a clumsy muddle, a fact that can be very easily demonstrated by examining one impossible sentence—one all too typical of the translation as a whole. The sentence actually has three relative clauses based on the word *kotoryi*, 'which, who': "the back wall *of which*," "three men *who*," "in a silence *which*." Now, in accordance with English grammar it is perfectly permissible to construct a sentence on multiple relative clauses. But as we all know, multiple *"kotoryi*-clauses" are extremely awkward in Russian. The Russian sentence has to be read aloud (without fail aloud!) in order to hear what nonsense has resulted from this maximally precise copy of the original foreign syntax. We have no right to blame Dickens for the clumsy phraseology here, because the sentence in the original is elegant, simple, and light:

> In an upper room of one of these houses—a detached house of fair size, ruinous in other respects, but strongly defended at door and window: of which house the back commanded a ditch in a manner already described—there were assembled three men, who, regarding each other now and then with looks expressive of perplexity and expectation, sat for some time in profound and gloomy silence.[4]

This translation was done by A.V. Krivtsova. Similar muddles of syntax in Russian, resulting from a direct conveyance of constructions permissible in English but not in Russian, can be found on every page of her translation. In one instance we find another *"kotoryi*-clause" used in an again impossible way to translate directly the sentence, "I, that know so much and could hang so many besides myself" (359). "I, that" is perfectly permissible in English, but a Russian sentence that begins with *Ia, kotoryi,* 'I, which,' is deplorable. In the translation of the sentence, "the gross air of the world has not had time to breathe upon the changing dust it hallowed" (149), we find an abuse of a demonstrative pronoun that again sounds terrible in Russian: *dlia toi griazi*, 'for the sake of *that* dust.' In the translation of the sentence, "Occasionally, when there was some more than usually interesting inquest upon a parish child who had been overlooked in turning up a bedstead, or inadvertently scalded to death. . ." (11), we again find a clumsy misuse of multiple relative clauses in Russian. Three clauses based on the pronoun "who" is simply not permissible in Russian. For the sentence, "the fist had been too often impressed upon his body not to be deeply impressed upon his recollection" (14), we again find a clumsy Russian syntax resulting from a direct conveyance of the original English syntax. Translated directly back into English it would read, "in order so as like not to be impressed upon." All of these constructions in the translation are fully permissible in accordance with the rules of English sentence formation, but they are deplorable in Russian. In each instance the precise imitation of foreign syntax caused the translator to violate the syntactic structure of her own language. Because of this system of translation we encounter awkward turns of speech throughout the Russian text.

Unhappily, in Moscow in the thirties there was a whole school of translators such as this, adherents all of a mechanistic method. The school was very influential. In addition to A.V. Krivtsova and Evgeny Lann, it included (with certain stipulations) I. Aksyonov, V. Yarkho, Georgy Shengeli, and many others. The school left a whole series of translations which are hopelessly ugly because they are based on a fallacious theory.

2 This school had numerous forebears in the nineteenth century. In the words of V.B. Obolevich in an article on the role of scientific knowledge in criticism of the translator in *Theory and Criticism of Translation* (162), these translators produced calques "word for word, sentence for sentence, clause for clause, with absolutely no creative thought given to imagery, characterization, style, the artistic fabric of original works. . . . Hundreds of colorless, mediocre translations flowed from the pens of these representatives of the 'precise' calque-translation who perverted . . . the truth of a writer, his talent, and the ideological and artistic bases of original works."

This pursuit of the phantom of external formalistic precision has been the ruin of many works translated into Russian, among them those translated by Evgeny Lann. Lann was a conscientious literary worker, an expert on language, but a literalist and pedant. He should have translated business documents or scientific pamphlets, which demand documentary precision, but at some fatal moment he decided to devote a whole year of his life, perhaps even more, to translating Dickens's *Pickwick Papers*, one of the most humerous books ever written. The translation, which was done with A.V. Krivtsova, was published in a very large printing (600,000) in the thirty-volume *Collected Works of Charles Dickens*, and although each line of the original text is reproduced with mathematical precision, not a trace has survived of Dickens's youthful, sparkling, stormy hilarity. The result is a ponderous, tedious book which no one has the strength to read to the end. Which is to say that it is the most imprecise of all existing translations, and perhaps even of all possible translations of this book. Instead of translating laughter into laughter and smiles into smiles, Lann and his accomplice Krivtsova translated each word and sentence like diligent schoolchildren, with no concern for reproducing the original's intonations of living speech or its emotional coloration.

This method of translation makes a great impression on people who know nothing about art. It seems to them that a method of this sort guarantees the translation will be adequate to the original. In actual fact—I repeat again—this straining for pedantic precision leads inescapably, irrevocably, to imprecision. It is impossible in reading Lann's translation not to be reminded of the old translation of *Pickwick Papers* done by Irinarkh Vvedensky. We will have something to say about Vvedensky later. Suffice it for now to say that even though there are more than a few concoctions and omissions in his translation it is still far more precise than Lann's because it conveys the most important thing—the humor. Vvedensky was himself a humorist, one of those young contemporaries of Gogol for whom *Dead Souls* was the greatest event in their lives. Vvedensky's *Pickwick Papers* reverberates with echoes of Gogol. This is why anyone who became acquainted with Vvedensky's *Pickwick Papers* in his youth will remember to his dying day Sam Waller, and Mr. Jingle, and Mrs. Bardell, and Mr. Snodgrass with the same grateful and enthusiastic laughter that he remembers Gogol's Manilov, Nozdryov, Selifan, and Korobochka. I do not claim that Vvedensky's translation is a perfect model. I repeat—it has many defects and it cannot be recommended to readers nowadays. I want to say only that it is immeasurably closer in all its spirit to the great original than the pedantically "precise," painstaking, but spiritless version put out by our late literalists.

And can there be any doubt that the immense success enjoyed by the Finnish writer Lassila's two satirical novellas *To Get Some Matches* and *Risen from the Dead* is a direct consequence of their being translated into Russian by Zoshchenko?[5] It is precisely because Zoshchenko was himself an extraordinary satirist, who hated with all his heart the idiocy of the philistine life against which his Finnish colleague also struggled, that he was able to translate the satires with such perfection.

3 We have just seen that there is absolutely no basis for the illusions of naive readers who imagine that the most artistic translation is that which most precisely copies the phraseology of the original. It is just as easy to prove that a precise reproduction of each individual word will fail as surely as calques of syntax to give an accurate impression of the original. In the first place, a word in one language has associations entirely different from those of the same word in another language. Every language has a hierarchy of words. The style of one and the same word even in two similar languages is completely different. Take even so universal a Slavic word as *mat'*, 'mother.' A precise translation of this simple word would not seem to offer any difficulty. But in fact there are instances where it is simply impossible to place an equal sign between the Russian word for mother and the Ukrainian word for mother. For the sake of experiment here, let's take the lines in Taras Shevchenko's poem *Kobzar* in which a serf maiden tenderly whispers the word three times: "Mati . . . mati . . . mati!" In Ukrainian the word sounds perfectly tender and romantic here. It would seem to be a very easy matter to translate this line into Russian, but not a single Russian translator has succeeded in doing it. The nineteenth-century poet L. A. Mey translated it as three exclamations, a conveyance which to me seems most strange considering that it is a whisper from the lips of a romantic maiden. Instead of the slow, grieving meditation of the original, it comes out as a shouted patter: "Mat'! Mat'! Mat'!"[6] Fyodor Sologub translated the same words in a different way, but with what seems to me the same lack of success. His serf maiden babbles out the inappropriately vulgar diminutive *matka*![7] It is easy to laugh at such translations, of course, but just how, in fact, is the Ukrainian word *mati* to be translated into Russian? Another poet, in his translation of *Topolya,* introduced the Ukrainian word *mamo* directly. This is hardly admissible, if only because the word *mamo* does not exist in Russian, but also because it is in the vocative case (which is also nonexistent in Russian) and is joined with the word for father in the nominative case, something which truly grammatical usage does not permit.

Artistic language, as we know, is entirely a matter of stylistic nuances and tonality. Shevchenko's poetry is difficult to translate into Russian because Ukrainian and Russian words seem to be similar and are identical in their roots, but their nuances and tonalities differ completely in style. There would seem to be no difference between the Russian word *mat'* and the Ukrainian word *mati*, but, as we have just seen, there are instances where words—or more precisely, the nuances which have been acquired by words in two languages—do not coincide. When a Ukrainian utters the words *mamo* or *mati*, the words are fully consonant in his linguistic consciousness with words of the highest style. Thus, in his imitation of the prophet Hosea, Shevchenko could use the word *mamo* in context with a most solemn biblical exclamation. But when Sologub translated this cry as "Rise, mama!" it became a parodistic vaudevillian mixture of styles, because in a Russian's linguistic consciousness the word *mama* is a private, intimate word, equally as inappropriate for solemn biblical speech as, for example, the too cute diminutives *mamasha* or *mamenka*: "Rise, mamenka!" The lack of stylistic adequacy between the two identical sounding words is obvious here: "Rise, mamasha!"

And just imagine what can be said for words in languages which do not have such a close kinship! Let's take as an example Russian and . . . Uzbek. As often as not it happens that the meaning of words can be identical in two different languages, but their stylistic coloration is different. In Russian the word for "liver" is perceived as a low-style word. It is often used in its scornful diminutive form, as in the folk sayings, "You stick in my liver," or, "Don't shout, you make my liver leap." Thus, when the most refined of Uzbek poets addresses his sweetheart and says, "Thy beauty wounds my liver," a verbatim translation would be utterly imprecise, because an Uzbek understands the word "liver" in a completely different way from a Russian. It is therefore impossible to place an equal sign between the words in the two languages. Or take the Russian word for "parrot." In our language the word is contemptuous: "You babble like a parrot." But in Uzbek the word for parrot is a canonical word of love for one's sweetheart. Uzbek has such constants as, "You are my adorable parrot," or, "I am ready to perish for a single glance from you, my cruel parrot," so that in this instance a verbatim translation would be imprecise, because a word which in the environment of one language evokes tenderness and endearment is in the environment of another language a contemptuous snort, a jeer. Or take the simple word in Russian for "aunt." In English this word is neutral. But in Russian its very sound—*tyo–tya*—places it in the ranks of comical words. Thus, if the line from Ben Jonson—"But my aunt is the Countess Esmund!"—were to be translated into Russian verbatim, the verbatim conveyance would be elusive because the style of one and the same word in two different languages is completely different. This applies to thousands and thousands of words. And not only with regard to style.

Not even the semantics of words in Russian and other languages very often coincide. For a Russian the word *pravda* has two different meanings—"truth" and "justice." When Pushkin's Salieri, in the little tragedy *Mozart and Salieri*, declaims: "It is said, there is no justice on this earth, / But neither is there justice on high," he uses the word *pravda* in its moral sense. But when we read in Pushkin's *Boris Godunov*, "The truth emerged from the fog," the word *pravda* has a quite different meaning—that something corresponds fully to reality.[8] But it is simply not possible to say that the first usage is devoid of a shadow of the meaning of the second or that the second lacks some nuance of the first. In a Russian's linguistic consciousness the triumph of truth is identical to the triumph of justice. In other languages, so far as I am aware, this concept does not have such an expansive, polysemantic word.

I have given an extreme example here, but there are multitudes of such examples. The English word "man" would seem to correspond perfectly to the Russian word *chelovek*, but the Russian word means "person" as well as "man." Just try translating a Russian sentence into English to the effect that a woman is a beautiful person using the English word "man." You will be laughed at, because in English the word "man" refers only to a male person. In English the sentence would come out as, "This woman is a beautiful man." Many people think that every Russian word has exactly the same meaning in other languages. Thus, if words were to be cast in the form of small discs, each French disc, let's say, would supposedly match its equivalent Russian disc fully and perfectly. In fact, this almost never happens. Take a disc and write the word *pravda* on it, then take another disc and write the French word *verité* on it. Now, try to place the one on top of the other. You will find that they do not match. One disc will cover a portion to one side of the other disc. The portion I have shaded in the diagram here is the portion covered; the rest remains untouched.

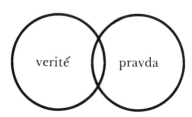

I borrowed this diagram from Admiral A.S. Shishkov's venerable book, *A Discourse on the Old and New Style of the Russian Language* (1803). Shishkov wrote:

One and the same word of one language in different parts of speech is expressed sometimes by the same word and sometimes by a different word of another language. We can explain this with examples. Let's suppose that a disc determining the designation of a French verb—for example, *toucher*—is A, and that this verb corresponds to, or its concept is represented by, the verb in the Russian language *trogat'*, the disc of designation of which will be B. Here, in the first place, it

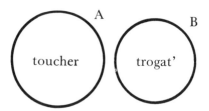

is necessary to note that these two discs will never be equal to each other in such a way that one of them, being placed on top of the other one, will completely cover it; but one will always be larger or smaller than the other one; and in fact they can never be evenly centered as shown here. But rather they will always transect each

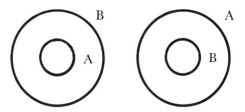

other and will be positioned as shown in the following diagram. C is the portion common to both discs, that is, that portion where the French verb *toucher* corresponds to the Russian verb *trogat'*, or can be expressed by it, as for example, in the following phrases: *toucher avec les mains* / *trogat' rukami*. E is the portion of the disc of the French

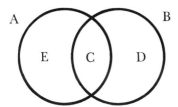

verb *toucher* located outside the disc B signifying the Russian verb *trogat'*, as for example in the following phrase: *toucher le clavacin.* Here the French verb *toucher* cannot be expressed by the Russian verb *trogat'*, for we do not say "touch the clavichord," but "play on the clavichord"; and therefore the French verb *toucher* corresponds here to the Russian verg *igrat'*, 'to play.' D is the portion of the disc of the Russian verb *trogat'* located outside disc A signifying the French verb *toucher,* as for example in the following phrase: *tronut'sia s mesta,* 'to get underway.' Here the Russian verb *trogat'* cannot be expressed by the French verb *toucher,* inasmuch as it is unnatural for the French to say: *Se toucher d'une place;* they explain this with the verb *partir.* And so, in this case the Russian verb *trogat'* corresponds to the French verb *partir.* Considered this way, it can be seen clearly that the units of speech in one language do not resemble the units of speech in another language, and that in any case words acquire their force and significance in the first place from the roots from which they originate and in the second place from usage. . . . Every people has its own units of speech and its own linkages of concepts.[9]

Everyone knows that Shishkov drew some highly ridiculous conclusions from his observations, but this does not at all mean that the observations themselves are not true. His idea applies to a multitude of words and emphasizes once again the idea that so-called precise (literal) translations are never and can never be precise, and that a servile copying of every single word is the most false of all translations. One of our most authoritative linguists, A.A. Reformatsky, in an article titled "Linguistic Problems of Translation," has stated this quite accurately:

> The Czech adverb *akorat* means "exactly," that is, more generally what we signify in Russian by *akkurat*. But the Czech *akorat* cannot be translated with the Russian *akkurat* in its meaning of "accurately" because in Russian this is a colloquialism and in Czech it is not. The Czech verb *znasz* coincides with surprising closeness with the Russian *znash'*, but in Russian the word is a dialectism and in Czech a literary form. And one other phonetic example: in Russian the word *andel* (instead of *angel*) is a phenomenon of Northern Great Russian dialects, while *andel* in Czech is a standard phonetic form of the literary language.[10]

The well-known Ukrainian theorist of the art of translation, Oleksy Kundzich, lists in an article in *The Craft of Translation* the mistakes and lapses of translators who naively hold to the belief in a conceptual equivalency of words which sound alike but are different in meaning. "The Ukrainian word *babka*," he reminds us, "is not at all the same as the Russian word *baba*, because Russian *baba* refers to any woman, while Ukrainian *babka* refers to an old woman. The title of the Ukrainian translation of Gogol's *Evenings on a Farm near Dikanka* uses not the direct equivalent for the Russian word *vechera*, which signifies both 'evenings' and evenings as 'parties' or 'celebrations,' but the Ukrainian word *vechornytsi*, which signifies only the second meaning." Kundzich concludes from this that "literalism is not only a disfiguration of words, a mutilation of phrases, and a violation of language, it is, in addition, a violation of artistic images and a distortion of the reality depicted in a work of art" (1959, 11).

A great many such testimonies could be cited here. An expert on Russian literature, the poet and translator Maurice Baring, has offered a correct observation about the Russian word *skuchno*, 'boring.' Commenting on two lines of Krylov's fable "The Two Pigeons," to the effect that the two pigeons were sometimes sad, but never bored, he noted that to a Russian the lines sound poetic, but to an Englishman the word "boring" is so prosaic that it could never be used in a translation of Krylov's fable. Baring had to translate the lines in an explanatory fashion: "Sadness they knew: / But weary of each other never grew."[11]

I knew Maurice Baring slightly. I met him in 1916 in Belgium at the front where he headed a squadron of British military pilots. I recall that we once had a chat about the English word "friend." He told me that it is as far from corresponding to the Russian word *drug* as the French word *ami*. A French movie star can quite freely scrawl *à mon ami* when autographing his picture for someone he has just met. And an Englishman considers it permissible to inscribe his book "to my friend so-and-so" when he gives a copy to a Russian he does not know very well. It would be absurd for a Russian to read into this word the same meaning it has in his native language. For an Englishman or a Frenchman the word is often likely to be more cold, reserved. To place an equal sign between these words and the Russian word *drug* is hardly ever possible. The same thing applies to the English word "dear," which to judge from all the dictionaries is equivalent to our word *dorogoi*. In fact, it is used in dry, official contexts, as in "Dear Sir," or "Dear Mr. Randall," and is more in keeping with out word *uvazhaemyi,* 'esteemed.' The translator who would translate this word precisely would be making a serious mistake.

4 Once, some time ago, I saw Molière's comedy *Tartuffe* at the Moscow Art Theater in a translation identified as "by an unknown poet." But after the first few lines I was overcome by a distant, familiar memory from my childhood. It was the same translation which, three-quarters of a century before, when I was five or six years old, I used when playing *Tartuffe* with my older sister. For me the best part of the whole play was of course the part where Orgon hides under the table and suddenly leaps out at the villainous Tartuffe. I was convinced this was the most important part of the whole play. When I leaped out from under the table I recited the lines where Orgon tells the good-for-nothing Tartuffe he can scarcely believe what he has just heard, and my sister would reply in rhymed lines that I had made my appearance too soon and should crawl back under the table to hear the rest. "How can a man be so dishonorable and base!" I would declaim, enraptured by the sound of the rhymes and shaking my six-year-old fist with immense enjoyment. And then I would throw myself at Tartuffe, grab him by the seat of the pants, and reproach him in a loud voice. It was especially this part that I recalled when I saw it on the stage of the Moscow Art Theater, and I enjoyed it as though I had just run into an old friend. I even confess to a bit of envy that now it was the actor Toropkov under the table instead of me. As it turned out, they were using the old translation by V.S. Likhachev, as I learned from the torn cover of the book from which I had played my favorite role three-quarters of a century before. In our time many would consider this translation imprecise, if only because it was done not in alexandrines, but in iambic lines of varying length à la Griboyedov in his play *Woe from Wit*. The original is composed in entirety of rhymed couplets alternating in strict order, while the translation violates this order by preserving or not preserving the rhymes in accordance with the translator's whim.

Another translation has been made of the same play by Mikhail Lozinsky. It conscientiously reproduces both the monotonous rhythm of the original and the alternation of rhymed couplets. It might be asked, therefore, why a theater with such a strong literary tradition, famed for its careful regard for texts, rejected Lozinsky's precise translation and preferred the "less precise" translation by Likhachev. After all, the indicators of precision are obvious in Lozinsky's modern translation: it is equirhythmic, it has the same number of lines, the same rhyme system, the same caesuras as the original, and it conveys the archaic quality of Molière's language. And yet, despite my esteem for Lozinsky's talent, I must say that I understand perfectly well why the Moscow Art Theater preferred Likhachev's translation to his. As surprising as it may seem, the old translation is more accurate, closer to the original, even though it lacks the indicators of precision which typify Lozinsky's. After all, when Molière's contemporaries saw the play on the stage, it did not sound in the least archaic to them. They were not separated from Molière by the wall of conventionally restored and stylized speech that resounds in Lozinsky's translation. In addition, in the context of French verse traditions, the alexandrine line does not seem in the least alien, stilted, bombastic. For a Frenchman it is perfectly natural. The French are as used to Molière's alexandrines as we are to, say, the rhythms of Nekrasov or the iambic tetrameter. As a result, there is no way that an equal sign can be placed between the way a poetic form was felt in France in the seventeenth century and the way it is felt by modern Soviet citizens. Implicit here is a diverse complex of historically conditioned feelings. What is the most important thing about Molière? The laughter, of course. The laughter, now funny, now bitter, that has sounded forth from the stage for four centuries the world over. Therefore, we must consider the most precise translation of Molière to be not that which pedantically conveys the stanzaic construction and rhythm of the original, but that which provokes the same youthful, infectious laughter as the original. And the truth is that Lozinsky's translation has none of this laughter. The work is somehow stiff, ponderous, forced. And so it is little wonder that when a vigorously alive theater needs to present a vigorously alive Molière on the stage—and not a musty restoration of Molière—

it turns to a translation which perhaps failed to preserve the illusory superficial conditions of precision, but conveyed in the most precise possible way the spiritual essence of Molière himself. I say this with full respect for Lozinsky, before whose great merits I am the first to bow. But I consider this instance regarding *Tartuffe* to be a very clear illustration of the chief thesis of this chapter, namely that any translator who strives for the most precise possible conveyance of an original text by following the dictates of exclusively formal principles, and who imagines that the most important thing in a translation of a poetic work is to convey only the stanzaic structure, the rhythm, the number of lines, the rhyme scheme, will never achieve precision, for poetic precision is not to be found in these things. Let's recall here Vasily Kurochkin's immortal translations of Béranger. Everyone knows he introduced a multitude of concoctions and personal fancies into his translations.[12] And then recall Vsevolod Rozhdestvensky, a highly experienced and cultured poet who reproduced in his own translations of Béranger the same number of lines as the original, and the meter, and the rhyme alternations, and the enjambment, and the character of the vocabulary, and many, many other elements of the original. And yet his translations are less precise, because they convey to a much lesser degree the poetic enchantment of Béranger's poetry, its musical character, its lyricism.

5   Or let's recall the translations of Samuil Marshak, translations which are all the more powerful because they are not done letter by letter, but with humor as humor and beauty as beauty. Let's take a look at his translation of Robert Burns's poem, "Is There for Honest Poverty." The first quatrain of the third stanza reads like this in the original:

> Ye see yon birkie ca'd "a lord,"
>   Wha struts, an' stares, an' a' that?
> Tho hundreds worship at his word,
>   He's but a cuif for a' that.[13]

If some literalist pedant happened to read Marshak's translation of this quatrain, he would be sure to shout to high heaven that the translator makes no mention whatsoever of the "birkie," or the way the author's despised aristocrat "struts, an' stares," or the "hundreds" who "worship at his word." He would complain that the translator turned "birkie" into "fool," and "lord" into "high-born lord."[14] But to anyone who loves poetry it is clear that Marshak's conveyance is as precise as possible: it conveys spendidly Burns's angrily contemptuous, sarcastic intonations, his hatred of haughty oppressors. Even more, it is a marvelous re-creation of the poem's swift aphoristic character. Marshak did an equally splendid job with the first quatrain of the second stanza:

> What though on hamely fare we dine,
>   Wear hoddin' grey, an' a' that?
> Gie fools their silks, and knaves their wine—
>   A man's a man for a' that.   (328)

Even though Marshak added "drink" to "dine" in the first line and changed "wear hoddin' grey" to "cover ourselves with rags" in the second—in order to make the rhyme *p'iom–trap'iom*—and even the imperative of the third line of the original is changed to the indicative in the translation, the ideas and emotions of the original are expressed with maximum precision. So also is the entire system of poetic images: fools and knaves still have their silks and wine, and a man is still a man for all that (183).

In my opinion, one of Marshak's greatest achievements is his translation of Burns's poem, "The Lass That Made the Bed." The subject of this poem is risqué, well calculated to outrage narrow-minded bigots raised on prudish parlor love songs. It is a frank tale, with no omissions, of a young traveler's nocturnal intimacy with an unknown lass who makes his bed. Every word is replete with unblushing, ardent passion. But there is so much purity, humanity, and tenderness in the passion, such a reverent delight with the lass, that one would have to be a boor to detect even a shadow of indecorum in it. The first quatrain of the second stanza reads like this in the original:

> I bow'd fu' low unto this maid,
>   And thank'd her for her courtesie,
> I bow'd fu' low unto this maid,
>   An' bade her mak a bed to me.   (397)

In Marshak's translation there is not a single departure from the original. Even the repeated line, "I bow'd fu' low unto this maid," is reproduced almost word for word. The second quatrain of the stanza reads like this:

> She made the bed baith large and wide,
>   Wi' twa white hands she spread it down,
> She put the cup to her rosy lips,
>   And drank:—"Young man, now sleep ye soun'."   (397)

In his translation of this quatrain Marshak cast out the "young man." In Russian this epithet has an ironic, vulgar character—"Hey, you, young man!" And although the original has a bed that is "baith large and wide," Marshak replaced this with the epithet "modest bed" in order to sustain in Russian the chaste tone that adorns the poem throughout. He also added the words "fine sheets" to the quatrain (the image does not appear in the original until the first quatrain of the last stanza), but on the other hand the lass's actions are conveyed in strict accordance with the original—albeit in different words. Further on in the poem the first quatrain of the fifth stanza reads like this:

> Her bosom was the driven snaw,
>   The drifted heaps sae fair to see;
> Her limbs the polish'd marble stane,
>   The lass that made the bed to me!   (398)

This quatrain is reproduced in the translation with a splendidly poetic boldness. Marshak replaced the third line with a reference to the breath of "early winter"; this epithet is so in harmony with the lass's youth that it is perfectly faithful to Burns even though not present in the original. And can one cavil that Marshak translates Burns's fourteen stanzas in fifteen, and that he adds two lines characterizing the lass as "pure as a mountain snowstorm" and another two lines that the years go by and snowstorms are followed by flowers?

The overall tone of the original—noble, crystal clear, translucent—is conveyed with amazing precision. The Russian reader of Marshak's "The Lass That Made the Bed" obtains the same impression from his bold and bright lines as an Englishman or Scotsman from the original. To some literalist the translator's twice-introduced simile between the lass's curls and intoxication, in place of Burns's line, "Her hair was like the links o' gowd," will seem an impermissible liberty. Marshak's translation does not have the lines, "Her teeth were like the ivorie," or, "Her limbs the polish'd marble stane," and his lass does not have rosy cheeks or white hands—in Russian these would be hackneyed clichés. He eliminated the recherché metaphor, "Her cheeks like lilies dipt in wine." In Russian the metaphor would sound pretentious and destroy the original poem's priceless simplicity. Such willfulness with the original can seem excessive. But Marshak is a poet, and in order for the poem to sound forth in his translation with all its music, he was right to sacrifice dozens of secondary details. One of the remarkable features of Burns's poem is the six-times repeated refrain, "The lass that made the bed to me!" In Marshak's version the refrain is repeated only four times. Nevertheless, I consider his translation to be ideal. Its merit is that it re-creates not Burns's lines per se, but Burns himself, his style, his pathos and humor, the very essence of his personality, his spirit.

Other translators have not detected Burns's multifaceted personality, they have not realized that this "farmer poet" had a command of the most diverse genres, the most diverse styles.

Marshak was the first to perceive this. He re-created Burns as just this universal genius, with a soul like a rich keyboard. His Burns is not just an idyllic plowman, not just a sweet singer of love, not just an apostle of freedom, universal brotherhood, and peace, but each and every one of these things, and in addition a humorist whose laughter—now mischievous, now noble, now angry—can be heard in *The Jolly Beggars*, and in *Tam o'Shanter*, and in *The Holy Fair* where bigots and zealots are given mighty boxes on the ear. It is thanks to Marshak alone that we have witnessed how easily a hearty, truly Shakespearian laughter gives way in Burns's poetry to a heroic pathos, to proud and splendid hymns to the glory of beautiful Scotland.

And it turns out to be complete nonsense that Burns was the dull simpleton, the composer of homemade, rough-hewn verses he has been made to seem by his Russian translators of previous times. Quite the contrary. Now he has stepped forth before us as one of the most refined stylists, a man of fine, irreproachable taste, a remarkable virtuoso of poetic forms. Marshak has succeeded in this because he is himself an artist of many styles who has done brilliant work in several seemingly incompatible genres—and is besides a highly skilled craftsman of the line, a remarkable master of the craft of words who is able to command the most unmanageable rhythms and rhymes. And of course, no skill could enable him to create such marvelous translations unless he was a poet. "Such versatility and fortuitous ingenuity in the use of the resources of the Russian language for the re-creation of the poetic fabric of another language," says Alexander Tvardovsky, "is of course to be explained not by the fact that S. Marshak is a skillfull virtuoso translator—in poetry it is not possible to be a specialist in the virtuoso—but by the fact that he is an authentic poet who possesses in full measure a vital creative regard for his own native word."[15] To this it must be added that brilliant literary technique plays a role here. Marshak is a poet. This is why Marshak's best translations of Burns do not sound like translations—they have such a high-quality texture, such vital naturalness in every gesture and intonation, such rich musical character, such light, free diction typical only of authentic original poetry, that the reader actually experiences the illusion that Burns is not a foreigner among us, but close kin.

This could never have happened if Marshak had renounced his creative methods to chase off in pursuit of literal precision. His translations would have turned into malicious distortions of the great original, as happened to Shelley's poetry when the tedious literalist V.D. Merkureva took it into her head to translate Shelley into Russian—thirty years after Balmont's translations which we discussed in the preceding chapter.

6 Merkureva's translations have none of that inflated Balmontism in them. Lightness is not among their qualities. Their solidness commands respect. Seemingly, the Soviet reader was finally offered the opportunity to become acquainted with the real poetry of the great revolutionary poet. The translator Merkureva has diligently met all of the strictest demands imposed on the translation of poetry by the sternest of pedants. The number of lines in her translations is always equal to the number of lines in the original text. The rhythm of the original and the order of the rhyme alternations are preserved most punctiliously. But there is not so much as a hint of the real Shelley here. Instead of Shelley we are given an unfortunate stutterer, a composer of unreadable doggerel whose meaning we have to guess at as in a charade:

> Be it calm,
> Blessed thy sleep,
> Like those who fell, not ours—through sobs.

Just imagine two hundred pages of poetry translated into such gibberish as this. Just who is it in this translation, that incomprehensible "not ours" who falls somewhere through mysterious sobs? The phraseology is so sluggish and confusing that one is obliged to force one's way as if through barbed wire to the meaning of almost every stanza. In the original poem, "Hellas," the lines read:

> Be thy sleep
> Calm and deep,
> Like theirs who fell—not ours who weep![16]

And this difficulty of access and tediousness of speech comes through in the translations as Shelley's *chief quality*, when in fact the quality could not be more unlike Shelley. Shelley is one of the most musical of all poets in all of world literature. The transparency of his style is fascinating. But in her translation of *Peter Bell the Third* Merkureva foisted her own impossibly phrased, crudely phonetic concoctions on Shelley: "the super-equatorial climate of Hades," "the butt of witticisms unable to withstand a hail of derision." She even threw in her own gratuitous references to Scaramouche and Othello where they do not exist in the original text. Every single line of the original is as clear as "the simple scales." The lines are additionally attractive because they are humorous. But Merkureva's translation offers not so much as a hint of a smile. And more important, no matter how you strain to decipher her translation, you will never fathom what she could possibly mean by such concoctions as that "butt of witticisms unable to withstand a hail of derision," or how the "climate" can wrap this butt of witticisms in a hail of derision (54).

All this seems particularly instructive to me. After all, there can be no doubt that while she worked on this translation Merkureva was sure she was creating the most precise possible copy of the original. And this delusion is quite understandable, because the translation exhibits every formal indicator of precision. But she forgot one indicator—the light and free poetic diction that is inherent to Shelley's lyricism. In her chief concern for preserving each and every one of the original rhyme schemes, she tries to cram the entire sum of Shelley's poetic ideas and images into cast-iron rhythm frames. These frames are so tight for the Russian verse line that the translator—whether she wishes it or not—is obliged to mangle and shred and mash the line in order to squeeze it into them. Merkureva pitilessly crams line after line into the unyielding scheme of Shelley's prosody and does not even want to notice that the operation fatally mutilates every line until there is not a breath of life or beauty left! Just imagine what her mutilations do to a poem like Shelley's "Hellas":

> Alas! if love, whose smile makes this obscure world splendid,
> Can change with its false times and tides,
>   Like hope and terror,—
>   Alas for love! (475)

In her translation Merkureva turns these fine lines into:

> Alas! Can love, whose smile makes the world shine,
> Betray, if she is lied to by
>   Fear and hope—
>   Alas for love! (111)

And these mutilations number in the thousands! The entire book is a virtual mortuary where the verses of a genius which have been loved for their peerless beauty and harmony are laid out in unnatural poses like bloodless, lifeless corpses.

For example, where Shelley has:

> In sacred Athens, near the fane
> Of wisdom, Pity's altar stood. (479)

the translator turns these lines into pure absurdity by cramming them into an unyielding rhyme scheme:

> In Athens—Wisdom is glorificator,
> And near it—Pity's altar. (102)

Lack of sense is nothing to this translator so long as she meets the demands of formalism! This sort of translation could be turned over to an electronic machine which no one would expect to convey the poetic charm of the original. As a matter of fact, I think that in another five years a machine will be perfected which can far surpass a translation such as this.

Like Byron, Shelley detested to the core of his very being the reactionary dictator of England, Lord Castlereagh. Lord Castlereagh's ally was Prince George (the future King George IV). Shelley dictated to these two foes of democracy a cruel satire titled "Similes for Two Political Characters of 1819." The satire contains these lines:

> As a shark and dogfish wait
> Under an Atlantic isle
> For the Negro-ship whose freight
> Is the theme of their debate,
> Wrinkling their red gill the while—   (573)

Gone from Merkureva's translation are the Atlantic isle, the dogfish, the red gill—everything that makes these lines concrete has been banished, and in their place we are given a pair of sharks, a vigilant watch, a booming ocean, and a tasty freight (163)! The translation leaves us wondering how one of the most musical of all English poets could resort to such cacophonic rhymes as *vakht– frakht*. Fortunately, there is at least a semblance of the intonations inherent in human speech in the translation of these lines, but Merkureva's version of the poem's opening lines sounds like something else entirely. The lines of the original go as follows:

> As from an ancestral oak
> Two empty ravens sound their clarion,
> Yell by yell and croak by croak,
> When they scent the noonday smoke
> Of fresh human carrion.   (573)

A niggardly crampedness can be felt in every line of Merkureva's translation. For the precise trochaic line, "When they scent the noonday smoke," she provided such a clumsy iambic phrase— "Chut' pákhnet pólden' zhárok"—that it is difficult to imagine how she could have done worse (163). By forcing the original phrase into her chosen metric scheme the translator not only excised the meaning, she even broke the cage into which she tried to cram it.[17]

Merkureva was led to this labored, soulless, and confusing diction—a diction completely unlike that of the original—by a worship of the fetish of equirhythms and equilinearity. Her labored diction results in large part from the extremes to which she goes to squeeze as many words as possible into every single line of her translations. How can we speak of musical character, naturalness of intonations, poetic quality, when the words of a translation are crammed so violently into such tight schemes? Take, for example, that terrible line, "Like those who fell, not ours— through sobs." In order to cram so many words into one line the translator had to use single-syllable words, and the result is *an unbroken string of eight single-syllable words*: "Kak tekh, kto pal, ne nash—skvoz' ston." This is offensive to the Russian ear: it imparts an antimusical, severe abruptness to the line. Such midget words turn lines of poetry into tongue twisters and deprive them of the breadth inherent to melodious poetic speech.

Poetic quality is also a criterion of no little significance for the appreciation of precision in a translation of poetry. If every single word of a text is conveyed with maximum precision, but its poetic quality is lost, the precision achieved is equal to zero. Here one can begin to appreciate that even the least successful of Konstantin Balmont's translations—those same translations which seemed to be so bad when we examined them in the preceding chapter—are a thousand times better than Merkureva's literalist renderings. There is a remarkable verse masterpiece by Shelley:

> One word is too often profaned
>   For me to profane it,
> One feeling too often disdained
>   For thee to disdain it.   (645)

In his translation of these lines Balmont departed drastically from the original.[18] Not even the rhythm is conveyed faithfully: where the original is in amphibrachs, the translation has six-foot alternating with three-foot anapests. And when we get to his version of the poem's second stanza we have to speak of concoctions rather than lines. And yet, in spite of this, the translation is true poetry. The lines are melodious—"ia egó ne khochú povtoriát'." They have poetic quality—the alternating rhymes *oskverniálos'* − *povtoriát'* − *vstrechálos'* − *prezirát'*. They have an irreproachable musical diction because they are translated by an authentic poet. Shelley does not sound here like the pitiful stutterer he is made to seem in Merkureva's versions.

7 External similarity between a translation and its original does not signify that the translation is of high quality. The Armenian writer Levon Mkrtchian was right about such supposedly precise translations, "When one reads translations of this sort . . . and compares them to their originals," he wrote in his study *Avetik Isaakyan and Russian Literature*, "one cannot help recalling the part in Tolstoy's *War and Peace* where he characterizes the charm of Helene in contrast to her brother Ippolit—'Ippolit bore a striking resemblance to his beautiful sister, and all the more so in that despite this resemblance he was strikingly ugly.' "[19] Just so "strikingly ugly" are those translations that "bear a striking resemblance" to their beautiful originals without reproducing their beauty. There is an amusing anecdote that furnishes sharp criticism of translations that maintain literal precision without conveying the poetic charm of their originals. The anecdote, which was related by the lexicographer Vladimir Dal, seems instructive to me here. I quote it from M.P. Alekseyev's *The Problem of Artistic Translation* (14):

> A traveling Greek was sitting by the seashore singing to himself, and suddenly he burst into tears. A Russian who happened by at the moment asked him to translate the song. The Greek translated it: "A little bird, I don't know what it's called in Russian, was sitting on a mountain, it sat for a long time and then stretched its wings and

flew far away, to the woods it flew, far away. . . . And so on. It doesn't sound like much in Russian, but in Greek it's very sad."

Just so are there many works of poetry which in the original make the reader "burst into tears," but seem like a collection of empty words in a "precise" literalist translation.

There was a time in our country when there were many defenders of translations that ignore the beauty and poetic quality of the original. One of the early translators of *Faust,* M. Vronchenko, even declared in the foreword to his translation that he was not in the least concerned with the poem's euphony. "In making this translation," he informed his readers, "primary attention was paid to the faithful and clear communication of ideas, then to power and brevity of expression, then to coherence and consistency of speech, so that *smoothness of verse* was not a first but a last concern."[20] (Emphasis is mine. K.Ch.) By "smoothness of verse" the translator meant Goethe's powerful phonetics. He imagined that Goethe's poetry could exist independently of its phonetics, that phonetics are a mere outer covering of poetry, not the first but the last concern. It did not even occur to him that by ignoring the phonetics he weakened a thousand times over the ideological aspect of Goethe's poetry he made so much fuss about.

The nineteenth-century poet A.A. Fet spoke out more than once in staunch defense of "graceless and rude" translations. The translator Fet in no way resembles the powerful master we have come to love in his lyric poetry. Even a scholar so well disposed to Fet as Professor V.F. Lazursky, in an article on "A.A. Fet as a Poet, Translator, and Thinker," was forced to acknowledge the ineptness of many of his translations:

> Right next to passages that closely resemble and poetically convey the meaning of the original we encounter lines so clumsy and inaccurate and sometimes even so totally incomprehensible that we are left wondering how a poet famed for the smoothness and beauty of his own verse could be capable of such lack of taste. . . . In his efforts to translate line for line and word for word (Fet) often fell into heavy and unintelligible literalism. In order not to depart a single step

from the original he had to resort to expressions and epithets not natural to Russian speech, misuse particles, do violence to stress patterns, and resort to irregularities both grammatical and metrical. In constructing such crude and dubious approximations of the original, Fet sometimes achieves effects so astounding that the Russian reader is obliged to turn to the original in order to decipher the puzzling meaning of some passages in his translations.[21]

Like all major poets who translate, Fet sometimes shows flashes of brilliance. But his translation methods are identical to, albeit not quite as extreme as, Merkureva's in her translations of Shelley. These translators belong to the same school. Fet claimed more than once that a painstaking reproduction of all the peculiarities of a translated text does not at all mean the translator is obliged to reproduce the artistic charm of the original. He did not deny that a reproduction of the "charm of form," as he expressed it, gives a translation great value, but he was convinced that it is permissible to do without the beauty of the original. In the foreword to his translation of *The Satires of Juvenal*, Fet openly proclaimed the translator's right to reproduce only the bare skeleton of a poetic creation without chasing after its vital beauty. He wrote:

The poorest photograph or musical instrument provides a greater possibility to become familiar with a Venus de Milo, or a Madonna, or a Norma, than any conceivable verbal description. The same can be said of a translation of a work of genius. Happy is the translator who achieves, if only in part, the overall charm of form which is an inseparable part of a work of genius. This is the highest possible happiness for both him and the reader. But the translator's chief task lies not in this but in the fullest possible literalness. No matter how graceless and rude the translation may seem in the new soil of an alien language, the reader will divine by instinct what makes for the power of the original, while in a translation which chases after a form which is familiar and beautiful to the reader, he will be reading what is for the most part the translator, not the original author.[22]

Fet's reasoning seems convincing at first glance, perhaps, but his own practice provides the best refutation of his anti-poetic theory. Anyone who has read *Faust* in his translation will find it impossible to understand why *Faust* is considered one of the finest works of poetry. In Fet's interpretation the famed tragedy became so inarticulate, clumsy, and rude that Goethe cannot but seem to the Russian reader the most inept of writers. In Fet's translations, Ovid, Virgil, Propertius, Juvenal, and Catullus seem to be mediocrities—so heavy, cacophonic, and fettered have their mellifluous works become. The whole of Fet's long practice as a translator proves that it is simply impossible to place the fetish of equilinearity and equirhythmics above the vital diction of human speech, above phonic expressiveness, because the "charm of form" is dependent on just these things. The critic Vsevolod Cheshikhin was right when he offered this estimation of Fet's translations of poets ancient and modern in his study *Zhukovsky as a Translator of Schiller*:

> Fet achieved his ideal at the cost of . . . violence against his own language. Even in the most precise of his Russian verse translations there is none of the poetic flavor that wins the reader over to Zhukovsky's translations, none of that grace that gives the impression of total control over all obstacles, no impression of magic, without which the reader's enthusiasm is unthinkable.[23]

The mechanistic quality of Fet's translation work is evident, for that matter, in the fact that he translated lines of Shakespeare without even understanding their meaning and, more important, without even attempting to understand them. Highly indicative here is his translation of these lines from *Julius Caesar*:

> For I have neither wit, nor words, nor worth,
> Action, nor utterance, nor the power of speech,
> To stir men's blood . . . .   (III, ii)

In Fet's version the first line begins, "I have nothing in writing." Totally indifferent to what this could possibly mean, he confused the English "wit" with "writ" without even wondering how Shakespeare could have written such patent nonsense.

Nor is this a random occurrence. It is a chief principle of his translations. "It is not my business to think and feel, my business is to translate word for word without worrying about meaning, beauty, or style"—this is the motto for Fet's translation practice. "In adhering to his method of preserving each letter without paying attention to meaning," Cheshikhin has noted, "Mr. Fet once translated the words, 'if you don't change your mind,' with the phrase, 'if you don't exchange your mind' " (171). In a word, the critic has detected in Fet's translations a profound disregard for meaning stemming from his exclusive concern with equivalence of lines and meter. The result of this attitude toward the artistic translation of Shakespeare is that not only has meaning perished, but also beauty, and poetic quality, and the animation of the original—what Cheshikhin calls "poetic flavor."

Of course, the days of amaturishness, dilettantism, and arbitrariness in translation are gone. The barbaric disregard of the style and rhythm of an original text that held sway over us beginning in the 1880s will never return. It gave way to a striving for equilinearity, for equirhythmics, for semantic and stylistic identity between a translation and its original, that is a lasting achievement of our culture. But now, when what we fought for in the 1920s has become the attainment of even the most ordinary translator, it is time for editors and critics to realize once and for all that the most precise translation of Goethe's "Uber allen Gipfeln" was given us by the violator of all literalist canons— Lermontov, of course—and not by the fetishists of precision who translated the same poem with the most scrupulous observance of rhythms, rhymes, and strophes. And while we are on this subject, equirhythmics are a conditional, unstable, almost metaphysical concept. For example, what meter would be used to translate Lermontov's poetry for Uzbek readers when the iambic tetrameter is an exotic phenomenon, one alien to their poetic perceptions? Equirhythmics would be completely out of the question here, because the iambic tetrameter has no place in the rich, refined, and complex traditions of the Uzbeks, who over many centuries have accumulated vast poetic experience, and comprehend European verse forms quite differently from the way we do. When, for example, the two remarkable Uzbek poets

Gafur Gulyam and Sheikhzade undertook to translate Lermontov's verse tale *Khadzhi Abrek,* they did not even try to reproduce the original iambs, because the effect of this meter on the Uzbek ear is not equivalent to its effect on the Russian. Gafur Gulyam translated Lermontov's iambic tetrameter into a thirteen-syllable line called a "barmak" (that is, syllabic verse), while Sheikhzade translated it into a nine-syllable barmak, and in the context of the tradition of Uzbek poetry this is the equivalent of our iambic tetrameter. The Kirghiz poet Alykul Osmonov translated Tatyana's letter to Onegin into an eleven-syllable line typical of Kirghiz poetry, and Kirghiz criticism confirms that so far as rhythm is concerned, this is the most precise translation possible.[24]

The concept of "precision" collapses into total bankruptcy here because this metric precision was achieved at the cost of most drastic departures from the original text. What the reader generally needs are translations that convey not only the external formal qualities of poets of another language (which is often not all that difficult), but first and foremost the internal beauty of the original (something that is achieved only by the very few). Modern translator-poets are keenly aware that they will not be saved by technical contrivances if they forget for even a moment that the chief quality of their translation must be without fail the poetic quality. Fortunately for our literature, the best masters of translation have proved in practice that a synthesis of refined technique and inspiration is not at all a utopian ideal.

I should mention the translator-poet V. Levik here. It is simply impossible to imagine he would violate any of the demands made on the translation of poetry nowadays. In his collection *From the European Poets of the Sixteenth through Nineteenth Centuries* he has preserved the sonnet form of Ronsard and the stanzas of *Childe Harold* with punctilious accuracy. And at the same time he manages by some miracle to reproduce the charm of the original too—that priceless something for which theorists and critics have not found an appropriate word, but which anyone who loves poetry will understand. Levik translates not only iambs as iambs and trochees as trochees, but also inspiration as inspiration and beauty as beauty. The form of Byron's *Childe Harold* is unimaginably difficult: each stanza is composed of nine lines alternating in strict order—ababbcbcc—in addition to which the ninth line is longer than the first eight. This scheme demands virtuoso technique from a translator: the fact that the second line must rhyme not only with the fourth and fifth lines but also with the seventh, makes a reproduction of this poem infinitely difficult, almost impossible. But Levik has handled this "Spenserian" stanza freely and easily, as if he were not even aware of the obstacles.[25] His translation is most definitely not a linear translation—not a single line of the translation matches the meaning of the corresponding lines of the celebrated original—but Byron's ideas are conveyed with amazing precision, the form is reproduced so punctiliously and the diction is so unconstrained that you seem to hear Byron's own voice.

Thanks to their natural diction, Levik's translations do not sound like translations: the speech flows as it does in the original, no matter to what genre the original may belong. This is attested by his volume of translations of Ronsard, whom he has made into a treasure of Russian Soviet poetry. Levik's translation of a poem in which Ronsard tells how he would like to be remembered after his death is so excellent that it seems perfect. It seems that if Ronsard had written in Russian he would surely have chosen the very same words for his proud epitaph. The translation says exactly what the original says. And the line lengths and the rhyme schemes are also identical: aabb aacc. Levik's translations of Ronsard's sonnets have the same lightness and naturalness of diction, regardless of whether they were written in a solemn, triumphal style or in the homely, everyday, intimate meter that Ronsard established in French poetry way back in the sixteenth century.

Levik's strength is his unconstrained diction and natural intonations. This is why, incidentally, his translation of Shakespeare's *Two Gentlemen from Verona* is so well suited for the stage. It is very easy for actors to declaim their monologues because the translation's syntax is flawless. A specialist in theory of translation, P. Toper, in an article in *The Craft of Translation* titled "The Renaissance of Poetry," has justifiably said about Levik:

V. Levik's talent is the talent of a true translator, the talent of reincarnation. He translates poets of the most diverse nationalities, ages, and sentiments, but he cannot be accused of an "omnivorous" lack of discrimination because the breadth of his interests is not a consequence of indifference. He has the capacity and the power for both the measured lines of Schiller's ballad *Hero und Leander* and the ironic intonations of Heine's "Die Söhne des Glückes beneid' ich nicht." It would be inappropriately simplistic to say that what we have before us are skillfully done Russian verses—we have to add without fail that these are the verses of Schiller, Heine, Ronsard, and Byron with their own exclusive and inherent, unrepeatable vision of the world and perception of life, their own exemplary means and system of expression, which the translator has fathomed, grasped, and conveyed by means of a Russian line become supple and all-embracing in his hands. Even without comparison to the original (which is of course indispensable to a detailed assessment) we are conquered by the sense of authenticity in these translations. From the very first stanza we begin to believe in their veracity—and this is an integral sign of realistic art, including the realistic art of translation. We might add that from the point of view of versification Levik's translations can withstand the most severe scrutiny of the Formalists—they are always "equilinear" (their translations have the same number of lines as the original), "equimetric" (they have the same meter), their enjambment, pauses, and intonational irregularities are in the overwhelming majority of instances fully correspondent to the enjambment, pauses, and intonational irregularities of the original. (1959, 200–201)

Levik's success as a translator is to be explained by the fact that by ignoring the sham precision for which the pedant-translators of the thirties strove so mightily (with such ill consequences), he translates in the most precise way the essence of the original—its style.

This principle of the translator's art was clearly formulated by the poet A. K. Tolstoy over a century ago. The poet overcame at that time great difficulties in working on his translation of Goethe's *Die Braut von Korinth*. "I am striving," he wrote to his wife, "to be as faithful to the original as possible, but only where *fidelity or precision do not harm the artistic impression*; and without so much as a moment's hesitation I depart from direct translation where this might give an impression in Russian that differs from the impression in German. I think it is not necessary to translate the *words*, and sometimes not even the *sense*, but it is essential to translate the *impression*. The reader of a translation must be carried into *the very same sphere* as the reader of the original, and the translation must act on the very same nerves."[26]

These words might serve as the epigraph to the present chapter.

FOUR

Vocabulary—Rich and Poor

1 Translators often suffer from a peculiar anemia of the brain that causes their texts to waste away. What a calamity for a Hemingway, or a Kipling, or a Thomas Mann, or some other full-blooded author to fall into the hands of these anemic invalids! It would be like turning their original works of genius over to them for a bloodletting.

I speak here about those translators whose vocabulary is wretchedly impoverished: a foreign word to them has only one lonely little meaning. Their supply of synonyms is scanty to the extreme. To them a horse is always a horse. Why not a steed, or a stallion, or a mount, or a jumper, or a trotter? A boat is always a boat to them, never a ship, a craft, a canoe, or a scow. A castle is always a castle. Why not a keep, a palace, a mansion, a strong-hold? Why is it that so many translators always write that a man is thin, not lean, spare, emaciated, frail, gaunt, or skinny? Why not chill instead of cold? Why not shanty or shack instead of hut? Why not chicanery or trickery instead of intrigue? Why is sad always sad, and never sorrow, melancholy, anguish, or grief? Many of these translators think that girls are only pretty, when in fact they are apt to be good-looking, cute, comely, attractive, not bad-looking—and a lot of other things too! To these translators a multitude is always a multitude. Why not a lot, heaps, a host, an enormous number? An obstacle is always an obstacle, never a hindrance, barrier, or impediment.

Vocabulary anemia needs treatment. Of course, if the disease has already been allowed to run its course, a complete cure is out of the question. Nevertheless, we have to take measures to ensure that the anemia does not become fatal, and in order to prevent this, such translators must be given a daily dose of synonyms. These translators must be made to read Dal's *Interpretive Dictionary of the Russian Language,*[1] along with the Russian writers who have the richest vocabulary: Krylov, Griboyedov, Pushkin, Lermontov, Sergey Aksakov, Tolstoy, Turgenev, Leskov, Chekhov, Gorky. When they read the classical Russian writers, these translators must memorize the words that can be of use to them in their translation work, they must assemble a huge collection of words—not words which are bizarre, florid, provincial, but the simplest, most ordinary words which, even though they are used in everyday Russian speech, are for some reason not typical of translators. I rarely encounter in translations of novels and stories such wonderfully colloquial words and phrases as "any old way," "off the mark," "stuck up," "flighty," "scary," "cowed," "all the way," "lazy," "easy as pie," "quick on his feet," "stuck on," "full of the dickens." To this very day there exists a breed of translators who inevitably say "madman" instead of "nut."

Not long ago I chanced upon a translation which can serve as a model and aid for young translators who wish to broaden the range of their speech. Scarcely had I opened the book when my eye met wonderfully colloquial words and phrases which, for all their simplicity and ordinariness, are almost never used by translators: "butter up," "savvy," "without batting an eye," "pretty scary," "messy," to say nothing of many other expressive words that are not easily found in an English-Russian dictionary. The nuances of human speech cannot be chased down in a dictionary. Therefore, the task of the translator, if he is an artist, consists of nothing less than finding as often as possible the equivalents for Russian and foreign words which cannot be located in a dictionary.

The translators about whom I am speaking here are S.P. Bobrov and M.P. Bogoslovskaya. The book they have translated is Charles Dickens's *A Tale of Two Cities*. I call their translation exemplary because their language is as rich as possible—keen, supple, abounding with fresh verbal colors. In the original, for example, the crude, vulgar Cruncher shouts at his son to be quiet: "Drop it!" According to the dictionary this means "stop it," or "leave off," or "don't." And this is what an ordinary translator would write. This would convey the sense of an angry shout with full accuracy, but it misses the stylistic coloration. Bobrov and Bogoslovskaya, taking into consideration Cruncher's character, translated it with the word *zatknis'!*—a marvelously apt equivalent based on the Russian verb "to plug," as in the expressions "plug your ears" or "plug your mouth shut."[2] And of course, in the context given, this is the most precise possible synonym. I have no doubt that if Cruncher were through some miracle to begin speaking Russian, he would certainly say *zatknis'*!

In just the same way, when in the very beginning of *A Tale of Two Cities* Dickens speaks of orators who eulogize their era or curse it, he calls them "the noisiest" (1), which according to all the English-Russian dictionaries means simply those who make the most noise or clamor the loudest, but (again in the context given) the epithet used in the Bobrov-Bogoslovskaya translation is far more expressive—*gorlastye* (9), meaning someone who bawls or makes a great fuss. Dickens says in the original that a mail coach is going "uphill" (5). The word is perfectly ordinary in any dictinoary, but since the incline is especially steep the translators preferred to use the more colorful Russian word *kosogor* (12), a word which can mean "uphill" but also conveys the idea of a more steep incline. And one cannot help thinking that were Dickens to have written it in Russian he would most certainly have used the word *kosogor*. And here is an even more graphic example. The same Cruncher, a stupid and superstitious tyrant, always keeps one eye out to see that his wife does not fall on her knees and pray to God to bring some misfortune down on his head. Whenever this happens he uses the expression "flop down": "If you must go flopping yourself down, flop down in favour of your husband and child, and not in opposition to 'em'' (70). He uses the expression several times, and always with comical effect. The translators found a very precise (and at the same time apt) equivalent for this expression—*bukhat'sia*, the perfect Russian verb equivalent to "thump down" (70).

Bukhat'sia, gorlastyi, zatknis', kosogor—hardly exotic words. They are simple, ordinary words, and their merit is to be found in the originality of their usage. They are unknown to ordinary translators. The same thing can be said about the word "vengeance." To judge from the dictionary, the word signifies "revenge." But our translators had to contend with the word "vengeance" in a particular context: "There was a time in my imprisonment when my desire for vengeance was unbearable" (190). And so they again circumvented the dictionary and came up with a synonym which is a more expressive and, I would say, more Russian word for "vengeance"—*rasprava* (190), which adds the fine nuance of settling a score. More important, these lofty masters of translation do not flaunt their wealth of vocabulary, they do not overload their text with forms of speech chosen deliberately for their freshness. Their mobilization of words and expressions beyond the bounds of the usual language of translation appears to be perfectly natural. When one encounters word after word after word in their translation which is untypical of the average translation style, it is impossible not to be convinced that this is the most precise possible reproduction of Dickens's style, the roots of which are watered with the envigorating juices of common, colloquial phraseology and lexicon.

This is why I term their translation superior. It does not follow from this, of course, that I consider it perfect. One might wish, for example, that their duplication of Cruncher's coarse speech had more departures from normal grammar—in the original the departures are extreme. One might wish that the first lines of the translation conformed to the poetic rhythms of the first lines of the original. But this is another subject, another concern. I speak here exclusively of the abundant supply of words commanded by these masters of translation. In this area Bogoslovskaya and Bobrov are millionaires.

2 I consider other translators who took part in the preparation of the new thirty-volume edition of Dickens millionaires too. N. Volzhina, N. Daruzes, E. Kalashnikova, T. Litvinova, M. Lorie, V. Toper, O. Kholmskaya—this "mighty coterie" of Anglists has worked up such a vast and flexible vocabulary that their best translations read like originals.[3] The translators belonging to this artel have already given Soviet readers excellent translations of Hemingway, Caldwell, Waldo Frank, Ambrose Bierce, and other American writers. *Fiesta* in V. Toper's translation, *A Farewell to Arms* and *To Have and to Have Not* in Evgenya Kalashinikova's translation belong among the highest achievements of the Soviet translator's art.[4] This is true also of the translation of Somerset Maugham done by M. Lorie.[5] One cannot admire enough the skill with which N. Volzhina has translated the English writer Graham Greene.[6]

At the present time, thanks to the skill and talent of these translators, Russian readers are being given brilliant translations of *Hard Times, Little Dorrit, Martin Chuzzlewit, Edwin Drood, The Old Curiosity Shop,* and *Great Expectations* such as they never had before. Previous translations of these novels should now be thrown out—every last one of them—so hopelessly poor and lacking in polish are they in comparison with these new ones. And these new translations—the ones I speak about here—can also be recommended with confidence to young translators who wish to perfect themselves in their difficult art. They can serve as textbooks for young people.

I also recommend that everyone get hold of John Steinbeck's book *Travels with Charley* in the translation of the same Natalya Volzhina.[7] It is one of the most talented translations I have ever had occasion to encounter in my long life. In style, and in wealth of spiritual tonalities, and in the brilliance of its idiomatic speech this translation—and I take full responsibility for saying this—yields not one whit to the magnificent original. Its idioms are unobtrusive, unconstrained, natural. For such descriptions of crowded American highways as "the roads squirmed with traffic" (95) and "the traffic rushed with murderous intensity" (162),

Volzhina finds such perfect equivalents as *dorogi, nabitye namertvo*, 'murderously jammed roads.' And there is a host of finely expressive Russian words (most certainly not to be gleaned from a dictionary, of course!) for such colloquial phrases as "such is my social cowardice" (75), "feel an uneasy sense of guilt" (76), "goes into a mild state of hysteria" (11), "I went into a state of flight" (140), "turkeys . . . roosted in clots" (115), and so on, and so on, and so on. And a very fine use of living Slavonicisms for such phrases as "may [he] live a thousand years and people the earth with his offspring" (167) and "that sweet local speech I mourn was the child of illiteracy and ignorance" (97). And the same skill in translating such bits of modern American slang as, "Fella camped here, kind of a nut" (100). For that Americanism "fella" Volzhina found the equivalent current Russian slang word *tip*, while for "nut" she used the word *psix*, not 'psycho' in its strong psychiatric sense, but precisely "nut" in our current slang usage.

In a word, from whatever angle one looks, this is a masterpiece of the "high art." Without the slightest sign of strain. A fresh, free breath of air. It is simply incredible that our reviewers and critics have not rushed to welcome this translation as one of the greatest achievements of our modern literature. They ought also to take heart from the growing skill of Tatyana Litvinova—her translations of John Cheever's latest stories.[8] And it would not be a bad idea if they were to welcome with warm praise the talent of Viktor Khinkis, who had to overcome thousands of obstacles to re-create John Updike's *The Centaur* in his native language.[9]

Yes, there are not just a few translations in existence now that can serve as models and textbooks—for example, the Russian translation of Harper Lee's *To Kill a Mockingbird* done by Nora Gal and Raisa Oblonskaya.[10] Evgenya Kalashnikova, a marvelous first-rate artist, has risen to a new level of skill with her translation of F. Scott Fitzgerald's *The Great Gatsby*.[11] You read, you delight in every line, and you think sadly: why is it that neither in the United States, nor in England, nor in France has a single translator been found who with such art and with such intense love would translate our Gogol, Lermontov, Griboyedov, Krylov, Mayakovsky, Pasternak, Mandelstam, and Blok?

It would be most helpful to a beginning translator to pick up the original text of, let's say, *Martin Chuzzlewit* and compare it line for line with the translation done by Nina Daruzes. The first impression is excellent—a colossal wealth of synonyms. In the original, for example, a young girl is called "a wild thing." According to the dictionary "wild" means "savage," "violent," "ungovernable," "frenzied," "irritable," "furious." But these words are hardly appropriate as a characterization of a young girl, and so it does one's heart good to find just the right synonym in the translation—*shal'naia,* 'capricious, mad' (62; X–XI, 156).[12] Or take the simple word "very," as in the line, "the passengers looked very frosty" (61). The dictionary gives only one equivalent for this common word, and this is just how some literalist would translate it. But Daruzes is an indefatigable foe of literalism; to her every word has many meanings, and she has translated the phrase with the unexpected word *poriadkom,* 'properly' (150), instead of the ordinary *ochen'.* And consider another line in the novel: "The anxiety of that one item . . . keeps the mind continually upon the stretch" (69). A literalist would translate this complaint by one of the novel's heroines as something like, "The anxiety keeps my mind continually in tension." This is the sort of translation jargon this group of masters resists. Instead of such a stiff conveyance of the colloquial phrase "upon the stretch," we find in the translation the expression *dusha ne na meste* (170), 'my soul is not in place,' but figuratively much closer to the original in style and meaning than the literal "keeps my mind continually in tension." Where a literalist would inevitably write, "great men readily give away what belongs to others," for, "great men . . . give away what belongs to other people" (2), Daruzes's translation says that "the great of this world give away (what belongs to others) right and left" (12). And although Dickens has neither "of this world" nor "right and left," the great writer's style and idea are conveyed far more precisely in these words in Russian than they would be by some literalist translator.

There is a paradox here. In many cases where it seems that the translator has been a bit too capricious in his attempts to broaden the limits of his vocabulary and has departed too far from the original, the departure is in fact a maximally close approximation of the original. At first glance a given line in Daruzes's translation can seem to be a distortion of the original text. Dickens uses the word "portal," for example (69). Daruzes, on the other hand, translates it as "the door into the holy of holies" (171). Since the original does not have the words "holy of holies," a pedant might call this a concoction. In fact this is the most precise possible reproduction of the author's thought. The door in question is tiny and leads into a squalid chamber where the first thing that meets the eye is the unmade bed of two young girls "in all its monstrous impropriety" (69). This is the mundane door that Dickens calls a "portal"—a term usually applied to the majestic entrance to a temple or the opulent gates of a church. So the ironic phrase "holy of holies" is perfectly appropriate here. Dickens says of an insurance firm that it started right off not as an "infant institution," but as a fully developed commercial establishment. According to V. K. Müller's *English-Russian Dictionary* the word "infant" means "elementary" or "rudimentary" in this context. Rejecting this anemic dictionary item, the translator found a meaning for "infant" that is not to be found in any dictionary—*zheltorotyi*, a Russian colloquial adjective close to the standard English meaning of "inexperienced" (XI, 13). And another example of this resourcefulness. In the original a rude boor shouts at his defenseless wife: "Why do you show your pale face?" (224). A literalist translation would handle this directly as "pale face," which would mean absolutely nothing to a Russian reader, but the conveyance we find with Daruzes is much closer to the original—"pious mug" (XI, 45). "Pious mug"—this is exactly what, to judge from the context, is said in the original. And in no dictionary will you ever learn that an "animal" is not only an "animal" but a *skotinka*, 'brute,' that "extravagant" is not only "extravagant" but "eccentric," that "a drink" is not only "a drink" but also "swill" (XI, 73, 114, 129; in the original text 247, 261, 268).

An unwritten law of this group of masters of translation is: "Translate not the word itself, but the sense and the style." This law is wise and fruitful, but it must be applied with great caution and tact. In most cases this is just what Daruzes does. Sometimes, however, she exceeds the limits of what is permissible and introduces images into the translation which would not make sense in the original. Such, for example, is the concoction, "a fountain of eloquence," introduced into the text of *Martin Chuzzlewit* where it does not exist in the original (61; 153). True, such concoctions are rare. As a general rule, the translation has none of the flagrant howlers with which prewar editions of Dickens abound, as when a "man-of-war" is turned into a person and a complexion into a build. In the entire two volumes of Daruzes's translation I found only one—and that quite minor—error. According to the translation, a man is "led out of the room by his ear," when in fact the original refers to a "box on his ear" (66; 164).

Recently readers have been in rapture over the rich language resources of Rita Rayt-Kovalyova in her brilliant translation of J.D. Salinger's celebrated novel *The Catcher in the Rye*.[13] The novel is written in a coarse but lively jargon commonly used among teenagers in the United States—and sometimes by our own teenagers too. The coarseness of this language does not prevent the teenager depicted in the novel from preserving romantically vital feelings somewhere deep in his heart or from striving toward humanity and truth. In adapting Salinger's remarkable work to the demands of Soviet morality, Rita Rayt-Kovalyova has slightly weakened the coarseness of the boy's language, but she has made an effort to convey the full expressiveness of his jargon, all the color and force of his speech. In so doing she has displayed an artistry that immediately ranks her among the finest masters of translation. For example, she translates the word "apiece" as *na brata*, colloquially 'per head,' the phrase "hot-shot guy" as *etakii khliust*, the word "stuff" as *vsia eta petrushka*, "has stolen" as *sper*, the past tense of the Russian verb "to filch, swipe," "to tiff" with the Russian colloquial verb "to bicker," "a stupid hill"—which an untalented literalist translator would convey directly, and thus meaninglessly—as (in complete agreement with the tonality of the original) *trekliataia gorka*, using the diminutive form of the Russian word *gora*, 'hill,' and a colloquial adjective signifying something closely akin to the American colloquial meaning "stupid," or "dumb," or "darned." Untalented translators would inevitably have the word "fighting" as a battle or a war or a conflict of some sort, but Rita Rayt-Kovalyova, applying all the richness of her vocabulary to the novel's vulgate style, used the pungent Russian word *bucha*. And when the hero uses a particular word to say that an advertisement is a fraud, the translator, faithful to the novel's style, writes the Russian equivalent to something like the English "pure manure."

Generally speaking, Rita Rayt-Kovalyova is a powerful and dependable talent. I have been speaking here only of her vocabulary, but it should not be overlooked that like the other translators I have mentioned in this chapter, she commands a wealth of rhythms, intonations, and syntactic forms. In her youth she translated Mayakovsky's poetry beautifully into German. Her biography of Robert Burns, issued in the series "Lives of Remarkable Persons," is one of the best books in this difficult genre.[14]

A propos, I recall that the same series has published Hesketh Pearson's biography of Charles Dickens. He has written quite a few biographies—*Oscar Wilde, Sydney Smith, Erasmus Darwin,* and *Samuel Johnson*.[15] These books have a brilliant, light, slightly humorous tone which is very difficult to convey in translation. The translator M. Kan has caught this tone excellently. Her translation fully matches the original in its rich emotative coloring.[16]

3 Nowadays, when in the tracks of M. Lozinsky, B. Pasternak, and S. Marshak a new generation of such great masters of verse translation has arisen as V. Levik, S. Lipkin, Leonid Martynov, Lev Ginzburg,

Tatyana Gnedich, N. Grebnev, Vera Zvyagintseva, Marya Petrovykh, Vera Potapova, A. Gitovich, M. Komarova, A. Adalis,
Lev Penkovsky, the reader will be easily convinced that despite
all the disparity of their talents they all have an inexhaustible
lexicon at their command—replete with gold mines of every
possible synonym and phraseological form. The individual words
of their translations far from always correspond to the
individual words of the original text, but the meaning, the
feeling, and the style are often conveyed with complete accuracy.
This is the most widely used method of translation at the present
time—a complete identity with the whole despite an absence of
similarity among individual elements. One triumph of this very
difficult method seems to me to be the translation of I.P. Kot-
lyarevsky's Ukrainian travesty of *The Aeneid* done by Vera
Potapova.[17] At long last Russian readers have been granted the
opportunity to feel all the turbulent beauty of this expansive,
hearty poem in which the voices of the Zaporozhian "Trojans"
have been heard for almost two centuries now—straightforward,
desperate, and invincibly hearty Cossacks. The translator needed
great creative boldness to resist calques of Ukrainian verses and
yet still convey their unbridled spirit with such force and truth.
She would never have been able to accomplish this had she not
possessed an unerring instinct for literary style, thanks to which
an external roughness has not deprived her translation of either
beauty or elegance. This instinct even enabled her to carefully
preserve the epic poem's Ukrainian coloration while at the same
time melting it down in a Russian stove and forging it into a truly
Russian colloquial language, thereby ensuring that it became a
work of Russian poetry.

Of course, it would have been useless for Vera Potapova to even
think about carrying out this difficult task if her lexicon was not
so rich. Freely ladling out words from her abundant vocabulary
supply, she again and again finds opportunity to re-create stanza
after stanza of the Ukrainian poem with the help of her own
words: these words may not exist in the original, but they are so
intimately near to it and so in harmony with its meaning and
style that they enable the reader to gain a more accurate impres-

sion of the original than had he been given a literal interlinear translation. She was particularly successful in her handling of the couplets which are encountered twice in each stanza. Precise and clear, like folk sayings, they are the most difficult part of the translation. True to her method of reshoeing the horse of a foreign text, the translator forges new shoes that flash and ring like the original. Take any ten-line stanza of *The Aeneid*, and you will find the translator has become an author, a creator of Russian poetic values. The translator was particularly successful in her handling of the poem's lines depicting hell. Here she has made many felicitous discoveries which fully convey the stylistic structure of the Ukrainian original.

Of course, a concept of style must take into consideration the flow of poetic speech dictated by its syntactic structure. Here again Potapova's outstanding strength can be felt: her lines flow lightly and freely, there are none of those swellings and dislocations of syntax which are inevitably encountered with translators who chase after the phantom of formalistic precision. These translators almost always doom their lines to a tongue-tied diction. Potapova does not suffer in the least from this speech affliction. Her line is perfectly equivalent to the original in its vital and natural intonations. Her translations of *The Aeneid* makes one want to read it aloud over and over again.

A translator needs a rich vocabulary precisely so that he need not translate word for word. This is a typical dialectical paradox: if you wish to approximate the original, you must depart as far as possible from it, ignore what is superficial about its words, and translate its essence—its meaning, its style, its pathos (as Belinsky used the word). A translation should not aim to duplicate the original letter for letter (I am prepared to repeat this a thousand times!), but smile for smile, music for music, emotional tone for emotional tone.

Literature records many funny anecdotes about the slips of miserable translators who have fallen flat on their face owing to an incomplete, one-sided knowledge of foreign vocabulary. A character in A.V. Druzhinin's nineteenth-century novel *Black Men* translates "The study in my apartment is very damp" into

"Mon logement est très fromage," because he takes the Russian short-form adjective *syr*, 'damp,' for the Russian noun *syr*, 'cheese.'[18] In his novel *At Daggers Drawn*, N.S. Leskov reports that one of his heroines translated the expression "canonisé par le Pape" as "cannoned by the Pope."[19] Not long ago an incredible ignoramous was ridiculed in a London journal because he understood the French slogan "à bas la tyrannie!" to mean "a stocking (*le bas*) is tyranny!"[20] In his well-known book *Remarkable Eccentrics and Originals*, M.I. Pilyaev tells the story of one of his eccentrics who, wishing to say, "Your horse is in a lather," said instead, "Votre cheval est dans le savon"![21]

Translators who do not know the phraseology of their foreign language are just such "remarkable eccentrics." Many of them know their foreign language only from the dictionary, and consequently do not know its most current idioms. They have never guessed that the English expression "God bless my soul" does not always signify literally what it says, but quite frequently just the opposite: "Devil take me." Or that to be "sent to Coventry" means to subject to ostracism, to ostracize. There is a need for a special dictionary of idioms. This dictionary would indicate that the expression "tall hat" signifies a "cylinder," that "evening dress" does not mean "evening toilet," but a "frock," that a "fair girl" is not a pretty girl, but a blonde, that a "traveler" is a salesman, not necessarily someone on a trip, that "minister" refers not only to a government minister but to a churchman. According to Ch. Vertinsky's book *Herzen*, the London journal *Critic* in 1855 said that "Herzen's supreme qualities are in the spirit of his genius." This is nonsense, of course. The reader has no reason to believe that the English in 1855 realized Herzen was a genius. The original probably used the term "genial spirit." Because he was not familiar with idioms, Vertinsky took the English word "genial" as an equivalent for our adjective *genial'nyi*, 'genius,' and turned a mild compliment into enraptured praise. The English language does not even have an adjective for its noun "genius."

In that regard, I know of a translation where the English word "smallpox" was turned into "little syphilis." If I were to collect the errors I have run into in the course of reading English books translated into Russian, I would have a list something like the following:

a "broadax" is not a wide ax, but a carpenter's ax;

a "red herring" is not red but smoked;

a "Dago" is not someone from Dagö, but a pejorative term for an Italian in America;

"sealing wax" is not wax for sealing, but a seal;

"night" refers not only to night, but to evening, and more often than not;

"China" is not only a country, but dishware;

a "highwayman" is not a tall man on a road, but a bandit;

"Old George" is not an old man named George, but the devil;

"Tower of Babel" is not a tower named after the Soviet writer; in a certain translation of a novel by Galsworthy we read: " 'Oh, Babel's tower!' she exclaimed";

a "compositor" is not equivalent to our word *kompozitor,* 'composer,' but is a typographer; in the translation of *The Adventures of Sherlock Holmes* published by Red Paper the famous detective notices that a man's hands are stained with printer's ink and deduces that he is a composer!

"chair" also signifies a chairman; we do not have this expression in Russian, so that when someone at a meeting in an English novel turns to the chairman and shouts "Chair! Chair!" we have to translate it as "chairman"; this is the way I translated it in my version of Chesterton's *Manalive*; another translator of the same work translated it literally and probably left even himself wondering why his hero shouts such nonsense;

a "public house" in England is hardly a place of ill repute but, rather, an inn or tavern;

"complexion" is not equivalent to our word *komplektsiia,* 'complex,' in the sense of "build (bodily) constitution, habit," but simply the color of one's skin;

a "scandal" is not public misbehavior or a street fight, as in Russian, but a socially shocking event;

"intelligent" does not signify an intellectual, but simply a smart person; when Paul Robeson's wife said on Moscow television that her little grandson was smart, the ignoramus interpreter obliged her to say ridiculously that "my tiny grandson is an intellectual";

a "novel" is not a novella, but is equivalent to our genre *roman;*

"gross" is not "great," but "rude, coarse, vulgar, repulsive"; we have already seen that Balmont took the English word "gross" for the German, and he is not the only one guilty of this error; the translator of Kipling's *Selected Stories* edited by Ivan Bunin understood the word in exactly the same way and translated it as "big" or "colossal";[22]

a translator of *Dombey and Son* did not understand the word "sweetheart" and translated it as "the mutual delight of our heart"!

Translators from French do not lag behind our translators from English. It turns out that they do not all know that:

"le telephone sans fil" does not mean a "wireless telephone," but a "radio";

"le pont" (on a ship) is not a "bridge," but a "deck";

"le trompe des journeaux" is not a "newspaper bugle," but the cry of newspaper sellers;

"la poudre" is not "powder," but "dust"; according to Gorky, one translator said of an old proletarian that he was "powdered and gloomy"; one would think that every out-of-work man in France used Coty perfume;

"les grains de beauté" are not "beauty spots" but "freckles";

"le trousseau de clefs" is not a "complete trousseau of keys," as one translator of Zola had it, but a "bunch of keys";

"l'adresse de singe" is not a "monkey's address" but a "monkey's agility";

by the same token, "peler des regimes de bananes" does not at all mean, "turn the usual life of bananas upside down" but simply, "peel a banana";

"le plongeur á l'hôtel" is not a "bather in a hotel," but a "dishwasher";

the French "artiste," like the English word "artist," is not an "actor," as in Russian, but a "painter."

I caught all of these blunders in reading translations from French in the mid-twenties. Nowadays such an abundant listing of errors is needless. But they are still encountered occasionally, chiefly in the work of inexperienced young translators, perhaps because there are still too few dictionaries of foreign phraseology, idioms, and so forth.

FIVE

Style

1 Still, the fact remains that a rich vocabulary is nothing if it is not subordinated to the style of the original. When a translator gathers his synonyms, he must not pile them up in a disorderly heap. He must arrange them carefully in accordance with their style, for every word has its own style—sentimental, majestic, humorous, commercial. Take so simple a verb as "to die." "He died" is one thing, "he postponed mortality" is quite another, and so are "he passed away," "he breathed his last," "he gave up the ghost," "he gathered unto his fathers," "he went the way of all flesh." Quite another matter are "he croaked," "he kicked the bucket," "he checked out," "he cashed in his chips," "he took the last count," and so forth.[1]

Academician Shcherba has divided the language into four stylistic levels:

solemn	neutral	informal	vulgar
countenance	face	mug	kisser
partake	eat	feed	gobble

The translator's art consists to a significant degree in being guided by a vital sense of style, of choosing from a variety of diverse synonyms the one which corresponds most closely to a synonym taken from the same level in the original language. If you are faced with a line such as, "Blonde Maid, was zagest du?" and you translate it as, "Saffron-haired wench, why d'you shiver?" instead of, "Fair maid, what makes thee tremble so?" the accuracy of your translation will be off the mark because you have taken four different synonyms from four different levels when they are all from the solemn level in the original. You will destroy the style of the original text just as surely if you take the Russian saying, "Heavy is the cap of Monomakh," and translate it as, "Oh, how weighted down I am by the royal hat of the Rurik dynasty!"[2] Carlyle's turbulent, fervent, prophetic style cannot possibly be conveyed by words taken from a stock-exchange report or notarial act. He who is insensitive to style has no right to undertake a translation: it would be like trying to reproduce an opera he has seen but not heard.

No amount of learning will cure a person of this deafness. What is required here is a well-developed aesthetic taste without which a translator might just as well gather unto his fathers. The deep scholarly erudition of the distinguished philologist Faddey Zelinsky cannot be doubted: he was an internationally prominent authority on the world of antiquity. But lack of literary taste made him totally insensitive to the noble, simple style of the ancient poetry he glorified. As a result, his translations are flawed. For example, in his reading of the simple and simple-hearted words addressed to Ulysses by Ovid's Penelope, "Certe ego quae fueram te discedent puella. / Protinus ut venias, facta videbor anus"—that is, "Of course, I who was at your departure a girl (young woman) will seem to you, if you return now, an old woman"—Zelinsky offered an offensively ornate Modernist interpretation: "I am after all thy pretty wench . . . should you come right now, you will say, / That the flowers of my youth have flown." Valery Bryusov, who noted this example, remarked gently that "We do not think the translator has a right to invent the metaphor 'the flowers of my youth have flown' for Ovid."[3]

Gentle treatment is hardly in order here, for the translation involves more than a mere metaphor. The translator also slandered Ovid by adding an elision to the first line, and he even added the phrase "pretty wench."

In Shakespeare's *Julius Caesar*, Brutus's wife reproaches her husband:

> You've ungently, Brutus,
> Stole from my bed: and yesternight, at supper,
> You suddenly rose, and walk'd about.   (II, i)

In his translation of the tragedy A.A. Fet used the word *nevezhlivo,* 'impolitely,' for "ungently," the colloquial word *vechor* instead of *vecher* for "yesternight," and the ultra-formal word *trapeza* for "supper." Critics of the time noted the disparity of style: "What a strange conjunction in three short lines of three words with such totally different nuances—polite, colloquial, and formal!"[4] Every age has its own style, and it would be intolerable for such words of the decadent nineties as "moods," "tribulations," "quests," and "superman" to be used in a tale of, let's say, the earlier thirties. For this reason I consider the translation of *Gulliver's Travels* done by A. Frankovsky to be fatally flawed, particularly by his introduction of words which clearly bear the mark of a later time—"talented," "moods," and so on.

It is intolerable that an English Jack or a Scottish Jock be given the name Yasha, a name strongly associated with a Russian (or Jewish) environment. But this is exactly what the early-nineteenth-century poet Karolina Pavlova did in her translation of the Scottish ballads of Sir Walter Scott, thereby ruining the entire translation (which is almost impeccable in other respects). It is simply terrible to hear what Pavlova says with reference to a Scottish lass in her translation of one ballad: "And yet her tears do flow—ever more dear is her Yasha to her."[5] It is intolerable for the slang diminutive *sestrenka* to be used for "sister" in formal verses addressed to Psyche. But in a recent translation of Edgar Allan Poe's mystical elegy "Ulalume," a work imbued with mysterious, uncanny images, Psyche is addressed with just this word.[6] To refer to Psyche as *sestrenka* is like calling Prometheus *bratishka* or Juno *mamasha*, using the vulgar diminutives for "brother" and "mother." It is impossible for Italian carbinieri or English lords to be forced to utter such ineffably Russian words as *tiaten'ka, mol, uzho, inda*. But Dickens's translator M.A. Shishmareva puts just such impossibly Russianate words in the mouths of her Englishmen. It is strange to read how British ladies and gentlemen tell each other *batiushka* and *tiu-tiu!* She even (unnoticed to herself) has them quote lines from Griboyedov's play *Woe from Wit*, which could hardly have been known in England.[7] And when Dickens's heroes sing "tippy tol li doll, tippy tol lo doll, tippy tol li doll dee!" E.G. Beketova translates it with the Russian refrain *Ai liuli! Ai liuli! Raz-liuliushen'ki!*[8] The result is as if Dickens's Mr. Squeers, and Lord Mulberry Hawk and Lord Verisopht were so many Ivan Trofimo-viches living in Kolomna and passing themselves off as Englishmen when they are really straight out of Saltykov-Shchedrin or Ostrovsky.

2 This Russification of foreign writers began a long time ago in our country. In his day the early-nineteenth-century poet Alexander Vostokov translated Friedrich Schiller's poem "Des Mädchens Klage" into a pseudo-folk Ryazan tune typified by all sorts of too cute folk diminutives.[9] In the 1820s translators were faced with the problem of how to translate the folk speech foreign writers were beginning to employ in their works. Some translators decided it should be translated with corresponding equivalents of Russian folk speech. Thus, for example, in the future Slavophile M.P. Pogodin's youthful translation of *Götz von Berlichingen* the character Sievers, a German, speaks like a peasant from Yaroslavl or Tula.[10] This became the norm for the conveyance of foreign folk speech. When attempts were made later in the century to inflict this "muzhikification" on translations of the ancient epics, many angry protests were raised. The attempts were proclaimed loudly, with a great deal of sensationalism. One announcement was particularly reckless and shocking, albeit made in the guise of a serious philological study. I speak here of a controversial article by O.I. Senkovsky (Baron Brambeus), "*The Odyssey* and Its Translations," published in Senkovksy's own journal *Library for Reading*.[11] The article, which is actually a deviously covert attack on Zhukovsky's translation, demanded that *The Odyssey* be translated not in the triumphal, oratorical language of the upper classes, but in a peasant, folk language. Professing to perceive "folk songs, the street music of pagan times" in *The Odyssey*, Senkovsky advanced a portentous thesis. "The colloquial speech of a language, no matter what language it might be," he asserted, "can be translated only with the colloquial speech of another language." Senkovsky was very much taken with colloquial speech. "Colloquial speech," he stated, "is the real language, the reflection in sound of the ordinary, constant manner of a people's thought—a language eternal, unchanging." For his own purposes Senkovsky placed the so-called literary language on a level below colloquial speech: "The refined, elegant language, the language of good society, is created artificially from folk speech . . . it is an invention, a caprice, an arbitrary mark of distinction, the conditional speech of a particular class. And like any caprice, it constantly changes." On the basis of this affected democratism Senkovsky insisted that the native poem of the ancient Greeks had to be translated not in a grandiloquent, flowery, "noble" language filled with Church Slavonicisms, but in a low peasant, folk language. He demanded that Nymph Calypso be named Silvermantle in Russian country bumpkin style, and that Zeus be called Allwise or Lord of the Heavens, Apollo—Shootafar, Polyphemos—Sharpeye, and so on, and so on, and he wanted Zeus to shout "Ekh, batiushka!" like some village elder, and the Homeric hexameter was to begin with the words "ba! ba! ba!" ($-\cup\cup$). He offered a sample folk translation of an excerpt from *The Odyssey*: ". . . Zhiv Godochislovich, most high-mighty ruler! The honorable Nymph Silvermantle who lives, like a *barynia*, in a shiny fretwork mansion, caught the poor fellow Runafar . . . that one who wants something fierce to be home to his wife, but the honorable Silvermantle insists—be a husband to her! right off!"

Up to this point Senkovsky's article preserves at least a superficial semblance of literary seriousness, but as always happens with him it now becomes patent nonsense. It turns out that ancient Troy should be translated as Troika! Agamemnon should be called Rasprebeshan Nevpopadovich, Clytemnestra—Drachunovna, Orestes—Grubian Rasprebeshanovich, and Antigones—Vyrodok Rasprebeshanovna. Which is to say that the names must be translated into preposterously Russified names with the endings for patronymics and surnames! This babbling philology even concludes with the incredible discovery that *The Odyssey* is an ancient Slavic work, and all its heroes are Slavs. Hercules is Yaroslav, Damocles—Meroslav, and so on. The article is written in such a farcical fashion that even the few sensible ideas found on the first pages seem to be outright lies. The critic A. V. Druzhinin responded promptly to it in Nekrasov's journal *The Contemporary*:

Just because we admire simplicity of language does not mean we can admire the "colloquial speech" proposed by Mr. Senkovsky. I will say even further that if Mr. Senkovsky were to translate Homer with phraseology from Russian fairy tales (which are far more seemly and simple than his colloquial speech), I would still not agree with him. Why should the primitive languages of two peoples who have nothing in common be forced to approximate each other? Our ancestors were not like Agamemnon of Atreus or Achilles, prince of the house of Peleus, and Homer was not some "muzhik in ragged clothing who sang for copper copecks and rolls at bazaars." Homer was a common man, but he was a Greek. The singer of *The Song of Igor's Campaign* was a Russian, and the two men lived in different climates, and among peoples who developed in totally different ways.[12]

Senkovsky's article appeared in 1849. In the same year (and in 1850) articles appeared in *Notes of the Fatherland* on Zhukovsky's translation of *The Odyssey*, written by the young scholar B.I.

Ordynsky, an erudite expert on ancient Greco-Roman culture. Ordynsky put forth the same demand as Senkovsky: the grandiloquent language used to translate Homer's epic should be lowered to the level of colloquial speech. "Generally speaking," Ordynsky wrote, "the language of our simple folk can greatly enrich our literary language." And here he offered samples of his own translation of *The Odyssey*—to the tune of a peasant song.

His translation has none of the crudely improvised bad taste which is so repulsive in Senkovsky's "colloquial speech," but all the same, his attempt turned into a complete fiasco. The most typical samples seem to be straight out of Russian folklore: "In reply to him said Achilles Swiftlegs—'Atreich most glorious, tsar of men, Agamemnon! If thou wishest gifts to give, so give them thou, and not chatter a chatter or dally a dally. . . .' "

But an authentic folk speech for literature had not yet been worked out at that time. For his time Ordynsky showed something of a flair for language: he managed to avoid the anecdotal extremes which fill Senkovsky's translation. It is even evident that he made an effort to "folklorize" not so much the lexicon as the syntax and intonations: "Oh, if only I were young, and had my former strength, like when it was we marched to siege on Troy . . . ahead marched Odysseus and Menelaeus . . . well, and all the others had on and with them their tunics and armor, but I, a fool, left my armor with friends in leaving the camp. . . ."[13] According to P. Shuisky in an article on "Russian Translations of *The Iliad*," a few years later Ordynsky published his "folk" translation of *The Iliad* with the intention of utterly devastating the "pompous Slavonicisms" of N.I. Gnedich's translation.[14] The translation was done very diligently, but it was not accepted by the reading public, and so his work of many years came to naught because the transformation of a monument of Greek antiquity into a work of Muscovy is a fallacious undertaking from start to finish. Ordynsky's antiartistic Russification was not met with sympathy by the critics.

This Russification of foreign writers reached epidemic proportions in the 1850s, and critics were obliged more than once to rise in protest against this vulgarized method of translation. In *The*

Contemporary, ridicule was heaped in one such translation, of Thackeray's *Vanity Fair*, in which English Johns and Johnsons speak in the dialect of Moscow corn dealers: "Yes, barin, be I allowed to judge it fair, that steward, Fletchers, is a sly one, barin. . . ." The reviewer for *The Contemporary* was indignant: "And this is called English folk speech! This is called preserving the color of the original? 'Barin!' It's unheard of!"[15]

3 And yet it seems to me that the style of a translation will not be ruined and need not deteriorate into "muzhikification" if we convey foreign folk saws and sayings with Russian sayings tactfully and cautiously, especially in cases where a literal translation would be awkward and prolix. Suppose, for example, a translator were to encounter the German saying, "Vom Regen in die Traufe kommen." He should not hesitate to translate it as, "Out of the frying pan into the fire." Although this method turns water into fire, the sense of the saying is conveyed precisely, and the style does not suffer in the least. The same thing goes for the English saying, "It's no use shedding tears over spilt milk." Nothing is to prevent a translator from replacing this with the Russian folk saying, "What falls from the cart is forever lost." This is all the more feasible in that the literal sense of a saying is almost never felt by those who use it in everyday conversation. It would be incongruous to translate the English saying, "No song, no supper," word for word when the same idea is expressed by a formula more natural to the Russian ear: "Water won't flow beneath a lying stone." That the original speaks of a song where the translation speaks of a stone should not deter the translator in the least, because, I repeat, the concrete images which comprise a given saying almost always remain beyond the awareness of those who have long grown used to it through everyday usage. A Russian who reproaches his companion for thoughtlessness or ingratitude by saying, "Don't spit in the well—you might want a drink later," is seldom aware he is employing the images "well" and "drink." We are seldom aware of the habitual formulas of our own figurative metaphorical speech. When, for example, a Russian says, "What's the use of waxing your skis?" he is not aware either of the skis or that they are not to be waxed. He is simply asking, "What's the use of doing that?" And when a mother turns to her son with the question, "Why are you hunched in three bunches?" neither she nor her son stops to wonder what bunches have to do with it and why there are three of them instead of two or five. She is simply telling him to stand up straight. I would call such expressions, the imagery of which is lost on both speaker and listener, "invisibles." These are fleeting images, deprived of substance. Included among them (as I have already had occasion to say) are such sayings as, "He won't so much as blow a goo-goo in one mustache." The person who says this is not even aware that what he is really saying is that some person is so stubborn that he will not do something silly to one of his mustaches. The attention of neither speaker nor listener is drawn for so much as an instant to the concrete images of this idiomatic expression. They comprehend it *beyond* its imagery, without reference to its images. It is indicative here that the saying is also applied to women, and no one even stops to think that women do not have mustaches.

In all these cases a literal translation is usually meaningless. Imagine that the heroine of a melodrama were to use one of these idiomatic invisibles at a crucial moment of the action. The spectators would immediately catch the inner meaning of the line without awareness of the unobtrusive metaphor which makes for it. But if a translator were to precisely reproduce the saying's imperceptible images—equal to zero—he would draw direct attention to them, and the spectators, struck by their unusualness, would gain an impression completely unlike the impression made by the saying in the original. In the original the metaphoricalness is equal to zero, but in a translation the zero would be apprehended as a vital metaphor. In his recent, highly significant monograph *Stylistics. Theory of Poetic Speech. Poetics*, Academician V. V. Vinogradov writes: "That which from the point of view of linguistic semantics functions as a metaphor, as a figurative expression . . . can in the sphere of the 'language of artistic literature' be totally deprived of its symbolic function and fulfill merely an expressive-characterological or characterizing role."[16]

Of course, in dictionaries and languages aids symbolic Russian expressions such as "He'd swallow a dog to get the job done" have to be translated literally. But since the imagery of this phrase has long since been lost to us in our everyday speech—has become an invisible, a fiction—a French translator who might encounter the phrase in a Russian story has a complete right, under appropriate circumstances, not to ascribe to some person a passion for swallowing dogs, but rather to replace the saying with a neutral expression in his own language. And when the same Frenchman says of a woman who has done something irreparable, "She mislaid her bonnet behind the windmill," the imagery of the saying is lost on him. For him both the bonnet and the windmill are invisibles. But if you, on the other hand, were to run into this saying while translating a French play or novel, and were to convey it word for word, both the bonnet and the windmill would enter your awareness in their concrete aspect, and would put a brake on your comprehension of the text, thereby diverting your thought into a different channel. For Frenchmen, both speakers and listeners, the saying plays an expressive role, but for us the images are glaring. My example here is taken from *Anna Karenina*, which has many such instances. They are treated by Academician Vinogradov in his monograph. I will not add to them. I assume his examples will do.

A thoughtful reader will, I am sure, confirm for himself that in the specific instances where a foreign saying hinges on fleeting, imperceptible images, it should be conveyed by a neutral saying based on similarly fleeting imperceptible imagery—without, of course, resorting to blatant Russianisms. I once happened to say of a successful doctor, "His chickens don't have to scratch for money," and was caught by surprise when a child asked him where he kept his chickens. In applying the saying to a particular everyday situation, I was not even aware of the image "chickens." Only a child not yet used to metaphorical speech notices the literalism of images that is almost never noticed by adults in our figures of speech. And if this is so, the translator is fully justified in conveying an indirect saying with one just as indirect, whose imagery has faded into oblivion. Pedantic literalism is unacceptable here too.

A literalist translator would convey the French saying, "Les beaux èsprits se recontrent," used in instances where two people say the same thing simultaneously, as something like "Kindred spirits find their kind." But when V.I. Lenin reproduced this saying in one of his works he conveyed it with a native Russian phrase: "Clever minds often meet." He did the same thing with the French saying, "A la guerre comme à la guerre," which a literalist translator would reproduce verbatim as, "In war as in war." Lenin reproduced the spirit instead of the letter here too: "If you must make war, be a war maker."[17] The Germans have a saying: "Den Sack schlagen und den Esel meinen." A literalist translator would reproduce this as, "Beat the sack and teach the ass." In his conclusion to *What Is to Be Done?* V.I. Lenin provided a Russian equivalent for this German saying: "Beat the cat, teach the bride."[18] Nowadays the practice in our dictionaries of not making calques of foreign folk sayings, but instead, seeking their semantic equivalents in Russian folklore, seems fully valid to me. In its listing for the German saying, "Mann und Weib, ein Unterleib," Nikolay Makarov's German-Russian dictionary suggests a Russian equivalent: "Man and wife are a single soul." Similarly, it translates the saying, "Arm wie eine Kirchenmaus," completely correctly as, "Naked as a hawk." The German saying, "Das Glück des einen ist das Unglück des andern," is translated in the dictionary as, "The patient dies and the doctor thrives."

These are all neutral sayings, without vividly expressed national coloration. But of course, under no circumstances should a Russian saying be used which is in any way associated with specific facts of Russian history or with realia of the Russian milieu. It is impossible, for example, to permit a squire in a translation from English to use many of our sayings involving our Russian stove, and he should certainly not be made to say something like, "Carry your samovar to Tula," because neither samovars nor Tula are typical of England. It is equally impermissible for the Spaniard Sancho Panza to say, "He fell like a Swede at Poltava!" or, "An uninvited guest is worst than a Tatar," and he could certainly not be made to use the Russian expression that announces St. George's Day to grandma as a way to say everything is lost, there's no hope. Because St. George's Day, and an uninvited Tatar, and that Battle of Poltava are all properties of Russian history. Sancho Panza would use these sayings only if he had been born and raised on the Oka or Volga.

In a word, there are no general rules here. Everything depends on concrete circumstances. Only one thing can be said with certainty: when substituting Russian for foreign sayings one should choose only those that are not characterized by historical or national coloration either in Russian or in foreign folklore. Thus, no one is prevented from using such utterances in a translation as, for example, "A bad peace is better than a good war," or, "Idleness is the mother of all evil," or, "Habit is second nature," or "He who laughs last, laughs best," because these are universal sayings which have entered into the folklore of all peoples in the world. If, for example, Heine says, "A scalded cat fears a boiling kettle," you may confidently write as an equivalent saying, "A once frightened crow fears even a bush," with complete assurance that a German who speaks about a scalded cat is no more aware of it than a Russian is aware of the crow in his own saying. In translating such utterances, you should translate the idea, not the imagery.

Sayings whose images are too sharp, unusual, and vivid are a quite different matter. One of Dickens's character says: "You might as well be hanged for a sheep as for a lamb." It seems to me that the translator made a great mistake by giving the reader an equivalent Russian saying: "You can't die twice, and you can't escape dying once!" because nothing can be felt in the translation of the wit, the picturesqueness, the freshness of the original. The translator should have preserved not only the lamb and the sheep, but also the smile of the saying, and the humorous tone so typical of English folklore. It is impossible to translate a saying whose images are fully felt with a saying whose images have already receded into oblivion and are no longer felt. By the same token, there is no reason to use ready Russian formulas to translate sayings which are too closely tied to realia of a foreign environment. Someone once translated the American saying, "A Negro needs soap like a fool needs advice," as, "You can't wash a black dog white." In my opinion, he translated it wrongly because references to Negroes are so typical of the folklore developed by inhabitants of the United States. And another example from the same direction. The English say jokingly of a dull-witted fellow: "He'll never set the Thames on fire!" Of course, the translator does not have the slightest right to replace the Thames with our Volga.

Before closing our discussion of translating sayings I would like to mention a most valuable article by I. Charikov on "Principles of Antonymical Translation" in *Translator's Notebooks* (1961, 35, 37). The article recommends a special method for translating sayings with the negative words "no" and "not." For example:

A word spoken is past recalling	A word is not a sparrow—once it's flown you won't catch it.
Let sleeping dogs lie.	Don't wake trouble when it's sleeping comfortable.
Every cloud has a silver lining.	There's no bad without good.
A bird in hand is worth two in the bush.	Don't promise a crane in the sky when you've a tomtit in the hand.

This method of translation is called antonymical. In an article on "The Translation of Stable Modular Word Conjunctions and Folk Sayings from Russian to English," A.V. Kunin says that it comprises "conveying a positive meaning with a negative, or a negative meaning with a positive."[19] But whatever the case—here as everywhere—the question should be decided with tact and taste —that is, in the final analysis, by a vital sense of style.

4 In the Middle Ages it seemed perfectly natural that the canvases of the Dutch masters depicted Christ and His Apostles and the ordinary inhabitants of Palestine in typical Dutch clothing, with typical

Dutch faces, with Dutch utensils, against the background of a Dutch landscape. Nowadays such nationalization of foreign subjects and characters is considered to be an impermissible device in art, especially the art of translation. If some translator were to depict Sam Waller (of Dickens's *Pickwick Papers*) as a Ryazan peasant with an accordion, it would be considered a malicious distortion of Dickens. Modern theory and practice of artistic translation generally reject arbitrary treatment of the national color of poetry, stories, and novels in translation. Contrary to this theory and practice, the English man of letters Sir Bernard Pares, in his translations of Krylov's fables, turned Krylov's Demyans and Trishkas into born-to-the-soil Englishmen and made them inhabitants of a British milieu.[20] In his translation of the fable "A Peasant Comes to Grief" the nameless Russian is turned by a whim of the translator into an English "Farmer White," and this "Farmer White" is visited by "old Thompson" in the company of "neighbor Soggs" and "Cousin Bill." In the translation of the well-known fable "The Casket" Krylov's again unnamed Russians appear throughout as John Brown, and Bill, and James, and Ned. Where Krylov has rubles, the translator has shillings, pounds sterling, and tuppence. Where Krylov has a house demon, the translator has an elf. Where Krylov has the words "matchmaker," "my little dove," "godfather," the translator always and inevitably has the Puritan word "friend." A Russian barin is called squire or sir, a Russian cat is "Pussy," and Russian kasha turns into rice pudding.

In a word, the translator has completely eradicated the historical and national character of Krylov's fables. And, unfortunately, he has done his job all too well. So that when Field Marshal Kutuzov, "Prince of Smolensk," makes an appearance in "Crow and Fowl," he seems like a foreigner who has strayed into a foreign country. Even Krylov's bears and rabbits are born-to-the-soil Russians from Kostroma and Kaluga, and when Pares turns these uniquely Russian beasts into typical Anglo-Saxons he prevents himself to a great extent from carrying out the task to which one would think that as a translator, historian, journalist, and professor he would have devoted his greatest efforts: the task of acquainting his compatriots with the mentality of Russians.

Let's recall here Turgenev's pertinent statement that "A foreigner who studies Krylov's fables thoroughly will gain a clearer idea of the Russian national character than if he were to read a mountain of works especially devoted to the subject."[21] But how is a foreigner to learn anything about the Russian national character if he has to gain his acquaintance with it from a version of Krylov's fables filled with English mores, English names, English miles, taverns, and elves?

Sir Bernard Pares's sins are not even exculpated by the individual successes of his translations. He shows great resourcefulness, wit, and sense of sound for example, by translating one phrase as, "But wise man Perkins / Has got no gherkins." " 'Our doughty Pug there's nothing daunts, / He barks at elephants!' " "Lean closer, and I'll breathe the burden of my tale, / Faint comes the song of nightingale / In Pussy's claws," "They chase me out of one, I fly into another"—each of these lines in Bernard Pares's translations is almost as dynamic as the original. And such successes are by no means rare. They can be encountered on every page. Little wonder he spent more than a quarter of a century on his translations. Fresh, original rhymes, variegated rhythms, many finely minted lines—these are the results of many years of work carried out with love and devotion. But the Anglicization he has systematically inflicted on Russians throughout his book greatly reduces the value of his labor. When Renaissance artists dressed their Madonnas, Christs, Josephs, and other Judaeans in the clothing of the Italian Middle Ages, their naive antihistoricism was fully explainable, but it is simply impossible to understand what impelled Pares to dress our peasants like Englishmen.

There was a time when such things could be explained by simple-hearted ignorance. For example, Russian translators who lived in the days of serfdom were simply unable to imagine that a Nicholas Nickleby could address his valet or coachman in the polite form. They therefore persistently obliged Englishmen to "thee-and-thou" their servants and inferiors. A translator of *David Copperfield* considered it permissible to have an Englishman shout at his coachman in the familiar form and to have the coachman reply, "At your command," in the respectful form.

The original, of course, has neither the shout in the familiar form nor the "At your command," because the event occurred in England, not Ordynka. The entire exchange was concocted by a translator living during the reign of Nicholas I, and at that time the concoction was understandable (although even then it was silly). But completely without point, the event was retained in the Soviet edition of Dickens published in the thirties. And in a translation of *Dombey and Son* it was hardly necessary to call the head of a banking house a *prikazchik* as if he were haggling on the corn exchange of the Brothers Khrenov in Moscow. In Irinarkh Vvedensky's translation of *David Copperfield* wonderfully English words are systematically replaced by native Russian words.[22] But these "Russianisms" were perfectly natural at the time. The old translator was unable to reject words and expressions that introduced realia typical of a Russian mileau of the time into English life of the time. He was not even aware of his oversight. But there have been cases where such "transplantations" of a translator's own natural realia into foreign works of poetry were done intentionally, consciously, with a specific aim—to make an original text more accessible and familiar to the mass reading public for which a translation is intended.

This is the case, for example, with the translations of Nekrasov's poetry by the Ukrainian poet M.P. Starytsky. Starytsky was a great translator, and he conveyed the very tonality of Nekrasov's poetry excellently, but he considered it necessary to adapt the poetry to Ukrainian mores and Ukrainian nature. Nekrasov, for example, says of a Russian soldier Ivan that he is built like a Russian hero (*bogatyr*). According to V.V. Koptylov in a study titled "The Language of M.P. Starytsky's Translations from M.Yu. Lermontov and N.A. Nekrasov," Starytsky translated this by saying the soldier is an eagle. The hero of Nekrasov's poem is light-haired, but Starytsky, in keeping with Ukrainian aesthetics, made him dark-browed. In order to bring Nekrasov's poetry closer to Ukrainian native folklore, Starytsky believed he had a right to turn Nekrasov's birches into linden trees.[23] In a study of "Mikhaylo Starytsky as a Translator of Pushkin," F.M. Neboryachok notes that in translating Lermontov's poem

"Homeland" Starytsky filled his entire translation with specifically Ukrainian images.[24]

Despite their esteem for Starytsky's literary legacy, Ukrainian translators of the Soviet period have totally renounced his principles of style. Working in Ukrainian literature at the present time are such remarkable masters of translation as Leonid Pervomaysky, Natalya Zabyla, and Boris Ten (who in 1963 published his magnificent translation of *The Odyssey*), and I do not recall a single instance where they have followed Starytsky's methods in their translations. Generally, Soviet translators are noted for a heightened sensitivity to the national style of the poets they translate. They are wonderfully conscious of their task: to use the means of their own language, their own poetic speech, to re-create the distinctive style of the original, reverently preserving its inherent national-cultural coloration. They are uniformly opposed to efforts to translate national poets into the blandish, styleless, cheap love-song, lady's-album language by means of which the translators of older times deprived original texts of all trace of national distinctiveness.

Included among these reactionary translators was, for example, the versifier Vasily Velichko, a hurrah patriot and chauvinist. It is as if Velichko took special pains to ensure that his translations from Georgian were left without so much as a trace of Georgian culture. One of his translations, disguised as "From the Georgian of Umtsiparidze," is so much banal doggerel, and even though the poem is titled "Georgian Lyre," the original author might just as easily have been French, or Portuguese, or Swedish.[25] The stylistic method of Velichko's translations of Baratashvili and Ilya Chavchavadze is of the same ilk. Fundamental to his method is a contemptuous attitude toward the people who gave rise to these poets.

I repeat: Soviet translators have totally rejected such methods. They are fully conscious that a failure in their translations to reflect any national feature peculiar to one of their brother nationalities would imply an immediate disrespect for other national cultures. And although a faithful interpretation of the style of a poetic work of a brother nationality often requires that they overcome colossal difficulties, they consider it their moral duty not to permit themselves the slightest indulgence and to bring each and every work to Russian readers in all the national distinctiveness of its poetic form. At times these forms are so complex, exotic, and fantastic that it would seem no one could be found adept enough to reproduce them with existing means of Russian speech and Russian prosody. But no other kind of translation is acceptable to the Soviet reader. He demands that a translation of native Daghestan verses correspond in rhythms, in stanzas, and in systems of consonance to the literary canons of Daghestan, and that a translation of native Kazakh verses corresponds the same way to Kazakh literary canons.

The difficulties faced by a translator in the reproduction of the national form of the Kirghiz folk epic *Manas* are many, because in addition to compound rhymes, each line has to begin with the same sound: *Semero—Segodnia—Smelo—Syplia—synovia—svyazannye*, or *Teper'—temnitsy—te steny—tiumeni — Tuda — Tam—Tysiacha*.[26] This translation is most certainly not Russified. Quite the contrary, its main tendency is a most precise reproduction of the stylistic distinctiveness of the foreign-language original. Even the showy reiteration of the initial-line sound, a peculiarity of Oriental poetics, is reproduced punctiliously. And although the Russian syntax is impeccable, the very movement of the line endows the syntax with a character natural to the original. The very way the words of each sentence are arranged, the play of alliteration and internal rhyme—*brat'ia—prokliatia – pechatiu, posmotri ty–vryti–obity*—betray an urge to bring to Soviet readers—as a great value—the national style of the Kirghiz epic.

The immortal Kazakh epic *Kozy–Korpesh and Bayan–Slyu* has been translated into Russian in the collection *The Kazakh Epic* by Vera Potapova in the full brilliance of its intricate sound patterns.[27] The first lines of the epic speak with great justification of "the golden traceries of ancient legends" which are woven the way a master weaver designs a carpet. The simplest model of these "golden traceries" is a quatrain woven of three end rhymes in an aaba pattern: *gonets–serdets–Sarybaia–otets*

(449). A more complex phonic tracery is created by three compound rhymes and one truncated end rhyme: *nevezhdy vy! — nadezhdy vy? —vezhdy! —odezhdy vy* (453). An even more complex tracery is based on the same construction, but with the addition of internal consonances with the ending of the third line:

```
. . . . . . ukradkoi . . . . . uletel
. . . kuropatkoi . . . . . . . uletel
. . . . . . . . . . . . . povadkoi
zagadkoi . . . . . . . . . . khotel   (455)
```

The original quatrain usually has seven external and internal rhymes in four lines. The translator considered herself obligated to construct each quatrain so that it has the same number of rhymes. This task would seem to be beyond human powers, particularly if we take into account that there are not two, not three, but hundreds of quatrains. Throughout the translation there can be felt the same rapture with the music of words, the same echoing of end and internal consonances:

```
. . . . . . . . . . . . . . . . svet!
. . . . . . . neveste . . . . . . ded
. . . gorestei . . . bed . . . vedai
. . . . . . . . . . vmeste . . . let   (497)
```

The entire translation is an overcoming of immense difficulties inspired by a passionate desire to re-create a remarkable monument of native Kazakh poetry in all the magnificence of its forms. Even when the translator encounters a text in the original which demands nine rhymes—nine rhymes, no less!—she does not retreat from her task and weaves her translation with all nine rhymes: *bagrets —prishlets —obrazets —ovets —tvorets —otets — ptenets — mudrets — serdets* (456–57).

Another long poem included in the same book, *Alpamys-batyr*, is offered in the translation of Yu. Novikova and A. Tarkovsky, who are equally faithful to the national canons of the Kazakh original. The rhythms of *Alpamys* are variable: a line of six syllables alternates in some instances with a three-syllable line. The translators reproduced even this distinctive feature of the original text. And when a variable number of feet alternates with a uniform pattern based on an identical number of feet, the translators considered it a matter of honor to reproduce this rhythmic pattern too. The translators were faced with the same immense difficulties in their translations of the Kabardinian epic, and they demonstrated the same powerful determination to overcome them through artistic creativity. Experts on Kabardinian legends and songs, organized under the common name *Narty*, define these difficulties as follows:

> The musical richness of the Kabardinian line is comprised of its internal consonances. The final syllables of a line are repeated by initial syllables of the next line and in the center of the third line, and they reoccur in the fifth or sixth line. The melodiousness of the line is reinforced by anaphoras; that is, by repeating similar words, sounds, syntactic constructions at the beginning of the line.[28]

The translators strove to translate these distinctive features of the Kabardinian line with maximum precision. Here is a representative excerpt from *The Legend of Narta Sosruko* in the translation of the remarkable master Semyon Lipkin:

```
. . . . . . . . . . . . rechi
O . . . . . . seche . . . . .
O putiakh . . . . . . . imykh
O koniakh . . . . . . . imykh
O . . . . . . . . . . . itykh
O dzhigitakh . . . . . . . .
Ob ubitykh velikanakh
O tumanakh . . . . . . . . .
O . . . . . . . . . uraganakh
V okeanakh bespredelnykh
O smertelnykh . . . strelakh
O . . . . . . smelykh . . . . .
. . . . . . . . . . velichavyi
. . . . . . slavy . . . . . . . . . .
```

The researchers have this to say about the excerpt:

In this excerpt almost all the features of the Kabardianian line are found in close conjunction: the peculiar pattern of zigzag rhyme— *itykh–dzhigitakh–ubitykh, velikanakh–tumanakh–okeanakh*—and the end rhyme (in conjunction with internal rhyme)—*O putiakh–imykh–O koniakh–imykh*—and the anaphors in the syntactic structure of the lines. The reader will of course notice that the word *rechi* at the end of the first line rhymes with the word *seche* in the center of the next line. The same can be seen with the rhymes *strelakh–smelykh* and *velichavyi–slavy*.   (17–18)

These line forms are peculiar not only to the Kabardinians. They are inherent to the majority of works in Oriental poetry. Lipkin has made them his own, native, as if he were himself a Kazakh or Kirghiz. By organically assimilating such difficult forms, he was able, after a quarter of a century of unrelenting labor, to re-create for the Russian reader the brilliant works of the East: *Leyli and Medzhnun, Manas, Dzhangar*. No matter to which page you open his translations of these ancient Eastern poems, you will find diamond-cut, jeweled, intricate lines. When the original demands it, Lipkin abstains from such excessively rich consonances, but he always preserves a lively, natural, clear-cut, unerringly accurate diction. The same classically sharp-cut line sounds forth in Lipkin's translation of the Uzbek poet-philosopher Alisher Navoi's famed long poem *The Seven Planets*.[29] In this poem Navoi praises the art of the jeweler, and likens the poet to him: the whole world marvels at the graceful beauty of the poet-jeweler's exquisite string of words. Lipkin seems to me to be a jeweler too, "a craftsman of gold and a cutter of diamonds" who makes priceless verse necklaces. The discoverer of the Eastern folk epic, Lipkin is enchanted by its beauty and communicates his enchantment to us. I would like to see the man so indifferent to poetry that he could put down *The Seven Planets* in Lipkin's translation without reading it to the end.

It is generally only in the Soviet period that the poetry of the Middle Eastern and Caucasian peoples has been revealed to the mass reading public in all its beauty and lofty human qualities. In order to re-create this poetry for Russian readers a whole group of Orientalist poets, "Easternists," has developed among Soviet masters of translation (beginning in the 1930s), including in addition to those already mentioned such masters as Ilya Selvinsky, Marya Petrovykh, Vera Zvyagintseva, Konstantin Lipskerov, Tatyana Spendyarova, Vladimir Derzhavin, Lev Penkovsky, Andrey Globa, Mark Tarlovsky, Pyotr Semynin, N. Grebnev, Ya. Kozlovsky, Valentina Dynnik, and many others. Many of them have devoted years of uninterrupted work to a single poetic monument. Thus, Valentina Dynnik has translated a complete volume, *Narta Legends* (Moscow, 1949), and Lev Penkovsky has translated the Uzbek poem *Alpamysh* (Moscow, 1958). Arseny Tarkovsky has conveyed with great artistry the monumental Karakalpak poem *The Forty Maidens* from the words of the singer Kurbanbay Tazhibayev.[30] The music of the lines, the variegation of the rhythms, the dynamic, passionate style which serves, so to speak, as a concentrate of all the most vivid distinctive features of the Eastern style—it is impossible to understand why critics have met this miraculous work (or for that matter *The Seven Planets* in Lipkin's translation) with such indifference.

5 Every great writer has not one, but several styles. These styles now alternate, now merge in bold and fanciful combinations, and the translator must reproduce this dynamic without which a work of art is lifeless. In the era of Boileau a mixture of styles was considered an unforgivable sin, but in our time it is considered one of the greatest merits of truly artistic prose.

Take, for example, the works of Kipling. He is a writer of very complex style in which biblical rhythms are combined paradoxically with newspaper jargon, and soldier vulgarisms with the melodies of old ballads. The majority of his works have several stylistic lines that are interlaced one with another in a most unexpected way. Yet Russian translators of Kipling have not even detected this multistyledness, and have translated him in styleless prose.

Unfortunately, in dealing with a multistyled author the majority of translators convey only one or another of his styles, and prove to be deaf and blind to the others. So many of Heine's poems have been rendered as pure lyrics, without the slightest nuance of the parodistic irony that is inherent to the original! The combination of several styles in one poem by Heine proved beyond the power of the majority of our translators, and for a long time they presented him to Russian readers as a most trivial, single-styled lyricist. However, the blame for this belongs not only to translators but to the readers who preferred just such translations.

Now that time is past. Translators of Heine (following the lead of Alexander Blok and Yury Tynyanov) are now coping rather well with this task.

But among the problems of the translator's art there is one which is exceptionally difficult. It has remained unsolved to this day, both in theory and in practice. For that matter, it is unlikely that a solution is possible, even though one is desperately needed.

The problem is this: how is one to translate colloquial speech? How is one to translate dialects? It is easy to say that dialects should be translated as dialects, colloquial speech as colloquial speech. But how does one actually fulfill this seemingly simple task?

At the present time hot debates are going on about this very subject among our translators. In order that the reader may picture more vividly what constitutes the essence of these debates, I thought it necessary, in the interest of clarity, to present on the following pages a show trial of those masters of translation who have disdained colloquial speech—an actual trial with prosecutor, defense attorney, and judge, so that thanks to a clash of opinions readers can get close to the truth. And so . . . .

6 (You enter the courtroom. A celebrated
case is being tried. The public is listening
intently to the ardent speech of the prosecutor. On the defendant's bench sits not a speculator, not a burglar, but an honored,
respected translator. The prosecutor is hurling thunder and
lightning at him.)

For this criminal (he is saying) there is and can be no excuse.
He has impoverished, diluted, and decolored the rich folk speech
of our people, washed away all its marvelous colors, deprived it of
its fine nuances and vital intonations; and by so doing he has
calumniated it. Having turned vividly artistic prose into soulless
official minutes—and this aggravates his crime all the more—he
has not even warned his readers of his willfulness, so that many
imagined they had before them a precise copy of the original,
that the wretched, moribund style of the translation corresponds
precisely to the style of the original text. I call this nothing less
than slander.

(Here the prosecutor swiftly seizes two little books from the
table before him—one in Russian, the other in English—
acrimoniously leafs through them, and turns angrily to the defendant.)

Here it is, the evidence of your heinous crime! The Russian
author has written, *Oi, liut' tam segodnia budet: dvadtsat' sem' s
veterkom i ni ukryva, ni greva!* But in your translation we read the
plain conveyance, "Oh, it'd be cruel there today: seventeen de-
grees below zero, and windy, no shelter, no fire." This translation
is glaringly imprecise. After all, the style of the Russian original
is folk, peasant. Here are *liut'*, a peasant colloquialism for a fierce
frost, and *ukryv*, another peasant colloquialism for a place of
concealment, often of stolen goods, and *grev*, a colloquial word
meaning to warm up or thaw out—words which are next of kin
to words Pushkin treated with reverence in his time. These are
born-to-the-soil Russian words. These words are ancient, distinctive, rare, and have never been entered into the so-called
literary lexicon. A translation which reproduces *liut'* as "cruel,"
ukryv as "shelter," and *grev* as "fire" does not give its readers the

slightest idea of the original. For only a translation in which the *style* of the original text is reproduced can be called artistically precise.

(The text about which the prosecutor is speaking is Alexander Solzhenitsyn's tale *One Day in the Life of Ivan Denisovich* in the English translation of Ralph Parker.)[31]

If the translator had taken special pains to slur over, erase, and destroy every stylistic distinction of the original, it must be admitted he achieved his aim brilliantly. In the original, for example, it is said, *I srazu shu–shu–shu po brigade*, 'And right off shoo–shoo–shoo through the brigade,' (29). But in the translation, "And at once a whisper ran through the squad" (36). That wonderful "shoo–shoo–shoo," which is Ivan Denisovich's little play on the sound of his own surname Shukhov—*shoo-khov*—is gone from the translation. In the original it says, *Fetiukov . . . podsosalsia*, 'Fetyukov horned in' or 'Fetyukov . . . came sidling up' (30). But in the translation, "Fetiukov . . . had come up closer" (37). The original mentions a "scorched felt shoe"—the unmistakably Russian *valenok* (58). But the translation has "mended boot" (77). Throughout the translation fresh, gleaming folk colors are replaced by banal and lackluster hues. The artistic distinctiveness of the original is not conveyed in a single line. It is as if it was translated not from Russian into English, but from rich into wretchedly poor.

When, for example, I encounter the words *konvoirov ponatykano*, 'guards all get out' or 'guards up the kazoo' (35), I can predict in advance we will read in the translator's version, "There were escort guards all over the place" (45). I can lay odds that in the translation such colorful phrases as *zafyrchal* (56), *ukryvishche* (56), *tabachinka* (30), *bushlat dereviannyi* (59), and *terpel'nik* (60) have been transformed into words of a standard educated style without so much as a blink of an eye: "hissed" (73), "shanty" (73), "pinch of tobacco" (37), "(a man) who has endured so much" (79), and so on. I particularly regret that *bushlat dereviannyi*. Among our people from time immemorial this has been the name for the coffin. "Coat of wood," "wooden jacket," "wooden overcoat"—this is a common metaphor in peasant speech.

Would it have been so difficult to translate the phrase as it is—"If you didn't sign—a wooden jacket for you"? But even here the translator showed himself faithful to his purpose—away with all this picturesque folk speech!—and replaced it with this insipid banality: "If he didn't sign (the confession of his guilt), he'd be shot" (78).

The text of the Russian tale is built completely on the internal monologue of a man from the country, a former collective farmer and soldier. And one need not be noted for too refined an ear to perceive that the text is dependent on an unobtrusive rhythm of folk narration:

> Oi, liút' tam segódnia búdet:
> dvádtsat' sém' s veterkóm,
> ni ukrý–va, ni gré–va!

The twice repeated *va* (in the last line) even underscores the melodiousness of narration. But the translator offers not so much as a hint of rhythm. If this English translation were translated back into Russian, the author would not even recognize his own tale. The translator-dilutor regularly and systematically expunged all the peculiarities of its astringent style and translated it back into the chemically pure—without color or smell—language of textbook and classroom exercises. In a word, only those readers who have neither artistic sense nor love for their own language will say this translation is precise. But anyone who is not completely indifferent to art will see here a ruthless distortion of the original. . . .

(The prosecutor pauses for a moment, and then, with renewed, even stormier fierceness, brings down righteous wrath on the defendant.)

In order that the court (he says) may picture more clearly what damage is inflicted on readers by the refusal of translators to reproduce folk style, I will introduce one of the most brazen examples—a translation of *The Inspector General* done in the United States by Mr. Bernard Guilbert Guerney.[32]

(This defendant is seated on the bench alongside his English colleague.)

Gogol's style is characterized first and foremost by startling verbal colors brought to such a dazzling shine that one delights in every line as a gift. And though you may know the entire text by heart, it is impossible to get used to its sustained revolt against the dull banality of predictably stereotyped speech and fixed, moribund forms. While rejecting "correct," colorless speech, Gogol tinted his entire comedy with folk lexical forms. It is not simply "ring all the bells" in *The Inspector General*, but *valiai v kolokola*, meaning to swing away at them. It is not "there's less to worry you," but "less worriedness," using the preposterous noun invention *zabotnost'*. It is not "get a big position," but "knock off a big promotion for yourself." Gogol uses not the simple word *p'ianitsa* for "drunkard," but the ridiculous diminutive *p'ianiushka*. This folk style ought to have colored Mr. Guerney's translation too.

If he had made an effort to make his translation artistic, he ought one way or another to have signaled his Anglo-American readers that in the original text we have not the standard word *obida* for "oppression," but the impossible *obizhatel'stvo*, and that equally impossible inventions were used for the phrases Guerney has translated in standard fashion as "go crazy," "wasted his money," "he went after the son of the merchant's wife." He ought to have introduced into his translation the expressiveness of the folk style of the original. He could not help but notice that the sergeant's widow does not say "flogged," but *otraportovali*, something closer to "they reported me so smartly I couldn't sit for two days." "Got in a free-for-all," "they caught me," and so on simply will not do for Gogol's play.

Mr. Guerney was honor bound to reflect all this revolt against dead blandscript in the language of his translation, because this is precisely where the essence of wonder-working Gogolian stylistics lies. Not to reproduce this essence means not to give foreign readers the slightest notion of what Gogol is about. What Russian when he speaks of *The Inspector General* does not delightedly recall his favorite Gogolisms, without which *The Inspector General* is not *The Inspector General* to him? There is good reason why immediately after the appearance of *The Inspector General* all his quotable expressions and words were immediately taken into the everyday language by progressive young people of the time. But Mr. Guerney deprives them of anything approaching quotability. When, for example, one of Gogol's characters says, *Vot ne bylo zaboty, tak podai!* Mr. Guerney envelops this laconic proverbial phrase in this thick, heavily worded concoction: "There hasn't been much trouble lately, so now we'll have plenty and to spare!" Where Gogol says, *Ek, kuda khvatili!* we read with Mr. Guerney: "You sure have taken in a lot of territory!" Is it any wonder that when they read such a translation foreigners, whatever their wishes, are unable to understand why the Russian people consider this gloomy author one of the greatest humorists who ever existed in Russia, why, even though Nicholas's Russia-of-the-knout has faded into the distant past, we accept *The Inspector General* not as a historical monument, but as a living work of art? As if just to destroy the color of the period and the nation once and for all, the translator has Khlestyakov say of a novel of the time—"Best seller"!!!

Mr. Guerney does not always understand the idioms of the text he has translated, but, I repeat, if he had not made a single error, even if he had not resorted to such concoctions, this would still be an erroneous translation of *The Inspector General* because the *style* of the brilliant comedy has not been conveyed.

I have purposely chosen as my example the work of one of the most qualified masters of translation. In addition to *The Inspector General*, Mr. Guerney has translated *Fathers and Children*, *The Three Sisters*, *The Song of Igor's Campaign*, *The Overcoat*, *The Bracelet of Garnets*, *The Lower Depths*, poems of Pushkin, Mayakovsky, and Blok, and he recently published in New York his *Anthology of Soviet Writers*. I repeat: this is an energetic and businesslike literary worker, and it is indicative that even he shirked his duty when it came to the re-creation of colloquial speech.

In general, foreign translators of Russian writers have not to this day worked out generally accepted principles for reproducing the variegated systems of colloquial speech they are bound to collide with in translating Gogol, Leskov, Saltykov-Shchedrin, Chekhov, Leonov, or Sholokhov. What, for example, are the

French likely to think about our "sorcerer of the Russian language" Nikolay Leskov should they happen to read his masterpiece "The Toupee Artist" in the French translation done in 1961 by Alisa Oran and Harold Lusternique?

(These translators are also made to take seats on the defendant's bench.)

The original tale artistically conveys the style of a former serf-theater actress whose phraseology departs in various ways from commonly accepted grammatical norms. The entire poetic value of Leskov's novella, all its charm and vivacity, lies in these capricious destructions of norms, in these touchingly comical verbal illegitimacies. But by forcing the old peasant woman to express herself in the colorless dialect of rather bad French textbooks, the translators have robbed Leskov blind, deprived him of the great mastery Gorky called "sorcery." Who needs a looted, tongueless, artificial Leskov who has nothing in common with the original Leskov? The story's heroine says, for example, *Graf . . . byl tak strashno nekhorosh cherez svoe vsegdashnee zlen'e.* Here in this single short excerpt, there are two departures from the norm. First, for the first part of the sentence, which the translators give literally as, "The count . . . was so terribly ugly," Leskov uses not the standard word *nekrasiv*, 'ugly,' but *nekhorosh*, an unexpectedly simple negation of the standard Russian word for "good." What Leskov has said here is something more like, "The count . . . wasn't all that pretty like. . . ." And second, instead of the translators' standard "due to being constantly angry," Leskov has made a substandard adjective out of the adverb *vsegda*, 'always,' and used the acutely colloquial noun *zlen'e* instead of the standard *zlost'* for "meanness" and substituted the preposition *cherez*, 'through,' for the expected "because" or "due to." The second part of Leskov's original sentence thus says something closer to "on account of his always being mean like." But the translators pay no heed to these whimsies of the Leskov style, and consider blandscript fully adequate to the Russian text: "The Count . . . was so terribly ugly due to being constantly angry." Citing this cruel violence inflicted on the writer by his French translators, E.G. Etkind, in an article in

Theory and Criticism of Translation (27–28), has justly observed: "N. Leskov is absent in the translation. . . . Everything distinctive, unexpected, stylistically witty has been removed" (which is to say "destroyed"—K. Ch.). The chief cause of this cruel violence against Leskov is that the translators' emaciated language is devoid of every last trace of folkishness.

Let the defendants not think to plead that their language does not have the resources needed for the translation of Russian poetry and prose. This argument is quite easily refuted by noting the undeniable achievements which have recently been appearing in the practice of some English and American masters of translation who are trying to re-create works of Russian literature in their own language. The poems of Pushkin, Lermontov, and Alexey Tolstoy in the translations of the late Maurice Baring, the stanzas of *Eugene Onegin* magnificently translated by Reginald Mainwaring Hewitt, Blok and Valery Bryusov in the translations of Professor Bowra, Sholokhov, Babel, and Zoshchenko in the translations of a gifted pleiad of young translators—all these are indisputable evidence that in England the period of mediocre translations of Russian literature which Tolstoy, Dostoyevsky, and Chekhov were obliged to endure in their time is already coming to an end. These translations show that the English language is not at all so unyielding to translations of Russian poetry and prose as one might think from reading the orders rushed out by some translators. . . .

(The prosecutor's impassioned speech has made an impression. Indeed, the facts he has revealed are all but irrefutable. To many of the public it even seems that the defendants' case is lost. What can the defense attorney possibly say in their defense?)

7 (But the defense attorney is not in the least dismayed. His appearance is bold and confident. Nor have the defendants themselves lost heart. The defense attorney begins his speech distantly.)

Yes (he says) in principle it is impossible to in any way condone the refusal of translators to reproduce slang, dialects, argot of every description, and the same thing goes for the various individual peculiarities of human speech which make up departures from the norm of literary style. The prosecutor is perfectly right: by introducing normative forms where they do not exist, translators wash away their brightest colors from the characters depicted by an author. After all, a speech characteristic is one of the most powerful figurative devices, and to abstain from it means to transform a living, warm-blooded human being into a soulless wax figure.

Yes, in principle it is impossible not to agree with the prosecutor.

But what is a translator to do in actual practice? As a matter of fact, it is not irrelevant here that our own best masters of translation commit the very same sins of which the prosecutor accuses their foreign colleagues.

Let's recall the kind and amusing Jim of Mark Twain's novel *The Adventures of Huckleberry Finn*. In the original his speech is a most violent departure from the norm. For every hundred words he utters there occur (I counted them) two score which sharply violate all norms of grammar. Instead of "going," he says "a-gwyne," instead of "dogs"—"dogst," instead of "I am"—"I is," and so on, and so on. How are these distortions to be reproduced in Russian? the defense attorney asks, turning caustically to the prosecutor. By what means is the Russian reader to be given some notion that the speech of the simple-hearted Jim is completely embellished with the bright colors of living and picturesque folk speech? By perhaps introducing such unmistakably Russian verbalisms as *ochinno, as', zavsegda, zhist', kufarka, kalidor, obnakovenno, idet'*? This would be insufferably bad taste.

The translator of this novel, N. Daruzes, refrained from such a barbaric mangling of words. And she did well, because all these Russian verbalisms would have imparted to Jim's speech a Ryazan or Kostroma coloration which does not correspond in the least to the lexicon and phraseology of the Negroes who lived in the nineteenth century on the banks of the Mississippi. The Jim of Daruzes's translation has a total command of educated, immaculately correct speech, and, in all truth, our Soviet readers have not lost a thing from it.

(Voices in the courtroom: "No, no, we have lost something. . . ." "No, we have not lost anything!" The chairman's bell. But the defense attorney remains imperturbably calm.)

It is very easy for the prosecutor to say, "Translate colloquial speech as colloquial speech," but just let him try to apply this demagogical slogan in practice. Either absolutely nothing will come of it, or it will turn out nonsense. So just how are these masters of translation he has attacked with such violent indignation to manage otherwise? Should they have translated the peasant-soldier-prison slang of Ivan Denisovich with the slang of Thomas Hardy's Wessex farmers? Or with the dialect of Walloon peasants? And just how else should the translators have handled the stories of Leskov? Are they to translate the mischievous whimsies of the Leskov style with the slang of Provençal wine makers? And can we hope there will ever be found an expert capable of correctly re-creating the stylistics of Rudyard Kipling's *Soldiers Three*, one of whom speaks in an Anglo-Scottish dialect, the second in an Anglo-Irish dialect, and the third in the street slang of East London? No, the problem of reproducing foreign slang, dialects, and argot in one's own language is very difficult and complex, and it will not be solved as offhandedly as my opponent would wish. So I invite him to look into this matter a bit more closely.

(The defense attorney takes a very handsome book from the table.)

Now, perhaps he would be so kind as to give some thought to the foreword with which Mark Twain prefaced his *Huckleberry Finn*. It is written as if to terrify translators. In it they can learn to their deep sorrow that the American writer used all of seven different dialects in his novel: the Missouri Negro dialect; the extremest form of the backwoods dialect of the Southwest; the standard dialect of a southern region of Mississippi; and four modified varieties of this last. However talented one may be, be one even a genius, one will never manage to reproduce a single one of these seven colorful dialects in translation, because the Russian language has not the slightest lexical means for the implementation of tasks like this. Rummage through Ozhegov's *Dictionary of the Russian Language* all the way from *abazhur* to *iashchur* and you will not find so much as a single equivalent, neither for the speech of Negroes living in the southern regions of the Mississippi nor for any one of its four variants. In our language, as in any other, you will find no correspondences whatsoever to the fractures and sprains of speech which saturate the original. An unavoidable trap lies in wait here for every translator, even the most skillful. Neither *deskat'*, nor *as'*, nor any other of your usual colloquialisms will help you here.

The heroine of Guy de Maupassant's *L'Odyssée d'une fille* says in the original *v'là* instead of *voilà, ben* instead of *bien, parlions* instead of *parlais*. Which is to say that in one way or another she departs from proper speech. As A. V. Fyodorov has noted in *On Artistic Translation* (136), the translator is completely helpless to convey these departures. The translator has only one way to avoid disaster here: to walk humbly in the path of those masters of translation who have completely refused to reproduce colloquial speech in translation. This is how *Huckleberry Finn* was translated by N. Daruzes—in a most pure, correct, neutral language, without straining after any dialects. And she did well! Very well! Marvelously!

(Voices in the courtroom: "No, badly!" "No, well!" The chairman's bell.)

I have here before me *Huckleberry Finn*, just published by the Children's State Publishing House in Daruzes's translation with the charming illustrations of Goryayev, and so far as I am familiar with the original, the entire book, from the first page to the last, is told in the person of a semiliterate, uneducated, half-wild boy who has not the slightest notion what proper speech is. In the translation this "wild" boy speaks in the bookish, grammatical language of cultured, educated people. True, this sometimes turns out a bit strangely. When you read one of the boy's nature descriptions, for example, it actually seems as if you are reading Turgenev: "Not a sound anywhere, complete silence, as if the whole world were sleeping . . ." and so on.[33] But is it really a matter of such petty details? Have these petty details prevented Soviet readers, children in particular, from falling in love with Twain's novel with all their hearts? They read precisely this translation with rapture and demand no other. And their love for this book is not a bit less than that of those children across the sea who read it in the original.

(Here the defense attorney falls into a lengthy silence. On the table before him, without the slightest haste, he spreads out a set of small green volumes—the novels of Dickens in the new edition of the State Literature Publishing House—and then he makes an extremely interesting observation. It turns out that in every one of Dickens's novels there is a "person of the lower class" with a plebeian, unpolished, but highly expressive speech. And—significantly!—all of our best translators of Dickens have presented this florid folk speech in an almost correct, colorless blandscript!)

Marya Lorie (the defense attorney continues) is justifiably considered one of our most talented, authoritative, and experienced masters of translation. She has to her credit the translation of Dickens's novel *Great Expectations*. A most artistic translation, exemplary. And here in the novel is the convict Magwitch, a vulgar savage whose speech fully expresses his crude psychology. But in Marya Lorie's translation he speaks almost literarily: "My dear boy," he says, "and you, comrade Pip, I will not presume to tell you the story of my life the way they write in books or sing in songs, but will explain it all briefly and clearly so that you will readily understand me . . ." and so on.[34] Again educated speech, without any plebeian tint. This is the way a person with a university education, a lawyer or a doctor, might speak, although in the original one hears from Magwitch's very first words the speech of an uneducated convict who has never been in a cultured milieu. Instead of "for" he says "fur," instead of "after"— "arter," instead of "someone"—"summun," and so on, and so on. Happily, these speech distortions are in no way reflected in the translation. Magwitch's "plebeianism" is conveyed excellently by intonations instead of lexicon. The same thing can be

said about the speech of another common man, Roger Riderhood, in the novel *Our Mutual Friend*, brilliantly translated by N.
Daruzes and N. Volzhina. Although in the original Riderhood
says not "he knew" but "he knowed," not "partner" but "pard-
ner," not "anything" but "anythink," these distortions of the
style standard found not a single reflection in the translation
(XXIV, 185–89).

So it is pointless for the prosecutor to attack Bernard Guilbert
Guerney and Ralph Parker with such unseemly fervor and to see
in their blandscript something so serious as sabotage. It is impossible to bring people to trial because they are not magicians and
cannot perform miracles! It is not without reason that masters of
translation—French, English, and Russian—distill foreign
speech in their translations. In fact, it is precisely because they
are masters that they do so. We ought not to put these translators
on trial for such "distillations," but thank them and salute them!
Here, in essence, is their great merit, which deserves every
praise!

Yes, not guilt, but merit!

What, more than anything else, impels them to replace foreign colloquial speech with blandscript? Their hatred of bad
taste and fraudulence. These masters recall with a shudder the
notorious Irinarkh Vvedensky, who in straining for colloquial
speech unpardonably Russified the originals and forced Anglo-
Saxons to use such markedy Russian words as *poddediulivat'* and
prishpandorivat' at each other, and even to use the word *naiarivat'*
at someone. They remember how it grated on their ears when
Dickens's Sam Waller, a most pure-blooded Londoner, addressed
his parent in translation as if speaking to some Ivan Susanin.[35]
And of course, the distillers are right: read Burns in the Russified
translation of Viktor Fedotov and it seems as if Burns is a dashing
balalaika player in a Ryazan amateur choir. Give a cloddish
translator like this a chance to introduce folk speech into his
translation, and he will load it up with so many phrases like
ai–liuli and *dolia–doliushka* that it will end up a sheer monstros-
ity. It is as if the sluice gates are opened for a flood of the most
coarse and tinselly bad taste. And then our readers will issue a

most friendly protest. "Better," they will say, "that translators give us a sketch of the plot, without even attempting to recreate foreign stylistics! Let them confine themselves to the modest task which, as we have seen, was advanced by Guerney and Parker— the task of informing their compatriots about the content (only the content!) of a work of Russian literature." It is a dread of coarse vulgarization that restrains translators from introducing folk speech into the texts of their translations. They are alarmed by the multitude of *mauvais ton* incidents perpetrated by translators in the past. This bad taste has even persuaded them to completely refrain from all attempts to re-create foreign colloquial speech.

And if this is the principled attitude of the most qualified of our masters of translation, why then, it may be asked, do we forbid their colleagues who translate Krylov, Griboyedov, Leskov, Solzhenitsyn, and Sholokhov from proceeding in the same way? It is possible that they were also stopped by the same hatred of tinselly vulgarization which would unavoidably creep into their translations if they started reproducing the colloquial speech of our classical authors with the aid of their own slang. We cannot make strict demands on them if only because they are already in the majority. Their translations are an everyday phenomenon. None of our critics reproaches them because when they wash away all the picturesque colors in a translated text, they deprive it of the powerful dynamic which acts so profoundly on the feelings and thoughts of readers. They are accustomed to this. This is considered to be in the order of things. And the same translator of *Ivan Denisovich* whom our prosecutor has attacked with such indignant wrath can say in his own defense that other translators of *Ivan Denisovich* have also distorted the text of the tale by not trying to re-create its style.

We know of four American editions of *Ivan Denisovich*. No matter which one of them you take, the same colorless official speech exists throughout. In the original, for example, it says, *Zakon on vyvorotnoi*, 'The law—it's a twistabout' (59). But Bela von Block translates it as, "They behaved with the law as it suited them."[36] And Max Hayward and Ronald Hingley: "They twisted the law any way they wanted."[37] And Thomas P. Whitney: "The law was the sort of thing they turned around as they saw fit."[38] The original has *Sen'ka Kloivshin uslyshal cherez glush' svoiu*, 'Senka Klyovshin caught it through his deafness' (60). But Bela von Block translates this as, "although he was deaf" (68), and Hayward and Hingley as, "Deaf as he was, Senka Klevshin could hear what they were talking about" (77). As you can see, there is a system here. It turns out that not only Ralph Parker, but everyone, absolutely every translator, has refused point-blank to translate colloquial speech. And they were joined in this by their Italian colleagues.

(Here the defense attorney holds up two Italian books.)

Both of these books have the same title: *Una giornata di Ivan Denisovic*. One was published in the translation of Giorgio Kraiski, the other in the translation of Raffaello Uboldi.[39] Both translators adhere to the same "protocol" method. With one that *shu—shu—shu* is "mormori," with the other "sussaro." This means that it is not at all a whimsy of one lone translator. It is a generally accepted, generally recognized method. No other method of translating *One Day* is possible, and for that matter, is there need of any other method? What is important in this tale is not the style but the plot. Yes, and even in *The Inspector General* we value the story above all else, and not a few silly words like *otraportovat'*.

(Here the defense attorney, thrusting his chest out confidently, begins elaborating on the idea that beauty of style and expressiveness of images appeal only to a few lonely epicureans anyway, and the general public prefers content. "The form of *The Inspector General*," he says, "is important only to the very few, while the vast majority of foreign and Russian readers value the immortal comedy's ideological tendencies. . . ." Shouts in the courtroom: "Lies! Demagoguery!" "Nonsense!" "It is impossible to separate content from form!" But the defense attorney is not daunted.)

Permit me to read you a certain document which proves in a most graphic way that the artistry of a translation is by no means such a priceless quality as the prosecutor would have us believe. It is a letter from the distinguished German writer Thomas Mann

quoted in an article in *The Craft of Translation*. In this letter
Thomas Mann says straight out that "if there is real substance in a
book, then even in a poor translation much will be preserved—
and that is enough." Here is the essence of the matter—much,
and it may even be said the very best, is preserved in a translation
even if it does not reproduce the original's stylistics. "I do not
know a word of Russian," Thomas Mann says in the same letter,
"and those German translations of the works of the great Russian
writers of the nineteenth century which I read in my youth were
very weak. But nevertheless, this reading belongs to the greatest
events in the story of my education."

In a word (the defense attorney concludes), the readers' losses
from a weak and colorless translation are by no means so great as
the prosecutor would like to convince us. And I hope that in the
light of these indisputably convincing arguments the court will
find it possible to acquit the defendants and not hinder them
from applying these same methods henceforth.

8 (But the most ancient judge agrees with
neither the defendants nor the plantiffs.)

No (he declares), the defense attorney is wrong in contending
that foreign colloquial speech cannot be translated into our native
language. Who will say that the Scottish coloration of Robert
Burns's poem "Tam o'Shanter" has suffered in the least from the
fact that Samuil Marshak, with the unerring taste that makes his
best translations classics, introduced into this translation such
Russian words as *narezat'sia, nakliukat'sia, pliukhnut'sia?* Everything depends on the translator's tact and skill.

And are there not perhaps examples of successful applications
of folk expressions and words which completely satisfy the most
refined tastes? Read, for example, *Japanese Folk Tales* in the marvelous translation of B. Beyko and V. Markova—not even the
severest of critics is jarred by the forms from Russian folklore

which are now and then encountered here. "Is it possible to think for even a moment," S. Petrov says about this translation in an article, "On the Use of Colloquial Speech" in *The Craft of Translation* (1963, 95), "that this is a translation, and one from an Eastern language besides? No, this is a genuine virtuoso assimilation of the Japanese folk tale into Russian. The entire language structure is from the Russian folk tale. . . . And despite this, the national coloration is so finely preserved! This is what it means to be able to use colloquial speech! Beyko and Markova have proven in practice here that Russification not only does not harm the material, but, on the contrary, makes it a true folk tale." This is the essence of the problem—sense of proportion, taste and tact. This is why the translators succeeded so well in accomplishing their literary miracle: by tinting their translation with the national coloration of Japan while using the colloquial speech of their native folklore. When you read their translation of *Japanese Folk Tales* about dragons, medusas, typhoons, and crabs the Russianisms they have woven into the verbal fabric seem perfectly natural. The miracle is that despite the Russianisms, the Japanese remain Japanese in translation and Japanese folklore does not become Russian folklore.

Or let's recall Romain Rolland's *Colas Breugnon* in the translation of Mikhail Lozinsky. The coloring of the French folk style is not in the slightest weakened by the fact that Lozinsky selects such Russian folk words and expressions for his recreation as *nekhrist', kaby, plutiaga,* and even *spinushka*.[40] Colas Breugnon does not in any way become a Tula or Ryazan peasant because of these Russian expressions and words. He remains a completely native Frenchman at all times, without losing his typical national traits for so much as an instant. Russian colloquial speech does not prevent him in the least from saving his Burgundy soul.

Just how is this miracle to be explained? Why, it may be asked, does a combination like this almost never succeed when used by others? Why should *spinushka* in the hands of other translators inevitably ruin an entire translation and leave not a single trace of Colas Breugnon's national character? Why is it that when Viktor Fedotov employs the very same Russianisms, he transforms a Scotsman into a Ryazan peasant, while *Colas Breugnon* in Mikhail Lozinsky's handling can even be permitted, so it would seem, an illegitimate combination of multistyled and heterogeneous words like the biblical name Delilah and the Russian folk exclamation *ai–liuli? Delilia! Delilia! Ai–liuli!*—this does not sound stylistically incongruous in the translation, nor does the word *ai–liuli* sound alien. We accept it as perfectly natural from the lips of a native-born Frenchman.

Why this occurs is not easy to say. I repeat: everything depends here on sense of proportion, talent, tact. Nowhere does Lozinsky overdo it, he never pumps his pedals, never overloads his text with outright Russian verbalisms—the result being that the vast majority have very light, barely perceptible touches of colloquial speech and not one is tied to the specific realia of our mode of existence. The important thing is that the stylistic aura of the entire text is so saturated with French colors that the very few (and cautiously chosen) Russian segments of folk speech merge organically without standing out against the general tone and without giving the impression of an illegitimate fusion of two styles.

The same Mikhail Lozinsky has to his credit still another, equally fruitful attempt to convey extraliterary speech in translation. I speak here of his translation of *The Life of Benvenuto Cellini.* In this case he ignored the lexicon of the original text and turned his attention exclusively to the syntax, well understanding that each of the personages who in one way or another departs from correct lexicon almost always has a highly undisciplined and chaotic syntax too. And nothing is to prevent translators who do not wish to resort to distortions of words from conveying the kinks of syntax of extraliterary speech. Lozinsky himself speaks of this in the foreword to his translation:

His [Benvenuto Cellini's] language is the living speech of the common man. The most painstaking translation is powerless to convey the dialectological peculiarities which lend to the original a large part of its charm. To strive to replace Cellini's solecisms with a system of Russian folk forms (*khochim, ittit'*) would be a profoundly false device. . . . But if Cellini's etymology is untranslatable, his syntax, the structure of his speech, can be translated more or less precisely. And we have perceived our basic task in following as closely as possible the curves, skips, and fractures of Cellini's style. . . . We have striven to ensure that every phrase of our text is *just as incorrect and in precisely the same way incorrect* as the phrasing of the original. (Emphasis mine—K. Ch.)[41]

At the time this was a sensational novelty. No translator had yet striven to intentionally distort syntax over an expanse of hundreds and hundreds of pages in translation. Of equal importance, the distortions were reproduced with a great sense of proportion, so that they are not glaring. There is nothing contrived in such rough clumsiness of style as: "Besides, the said Francesco said and he swore definitely that if he could have, that he would have stolen the gilt from this medal," or: "Trusting to my boots that they were very high, when I put my foot forward the soil parted," or: "My Benvenuto, that mean thing which was with you, I felt real sorry for him" (294, 296, 537). These barely perceptible, microscopic faults were sufficient to signal us that, as Lozinsky says in his foreword, "Cellini was not a grammarian," that "he wrote picturesquely, passionately, but clumsily," and that his prose is "an unbroken chain of unrelated clauses . . . or conjunctions which lead one astray" (42).

It follows from all this that translators always have the opportunity of reproducing a few—true, not all—peculiarities of colloquial speech, of extraliterary language, and consequently, the matter is not at all as hopeless as it seems to the defense attorney. Let's take, for example, the English novel *Martin Chuzzlewit* in the translation of N. Daruzes. This particular novel is dear to readers chiefly because of the grotesque figure, excellently drawn by Dickens, who stands at the peak of his genius for humor and powerful force of depiction—the figure of the base bigot and sly old vixen Mrs. Gamp, a living embodiment of toadyism, cunning, and falseness. Much in the literary heritage of this great novelist has begun to fade with time, many pages of his books which so passionately stirred his contemporaries have become so old fashioned that they are regarded by the present generation of readers as unnecessary ballast (particularly those embellished by sentimental rhetoric). But the image of Mrs. Gamp, the London sick nurse, lives and delights us to this very day. Her every appearance in the novel is greeted by readers with renewed laughter—chiefly becuase of her typically muddled London Cockney dialect. This slang has a heavy tinting of "lower-class" character, but since in her capacity as midwife and sick nurse Mrs. Gamp has been accustomed to mingling with the so-called upper class from early youth, her colloquial speech is saturated with words of a more cultured milieu which she mangles most amusingly. She pronounces the word "surprise" as "surprige," the word "excuse" as "excuge," the word "suppose" as "suppoge," the word "individual" as "indiwidgle," the word "situation" as "sitiwation." She is even unable to pronounce her own name, Sara. With her it comes out as "Sairey." The wildness of her concept of language reaches the point where she confuses the words "guardian" and "garden." How is one to convey this wildness into Russian when the Russian equivalents—*opekun* and *sad*—are not even remotely similar? This talented translator does not even try to find Russian equivalents, since she is well aware that no such equivalents exist. In the original Mrs. Gamp speaks like this:

> "Why, goodness me!" she said, "Mrs. Chuzzlewit! To think as I should see beneath this blessed ouse, which well I know it, Miss Pecksniff, my sweet young lady, to be a ouse as there is not many a like, worse luck, and wishin' it ware not so, which then this tearfull walley would be changed into a flowerin' guardian, Mr. Chuffey. . . ."

But with Daruzes Mrs. Gamp speaks perfectly correctly:

> "Ah lord, Mrs. Chuzzlewit! Who would have ever thought that I would see in this blessed house, Miss Pecksniff, my dear mistress, after all I know perfectly well that such homes are few, more's the pity, and one would wish there were a few more, then this, Mr. Chuffey, would not be a vale of tears, but a garden of Eden. . . ."[42]

Not a single departure from correct speech! While in the original there are five outright departures: "ouse," "ware," "guardian," and so on, and all these departures make up a unified system which cannot be re-created in another language.

And yet, despite all this, Russian readers still feel in Daruzes's bland translation—true, not quite clearly—what the style of Mrs. Gamp's verbal effusions really is. The translator still managed to find a sure and promising device to signal readers that Mrs. Gamp's speech departs from the normal speech standard. True, this apt device is applied too timidly, but nevertheless, the specific character of Mrs. Gamp's verbal effusions is revealed with sufficient clarity. Try carefully to get to the gist of this tirade, for example:

> "I know a lady, Harris is her name, I will not try to deceive you, Mrs. Chuzzlewit, she has a brother besides, that is, her husband has a brother besides, six feet three inches in height, and on his left arm he has a birthmark—a mad bull in Wellington boots, because his dear mama was chased into a shoe shop by a bull when she was in a certain condition: and happy is the one whose family is growing, as I have told my husband so many times when, as it would happen, we had a quarrel over the expenses, and often, as it would happen, I said to Mrs. Harris, 'Akh, Mrs. Harris, my lady! Your little face is simply angelic." And it would be angelic too, were it not for the pimples." (XI, 333)

No one would ever say this is correct, normal speech, because even though it is devoid of departures from normal speech, the syntax is chaotic. And herein lies one of the devices by which a translator can always give the reader at least some vague idea of the distinctive style of the original without resorting to inappropriate Russianisms. The translation is not at all too far removed from the original:

> "I know a lady, which her name, I'll not deceive you, Mrs. Chuzzlewit, is Harris, her husband's brother bein' six foot three, and marked with a mad bull in Wellington boots upon his left arm, on account of his precious mother havin' been worried by one into a

shoemaker's shop, when in a sitiwation which blessed is the man as
has his quiver full of sech, as many times I've said to Gamp when
words has roge betwixt us on account of the expense—and often
have I said to Mrs. Harris, 'Oh, Mrs. Harris, ma'am! your counte-
nance is quite a angel's.' Which, but for the pimples, it would
be." (698)

In addition to these fractures of syntax the translator
introduces—again too infrequently, unfortunately—a few random transformations in Mrs. Gamp's vocabulary, causing her, for
example, to use the word *serviz,* 'service,' for "surprise" (XI,
333). And instead of *deviz,* 'motto,' she uses the word *serviz* again
(XI, 249).

But if the opportunity had arisen to resort to Russianisms,
there would certainly have been no great defect in it. For the time
has long since passed for placing too severe a ban on slang and
dialectical verbalisms. Just because bad translators use them
clumsily, it does not follow that good translators must declare a
total boycott on them. Yes, with bad translators every sort of
vcheras' and *pokeda,* used irrelevantly, out of place, produces an
impression of falseness. But why should we make comparisons
with bad translators?

This subject is discussed most eloquently in the previously
quoted article by S. Petrov. The court considers this article urgent, stirring, burning. It is titled "On the Use of Colloquial
Speech." Its author argues passionately for the right of translators
to reproduce foreign colloquial speech with their own colloquial
speech—not literally, of course, but with commensurate tact and
creativity, without fearing accusations of tinselry. "It is necessary," he says, "to transplant a foreign work carefully and conscientiously onto Russian soil, and not mutilate it by distilling
and preparing it to please just any taste. . . . Ideally, a translation must elicit from readers the same *stylistic impression* experienced by the readers of the original" (95). Golden words, and
they will not be refuted by sophisms.

Do the translations of Mr. Parker and Mr. Guerney make the
same stylistic impression on the English reader as the original on

its readers? Not in the least. We may apply the term *distilled* to their translations, because their translations are cleansed of all the elements of artistry. The "stylistic impression" they convey is exactly the same as that we experience in reading a newspaper report or the minutes of a meeting. "First Ivan Denisovich did this, then he went there," and so on. When he translated Gogol's powerful comedy Mr. Guerney had the opportunity—true, only a small one—of reproducing its style in his own language. Of course, it should by no means be demanded that he lend a particular stylistic coloration by using the same words with which it is conveyed in the original. He should choose other words for a similar coloration of *The Inspector General*. But to refrain completely from reproducing the billiant canvas of the comedy means to refrain from all pretensions to the art of translation. If he is unable to translate the words *p'ianiushka* and *obizhatel'stvo* into English, then let them simply become "drunkard" and "oppressive." But in this case it follows that he should have revealed these deformations with some adjoining words introduced into the text, so that Anglo-American readers could feel at least partly what Gogol's stylistic coloration is like.

For that matter, if one looks closely at the texts of the five translators of *Ivan Denisovich* one encounters, now with one, now with another, an occasional expression which slipped in almost inadvertently, seemingly unintentionally, but which fully corresponds to the style of the original. Bela von Block, for example, translated *Oi, liut' tam segodnia budet* with the very precise colloquial equivalent, "It'd be murder out there" (31), and she found for *podsosat'sia* the very close equivalent in American slang "to horn in" (33). Thomas Whitney considered it possible to translate *dereviannyi bushlat* directly as "wooden overcoat" (70), and in this way saved several lines of his translation from banality. It was he who ventured to translate *vilami po vode,* 'with a fork through water,' with the equally picturesque expression, "to paddle a canoe with a pitchfork" (69). And this convinces me that there are many possibilities hidden in English speech for a translation that conveys more precisely the colloquial speech of the original. Nikolay Zabolotsky has said with great truth in *The Craft of*

Translation (1959, 252): "Blandscript is our personal enemy. Blandscript bespeaks an indifference of the heart and a disdain for the reader."

And should we perhaps prefer that Boris Pasternak did not resort in his translation of Hans Sachs's folk poetry to such expressions as *gliadi-kos'* and *pravednik kakoi?* (See Petrov, 93.) And who would criticize such a powerful master as M.N. Lyubimov because our folk speech sounds forth in his *Don Quixote* and *Pantagruel,* as a result of which neither Spaniards nor Frenchmen have become Russians in disguise, but assert their own national qualities even more powerfully in the minds of Russian readers? In comparison with these translations, the translations of this or that folk text done with the help of normalized blandscript seem even more pallid, more anemic to us. Call these translations "information translations" if you wish, or "distillery translations," or "protocol translations," but do not call them works of art.

And since an artistic translation is always and in all cases a creative act, we condemn these protocol translations of great works of art and find the defendants *guilty,* albeit deserving of clemency in view of the fact that their harmful actions were committed with the open complicity of the critics. This verdict is by no means final and is of course subject to appeal.

The reader who examines this court hearing intently will, I hope, be quickly persuaded that it is impossible to apply sweeping rules here. Precisely because it is a matter of art, such rules do not generally exist. There are no universal recipes here. Everything depends on individual circumstances. In the final analysis the fate of a translation is always decided by the translator's *talent,* his *cultural level,* his *taste,* his *tact.*

I have devised this trial in order to give readers a clear idea of how difficult and complex are the problems connected with the practice of translation and questions of style.

SIX

The Translator's Hearing. Rhythm.
Sound Patterns

BEFORE the translator undertakes to do a translation of a foreign author he must determine for himself precisely what the author's style is—his system of images, his rhythms.

The translator must read the author aloud as often as possible in order to catch the tempo and cadences which are as essential to artistic prose as they are to poetry. It is not possible, for example, to translate Ossian without reproducing his inner music. It is not possible to convey John Ruskin, or Walter Pater, or other masters of rhythmic ornamental prose without reproducing the variegated rhythmic pulsations that are the chief charm of these writers. It is indicative that of the four early translators of Charles Dickens's *A Tale of Two Cities* not one noticed that the novel's opening lines are essentially a poem in prose.

Many prose writers turn to the same methods used by poets for achieving artistic effects. Artistic prose aspires far more often than we realize to cadences, to the rhythmic sequences of the rise and fall of the voice, to alliteration and internal rhyme. The prose of Andrey Bely is subordinated even in his memoirs to a rhythmic structure, most often to an anapestic rhythm. The same thing can be said of Melnikov-Pechersky's two novels, *In the Woods* and *In the Mountains.* Even with such "prosaic prosists" as Charles Reed and Anthony Trollope it is not a rarity to find symmetrical sentence structures, alliteration, refrains, and other accessories of verse methods. The phenomena of artistic prose can be caught only by the most refined, attentive hearing, and every translator must develop his hearing by any means he can.

In her translation of Dickens's novel *Our Mutual Friend* M.A. Shishmareva translated a certain sentence this way: "All their furniture, all their friends, all their servants, their plate, their carriage, and they themselves were spic and span new." The original, on the other hand, says: "Everything about the Veneerings were spic and span new. All their furniture was new, all their friends were new, all their servants were new, their plate was new, their carriage was new, their horses were new, their pictures were new, they themselves were new. . . ."[1] The author was pleased to repeat the same verb nine times and the same adjective with nine nouns. The translator, on the other hand, obviously devoid of hearing, ignored this insistent, nine-times repeated refrain, and thus impoverished and diminished the entire sentence and robbed it of its rhythm. Dickens generally loved phonic adornments like this in which the same word is repeated with intrusive frequency. A sentence typical for him reads: "(We) went past . . . boat-builders' yards, shipwrights' yards, shipbreakers' yards, calkers' yards. . . ."[2] Yet in the translation of the same sentence in *David Copperfield* by Shishmareva we read: "We went past boat and ship yards" (31). An even more striking example of this careless disregard of rhythm can be observed, as already mentioned, in a translation of another novel by Dickens—*A Tale of Two Cities.* Dickens's novel begins like this:

It was the best of times, it was the worse of times, it was the age of wisdom, it was the age of foolishness, it was the epoch of belief, it was the epoch of incredulity, it was the season of light, it was the season of darkness, it was the spring of hope, it was the winter of despair, we had everything before us, we had nothing before us, we were all going to heaven, we were all going direct the other way. . . .

There is an almost poetic cadence in this excerpt. The sound symmetry conveys its ironic tone extremely well. But the translators, deaf to the charms of rhythm, preferred to translate it this way:

> It was the best and worst of times, it was the age of wisdom and foolishness, the epoch of belief and incredulity, the time of enlightenment and ignorance, the spring of hope and the winter of despair.[3]

Which is to say, they did not catch the author's intonations and thus robbed his words of the dynamism stemming from the rhythm.

I speak here only of word repetitions which organize the rhythmic structure of prose. By no means does repetition always fulfill this function. There is no relationship to rhythm in this sentence by Tolstoy, for example: "By the porch stood a carriage *tightly* bound in iron and leather with a well-fed horse *tightly* harnessed to a wide bowshaft, in the carriage sat a *tightly* belted steward with his eyes *tightly* shut."[4] Of course, a translation has to reproduce repetitions like this too. This chapter is not about this type of repetition, however, but about symmetrically arranged verbal constructs in which it is precisely the symmetry that imparts a rhythmic pattern to the whole sentence. And of course, the symmetrical construction of parallel semantic units in an extract of artistic prose is important not in and of itself, and not because of a particular verbal ornament is of value to us for aesthetic reasons, but solely because the verbal ornament heightens the emotional force of a given conjunction of words.

The rhythmic patterns of prose differ greatly from the rhythms of poetry. "The basic indicator of rhythm," says Professor L. Timofeyev in his study *Theory of the Verse Line,* "is above all a natural repetition of homogeneous phenomena; hence the attribute of prose rhythm is perceived in terms of the establishment of repetition. However, in prose rhythm we deal only with an elementary rhythmicity which does not approach the rhythm of a distinct construction" (58). And he quotes the French scholar P.

Vérier: "Prose rhythm is only a rudimentary rhythm" (58). The more difficult it is to detect the rhythm, the more refined the translator's hearing must be. Prose rhythm, says Andrey Fyodorov in *On Artistic Translation* (121), "is achieved not so much by a regular alternation of phonetic units (for example, stressed and unstressed syllables, whole groupings of syllables, masculine- and feminine-end words) as by a regulated arrangement of larger semantic and syntactic speech elements, by their dispersement in a defined order by means of word repetition, parallelism, contrast, symmetry, and the character of phrase and sentence linkages. In addition, prose rhythm is conditioned by emotional impulses, distribution of emotional forces, the nuances of feeling associated with a given speech extract." As an example, Fyodorov presents an excerpt in Russian from the prose of Heine which even in translation retains its rhythmic patterns. "In this translation," he notes, "the most important thing has been conveyed: the character of the phrase connections, the symmetrical correspondences and contrasts established among them, their linkages and the semantic echoes among the separate parts stemming from verbal repetition."

> My friends shall lie in half-ruined graves,
> while I remain, a lonely stalk of grain the
> reaper left,
> amidst a *new* generation grown up around me,
> with *new* desires and *new* ideas,
> with awe I'll hear their *new* names and *new* songs,
> *forgotten* the names of old,
> *forgotten* even I,
> esteemed, perhaps, by very *few*,
> despised by more than *few*,
> and loved by none. (121–22)

Verbal repetitions and semantic echoes like these can be detected only by an attentive hearing.

Romain Rolland's famous novel *Colas Breugnon* is sustained by a rhythm which is quite similar to the Russian *raioshnik*, folk verses with lines organized solely by striking end rhymes. The novel's hero, a jovial Burgundy winemaker, sprinkles his glib colloquial speech with facetious sayings and ringing rhymes which the remarkable master of translation Mikhail Lozinsky tried to reproduce in his translation. When any part of the translation, chosen at random, is cast out in lines, the rhymes become readily apparent:

> I am Colas Breugnon, a wise old bird,
> of Burgundy birth,
> a man of the earth,
> vast in girth . . .
> a giant man—a man of worth!
> I'm a stuffed old sack
> of tricks and smiles,
> mistakes and wiles,
> of all a man can want,
> and much he'd better want. . . .[5]

Some twenty years earlier the same novel was translated by M. Elagina (Ryzhkina-Pambe). An attempt was made to convey the *raioshnik* form in her translation too. In one instance Colas Breugnon says of himself that he is

> a forthright creature
> of simple nature,

but later on the translator all but rejects attempts to reproduce the verse structure of Rolland's novel and translates the same excerpt as, "How we did stuff that old sack with joys and sorrows, tricks, wiles, and inanities," and so on.[6] In Lozinsky's translation Colas Breugnon says:

> If you want to know the moral of the thing:
> do for yourself and be done by the King.

In Elagina's translation the idea is expressed in prose: "The moral of all this is : help yourself and the King will help you." There is not even a feeble attempt at rhyme here. At times, in order to emphasize the poetic quality of the novel's intricate prose, Lozinsky hits upon wondrous, curious rhymes where Elagina offers none at all. Elagina's translation is conscientious and talented, but it has lost a great deal by her disregard for the phonic distinctiveness of the original.

An instinct for rhythm, a musical instinct, is indispensable to the translator not only in those instances where he must deal with rhythmic prose, but also when he is presented with the task of translating ordinary, everyday prose which has no pretensions to verse rhythms. In *The Adventures of Huckleberry Finn* Mark Twain depicts a prim, tedious woman who torments the boy with her attempts at pedagogy. In order to characterize the relentless way she pesters poor Huckleberry, the author has her repeat his name three times: "Don't put your feet up there, Huckleberry . . . don't scrunch up like that, Huckleberry . . . don't gap and stretch like that, Huckleberry. . . ." But the translator, devoid of a refined hearing, did not even notice this triple repetition, did not understand the role it was assigned by the author, and translated the entire passage with a gingerly rendition: "Don't put your feet up there, Finn! Don't stretch, don't scrunch up, Huckleberry!"[7] The psychological value of the passage was completely lost.

If phonic perception of a text is so necessary to the translator of prose, just think how much more important it is to the translator of poetry. Just think what a richly refined hearing must be possessed by, for example, the translator of Virgil! After all, the chief power of *The Aeneid* is to be found in its magnificent acoustics, its sound patterns. "No one," Valery Bryusov has written in an article in the journal *Hermes*:

no one among all the poets of all ages and all nations was able to paint pictures with sound more perfectly than Virgil. For every picture, for every image, for every idea, Virgil finds words which communicate them, interpret them, suggest them to the reader by their sound. Virgil's sound patterns turn his poetry now into a painting, now into a work of sculpture, now into music. We see as well as hear, what the poet says. Where necessary, Virgil's sound patterns become onomatopeic. To this must be added his lofty power over the rhythm of the line—equally important to the way he turns the content into a painting—his unusual ability to play with caesuras, and finally his special artistry in arranging words so that some ideas move to the forefront, others remain in the background, and still others manifest themselves unexpectedly. All of this turns a reading of *The Aeneid* in the original into something beyond artistic pleasure to continual wonderment over the artist's exceptional skill.[8]

Which means that the translator who is insensitive to the delights and meaning of sounds must never undertake to translate *The Aeneid*. There are some minds for which words mean only what they learn about them in dictionaries. Such minds are able to create excellent scientific works, but the translation of even so much as a single line of *The Aeneid,* or *Metamorphoses,* or the ballads of Coleridge, or Victor Hugo's *La légende des siècles* is a task beyond them. The verbal music that exists in every original work of poetry is only more noticeable and, so to speak, naked in *The Aeneid*. "Sound patterns, the sounds of words in poetry," says M. Lozinsky in an article titled "The Art of Verse Translation,"

act upon our emotions more sharply than any other phenomenon. These are not simply musical sounds which agitate us. These are the sounds of words, and words are bearers of ideas, images, conceptions, feelings. And these ideas, images, conceptions, and feelings are endowed with a light that can be heard. They join together into a complex echoing, their sounds mingle them in some mysterious fashion, they create complex networks of semantic and emotional associations for us. Imagine that you have two lines of poetry before you. They acquire their life from the reverberating light of sounds. Change the sound of one of the words of the first line, and instantaneously a sound you cannot catch in the second line, a sound which was replete with a disturbing idea, perishes. It becomes blind and inexpressive because the sound echoing it in the first line has perished.[9]

Sound patterns are of course very important in the work of a poet like Nekrasov, about whom legend has survived among esthetes that his verses are clumsy, prosaic, and of little artistic value. In his remarkable couplet:

> VOlga, VOlga, vesnoi mnogoVOdnoi,
> Ty ne tAk zAlivAesh' poliA. . .

the first line is founded from start to finish on the repeated sound *VO,* while the second is founded on the sound *A.* But in the French translation, these lines are conveyed with utter contempt for the sound patterns:

> Volga! Volga! même grossie des pluies [sic] du
>   printemps,
> Tu couvres moins nos champs . . .[10]

True, the meaning of these brilliant lines is not so offensively distorted as the sound patterns. (Although the meaning is in fact distorted: Russian rivers are fed by melting snows, not rain.) But after all, sound patterns "enable the poet to say more than mere words can say," and to deprive him of this power is to deprive him of his most powerful means of acting on the reader's psyche.

The same deafness was revealed by the translator Vorony, who attempted to offer a Ukrainian version of a well-known couplet by Fet:

> I know not what I will
> Sing, but only that the song is ready.

The most important thing about the structure of Fet's couplet is the unusual break between the words "will" and "sing"—the enjambment preceding the word "sing" at the start of the second line—which creates a disruption of the syntax corresponding to a lack of awareness as yet about the song Fet will sing. But the translator completely omits the disruption and gives only a most ordinary "occasional" rhythm:

> What I will sing, I know not,
> But what I will sing is ready.

The same deafness was revealed by the translator of Shakespeare, Sokolovsky, when he transformed Queen Margaret's monotonous plaint in *Richard III* into these variegated lines:

> Killed
> Were my spouse and my son by Richard. Thou also
> Were of Richard and Edward deprived,
> Killed in battle by the same Richard.

This deafness became especially apparent after the appearance of Anna Radlova's translation of the same tragedy. Her translation is very weak, filled with scores of imprecise usages, but the stern rhythm of Queen Margaret's plaint is conveyed with maximum approximation to the original:

> I had an Edward, till a Richard kill'd him;
> I had a Harry, till a Richard kill'd him:
> Thou hadst an Edward, till a Richard kill'd him;
> Thou hadst a Richard, till a Richard kill'd
> him.   (IV, 4)[11]

The four-times repeated combination of identical words ("till a Richard kill'd him") is reproduced exactly in the translation. Other translators—as a direct consequence of their deafness— attempted to impart variations to the unfailingly repeated words "kill'd him": "perished," "destroyed," "deprived of life," and so forth, and so forth. This variation of verbs resulted in a variation of rhythm, when in fact a correspondence to the original demanded the monotonous repetition of the identically structured lines.

The translator could have caught this monotonous repetition by sight, if not by hearing, for the identity of the syntactical structure of all four lines, following as they do one after the other, is evident here even from a careless reading. After all, it is possible to be a poor musician, but still be able to read notes to perfection. Even those translators who do not have a refined hearing for verse can detect the syntactic-rhythmic forms of poetry visually and make an effort to reproduce them in translation. Let's suppose that Shishmareva really was deaf to Dickens's intonations. Even so, the intonations cannot only be heard, they are immediately apparent to the eyes, and no one prevented the translator from seeing what she could not hear.

Precisely because such an immense role is played in a work of verbal art by repetitions of sound which cannot be reproduced in another language, many writers have from ancient times expressed a conviction that a precise translation of such works is generally impossible. Indeed, listen for a moment to the music of these lines by Pushkin, adorned with the swift repetition of the sound *u*:

> BrozhU li ia vdol' Ulits shUmnykh,
> VkhozhU l' vo mnogoliUdnyi khram,
> SizhU l' mezh iUnoshei bezUmnykh,
> Ia predaiUs' moim mechtam.[12]

Without its phonetic intricacy, this poem would not be poetry. The very arrangement of the sound *u* is far from accidental here. In order to act upon the emotions of his Russian readers, the poet had to ensure that the sound *u* was heard three times in the odd lines, and once or twice in the even lines (3–2–3–1). Now imagine that a Spanish poet wishes to reproduce this poem by Pushkin in his own language. Since the poem's form is inseparable from its content, the translator would have to consider himself bound to convey the aural repetition. But Spanish does not have verbs ending with the sound *u* such as Russian verbs (*brozhU, vkhozhU, sizhU*), and in Spanish the words for *bezUmnyi, mnogoliUdnyj,* and *shUmnyi* do not have the sound *u* either. Thus, no matter how the translator might rack his brains, he would be able to do what is required. And even were he to manage by some miracle to reproduce the music of the lines, his translation would still not be sufficiently precise, because the sound *u* has a completely different effect on a Spaniard's ear than on a Russian's.

The impossibility of conveying the musical form of poetry from one language to another has driven a great many translators to despair, and it has been said more than once that a precise translation of a work of poetry is a hopeless undertaking doomed to failure in advance. "Hence the language of poets," said Percy

Bysshe Shelley, "has ever affected a certain uniform and harmonious recurrence of sound, without which it were not poetry, and which is scarcely less indispensable to the communication of its action than the words themselves without reference to that peculiar order. Hence the vanity of translation. . . ." And Shelley reinforces his thought with a remarkable comparison: ". . . it were as wise to cast a violet into a crucible that you might discover the formal principle of its colour and odour, as to seek to transfuse from one language into another the creations of a poet."[13] The very same thing was said five hundred years before by Dante. "Let every man know," he wrote, "that nought involving the aims of harmony in the musical bases of poetry can be translated from one language to another without destroying its harmony and charm." This same thought was expressed by the modern Soviet poet Al. Mezhirov, who wrote verse lines "On the Margins of a Translation" to the effect that poetry is eternally impossible to translate because it remains "ever faithful to its native language."[14] I encountered the idea again not long ago in a recent publication on the art of translation in the United States. A professor from the University of Texas, Werner Winter, even titled his article "Impossibilities of Translation." The article begins with these words:

> It seems to me that we may compare the work of a translator with that of an artist who is asked to create an exact replica of a marble statue, but who cannot secure any marble. He may find some other stone or some wood, or he may have to use a brush or a pencil and a sheet of paper. Whatever his material, if he is a good craftsman, his work may be good or even great; it may indeed even surpass the original, but it will never be what he set out to produce, an exact replica of the original.[15]

Boris Pasternak says the same thing: ". . . translations are not realizable because the chief charm of a work of art is its unrepeatability. How can a translation expect to repeat it?"[16] The well-known English poet and critic Robert Graves, author of numerous historical novels translated into other languages, and himself an indefatigable translator, summed up his great experience as a translator in these words: "Finally he [the translator] must realize that translation is a polite lie, but nevertheless a lie. . . ." The writer provides a most simple example:

> *Ein Stückchen Brot, un morceau de pain, un trozito de pan,* are all similarly rendered in English as "a morsel of bread." But the altogether different sounds of these words convey immense variations in shape, colour, size, weight and taste of the breadstuff to which they refer, and in the eater's attitude to them.[17]

The American poet Robert Frost said that poetry is "what gets lost in translation." These words deprive translators of all hope, and even of the right to exist. The seventeenth-century English poet James Howell expressed in a poem the very same joyless thought. He compares a verse original with an opulent Turkish rug. When one looks at the gray reverse side of the rug one would never guess the fantastic and brilliant traceries that adorn its front side. A translation is just such reverse side of a rug which gives not the slightest notion of what the rug—that is, the original verse—is really like.

Sometimes it seems there is good reason for such pessimism. But then one recalls Schiller's *Der Taucher* and Sir Walter Scott's *The Eve of St. John* in Zhukovsky's translations, one recalls Mickiewicz's *Budrys* as translated by Pushkin, Lermontov's "Uber allen Gipfeln" from Goethe, Alexey Tolstoy's *Die Braut von Korinth* from Goethe, and the scores of other masterpieces of modern masters of translation, and then all these bitter thoughts about the impossibility of translation evaporate. In the end Boris Pasternak came around to the same optimistic view, although admittedly on different grounds. "Translations are conceivable," he writes, "because ideally even they must be works of art and in their common character as texts come up to par with their originals in their own unrepeatability. Translations are conceivable because through the ages they have translated whole literatures to each other, and translations are not a means for the familiarization of individual works but a way for the centuries old contact among cultures and peoples" (166).

SEVEN

Syntax. Intonation. Toward a Method of Translating Shakespeare

1 The exact reproduction of foreign syntax in all its specific features is of course impossible. It is impossible to conceive of an exact copy of the phraseology of another language, because each language has its own syntax. But in cases where the syntax of the original text employs repetition, parallelisms, anaphoras, or symmetrical verbal constructions which facilitate the organization of a marked poetic or prose rhythm and can easily be conveyed by available Russian syntactical means, the reproduction of these syntactic forms in a translation into another language is obligatory.

It does not follow from this, however, that the syntax of our Russian translations should sound un-Russian. A good translator, even when he has the foreign text right before him, thinks consistently in his own language and only in his own language, without surrendering for so much as one instant to the influence of foreign expressions which are alien to the syntactical rules of his own language. The Russian translator must make every effort to ensure that each translated sentence sounds Russian by adhering to the logic and aesthetics of his own language.

At one time fierce debates were conducted on this subject. The distinguished English critic, poet, and philosopher Matthew Arnold summed them up this way:

On one side it is said that the translation ought to be such "that the reader should, if possible, forget that it is a translation at all, and be lulled into the illusion that he is reading an original work,— something original" (if the translation be in English) "from an English hand. . . ." On the other hand [another] declares that he "aims at precisely the opposite: to retain every peculiarity of the original, so far as he is able, *with the greater care the more foreign it may happen to be*"; so that it may "never be forgotten that he is imitating, and imitating in a different material."[1]

Modern masters of translation subscribe to the first of these two mutually exclusive methods of translation. The syntax of the original, they insist, ought not to take control of the translator. The translator must keep full control of the syntax of his native language. In this regard, it is simply impossible to translate directly into Russian such English sentences as, "He walked *with his eyes* turned to the ground and *with his arms* folded across his chest," or, "He looked like a Spaniard *with his swarthy skin,*" or, "The groom looked like a dandy *with his draped spats and his round face.*" In English these sentences mean, "while he was walking, his eyes were turned to the ground and his arms were folded across his chest," "he looked like a Spaniard because of his swarthy skin," and "the groom's draped spats and his round face made him look like a dandy." Were these sentences to be translated directly into Russian with the preposition "with" [*s, so*], they would turn out to mean, "he *and* his eyes turned to the ground *and* his arms folded across his chest walked together," "he *and* his swarthy skin looked like a Spaniard," and "the groom, his draped spats, and his round face looked like dandies." Nevertheless, I have found just such direct incorporations of English syntax into Russian, and unfortunately they have become an all too common phenomenon. Even in the works of Anatole France, which appeared in Russian translation under the editorship of A.V. Lunacharsky, we find such expressions as, for example, "He found her very pretty *with her tiny nose* " In French, this means that he found her to be pretty because her nose was tiny. Translated directly into Russian, it means, "He found her pretty in the company of her tiny nose."[2]

Generally in our literature, a peculiar, conventional language of translation has arisen which has nothing in common with correct Russian. Three examples of our translators' pet lexical items are the word *massa*, 'mass,' as an attempt to convey the English expression "a lot of," *para*, 'pair,' as an equivalent for the English expression "a couple of (hours)," and *chleny*, 'members,' for "arms and legs," even though the plural *chleny* does not mean "members" in the sense of "arms and legs" in Russian. It is a peculiarity of Russian syntax to replace possessive pronouns with prepositional constructions. Under the influence of English, translators have begun to use possessive pronouns incorrectly. English speakers can say either "her eyes are green" or "she has green eyes," but only the latter, constructed in Russian with the preposition *u* and the regular pronoun, is correct for our possessive. In many recent translations we encounter such expressions as, "I would have saved him, but I lacked the courage *to do it*," or, "He treats us well, I don't understand why *he does it*," when the sentences would sound much better without the awkwardly dangling words at the end. Syntactic calques are used with particular zeal by the well-known advocate of verbal precision (that is, literalism) Evgeny Lann. We are likely to encounter in his translations direct, and thus incorrect, conveyances of English phrases such as "with his face expressing lively satisfaction."[3] As I have pointed out, the Russian preposition "with" cannot be used as it is used here in English. His direct conveyance means, "He and his face were expressing lively satisfaction."

Russian syntax does not permit the use of an adverbial subordinate clause if its subject does not agree with the subject of the main clause. And yet, when our translators encounter an English sentence such as, "Because I was a tramp, all sorts of acts of vandalism were blamed on me," they are apt to translate it directly into Russian, the result being a non sequitur: "While being in the capacity of a tramp, all sorts of acts of vandalism were blamed on me." Or they translate "While I was lying in the ditch, it seemed impossible that I would be rescued" directly and thus incorrectly as "Lying in the ditch, rescue seemed impossible to me." R. O. Shor has justly remarked that a servile reproduction of foreign grammatical forms stems chiefly from "the translator's trembling worship of grammatical forms whose fundamental bases are beyond his comprehension." She continues: "Because he is ignorant of the fundamental bases of either the foreign language or his own, he is unable to find syntactical equivalents and slavishly copies syntactical expressions which are alien to his own language. This is what gives rise to such non sequiturs as, 'With her graceful young girl's waist she listened to his poems.' "[4]

Similarly, translators forget that in Russian the accusative case for the direct object becomes genitive only if the negative particle *ne* is related to the verb which governs the object. They introduce the genitive case even when the negative particle is joined to verbs having no direct relation to the direct object. They write, "I don't want to describe the diverse feelings," and put "diverse feelings" in the genitive instead of the accusative, forgetting that the negative particle is connected to the verb "want," not the verb "to describe." This rule is violated more often than any other. Even good translators write, "A match cannot produce lightning," putting "lightning" in the genitive instead of the accusative, and "That couldn't have happened," using the genitive *etogo* for "that" instead of the nominative *eto*.[5]

When they bow to the syntax of another language, translators sometimes add superfluous words which make their sentences heavy and awkward. Russian translators consider it permissible to compose such sentences as, "What was worst of all—that was when we stopped praying," when it would have been much simpler to write, "Worst of all, having finished our prayers. . . ." As a general rule, Russian translators should do their utmost to ensure that a foreign author's phraseology does not lose its dynamism and lightness, and that laconic phrases do not become waterlogged and swollen. It is well known that a huge majority of words in the English language (especially in its latest forms) are monosyllabic. On the average, English words are half the length of their Russian equivalents. This shortness imparts a particular power and concentratedness to English speech. It is unavoidable that in a translation into Russian an energetic passage of seven lines will turn into a limpid eleven or twelve lines. This is fatal for a language which has the monosyllabic word "crime" instead of our five-syllable *prestuplenie,* "bus" instead of *omnibus,* "wee" instead of *maliusen'kii,* and in which sentences often do without connectives. Interesting here is a table comparing the length of words in English, German, and Russian (based on a text of one thousand words):[6]

Number of Syllables	1	2	3	4	5	6	Average
English	824	139	30	6	1	—	1.22
German	428	342	121	41	8	—	1.74
Russian	328	288	237	121	19	6	2.24

In order to somehow unburden a translation of an English text, it is necessary wherever possible, especially in conversational speech, to excise all superfluous words. This will at least in some small part convey to the translation some of the lightness that marks the original text thanks to the shortness of English words and the simplicity of English syntax. In an old translation of *Barnaby Rudge* we read: "I was, I can no longer be it." Throw out the last word, and the sentence becomes significantly lighter: "I was, I can no longer be." In the same translation, it is said that the buds of the trees opened up into leaves. Throw out the last words "up into leaves," and you spare the sentence from awkwardness, banality, and three superfluous words. In another place it is written, "She was exactly the person whom he wanted to see." The sentence can easily be reduced by eliminating "whom," the result being, "She was exactly the person he wanted to see." Why say, "I don't pay any attention to that circumstance," when "I pay no attention" will do so much better?[7]

Of course, in attempting to unburden the syntax in this way, it is necessary to cast out only the truly superfluous, that which the sentence can do without, that which doing without will make as free, colloquial, and unpedantic as the original. On the other hand, casting out as unnecessary ballast the important elements of the text which were cast out by certain translators of Shakespeare is not recommended under any circumstances, because this leads directly to distortions of the original. After all, the intonations of speech—its emotive, expressive level, its very soul—are directly linked with rules of syntax.

2 This is especially noticeable in translations of poetry. Intonations are the prime basis of the line. A line without intonations is not a line. Among the Russian translators of Shakespeare there was once a whole group who for the sake of a "precise" reproduction of rhythms, mangled (or more correctly, completely destroyed) the intonations of Shakespeare's lines. In *Othello,* for example, Desdemona says before her death: ". . . why I should fear, I know not, / Since guiltiness I know not; but yet I feel I fear" (V, ii). In place of this concise and coherent, logically clear sentence the translator Anna Radlova forced Desdemona to shriek three abrupt utterances: "I fear . . . / Why should I?—[I am] without guilt."[8] It is as if Desdemona had asthma or a shortness of breath, and were gasping after each utterance: "I fear [pause] Why should I? [pause] Without guilt." If you have asthma, you have no breath left to articulate your lines with expression. To judge from this translation one would think that every character in *Othello* suffered from the same serious disorder. Cassio ought to say, according to Shakespeare, concisely and coherently: "You are jealous now. / That this is from some mistress, some remembrance . . ." (III, iv). But asthma forces him to shout three abrupt utterances in succession: "Really, you've become jealous! Really, as if from a mistress! Really, from some remembrance!" The thrice-repeated "Really!"—*Uzh! Uzh! Uzh!*—emphasizes even more strongly the abruptness of asthmatic speech. The original does not have the "Really!" or the exclamation marks, or the pause after each exclamation.

Even the Moor of Venice himself turns out to have asthma. In the original, for example, he says with utmost smoothness and coherence: "I'll see before I doubt; when I doubt, prove" (III, iii). In Radlova's translation he utters three abrupt verbs: "To see, to doubt, to prove!" The Duke suffers from the same ailment. According to Shakespeare he ought to ask the Senators, "How say you by this change?" (I, iii). In the translation he can barely catch his breath long enough to declare, "What a change!" Sufferers from asthma are not up to eloquence—they are more likely to gasp out a thought as abruptly as possible.

In the process of chopping the vast majority of Shakespeare's lines down to bare stumps, the translator just as often chops out words without which the lines become incomprehensible, and sometimes even senseless. What, for example, is the meaning of such a rebus as "Otherwise I say you have become wrath— / You are no longer a man," or: "I beg you in your report . . . / To say who I am, nothing weakening, / Not adding maliciously," or: "But she must die—she will betray others," or: "This will not be believed in Venice, General, / Though I will swear I saw it myself. It is excessive!" These amputations of human speech, deprived as they are of vital intonations, have nothing in common with Shakespeare's poetry, of course. They are the result of the translator throwing out some of the most important words and printing whatever odd bits and pieces were left after the operation with the pretense they are Shakespeare's own lines.

Some words can be quite easily cut out—those words whose absence does not destroy the structure of the syntax. The excision of such words does not do any particular harm to the text being translated. If Shakespeare has "the general's surgeon" (V, i), and the translator writes "surgeon," the reader loses comparatively little, for the basic speech construction is untouched. The reader's loss is equally significant if instead of the phrase, "Those charms, thine eyes" (V, i), the translator gives only, "Those charms." These losses are in the nature of things; it is not of such petty details I am speaking here. I am speaking about those invalids of human speech which have had their arms and legs chopped off and have thereby lost all resemblance to the original

poetry of Shakespeare. I could offer fifty or a hundred such invalids from Radlova's translation. Here are six:

> The devil! You're robbed! Shame! Dress yourself!
> Your heart is broken, half your soul lost!
>
> They point out—a hundred and seven galleys. . . .
>
> [She] knows how to think and knows how to hide it.
>
> Whether foolish and fair, this is a delicate matter.
>
> He could command; but here's a defect!
>
> It seemed, the thrill of your glance,
> And nevertheless, she loved.

And they go on and on. Compare any of these half-mean-
ingless sentences with the original and you will see how Radlova,
deaf as she is to intonations, has utterly devastated Shakespeare's
phraseology. The reader will strive in vain to divine what is meant
by the Senator's enigmatic statement, "They point out—a
hundred and seven galleys." How can galleys moored off the
island of Cyprus be "pointed out" from Venice? The phrase
"point out" has no resemblance whatsoever to the original, for
the original reads: "My letters say a hundred and seven galleys"
(I, iii). Shakespeare does not say, "The devil! You're robbed!. . ."
and so on as Radlova's translation has it. He says: "Zounds, sir,
you're robbed; for shame, put on your gown; / Your heart is
burst, you have lost half your soul" (I, i). In the original, Shakespeare says: "She that could think and ne'er disclose her mind"
(II, i), and: "She never yet was foolish that was fair" (II, i), and:
"And when she seemed to shake and fear your looks, / She loved
them most" (III, iii). He does not say, As Radlova has it: "Otherwise I say you have become wrath— / You are no longer a man,"
or: "But she must die—she will betray others." He says: "Or I
shall say you are in a spleen, / And nothing of a man" (IV, i), and:
"Yet she must die, else she'll betray more men" (V, ii).
    This abruptness and lack of precision oblige the reader to

attack almost every line with questions. Where? How? Why? When? When, for example, the reader encounters, "She gave him," the reader of course asks what, and to whom? When he reads, "Hatred the only consolation," he asks whose consolation and hatred for whom or what? Readings like these have to be interrupted every moment with questions. "I do not believe." Believe what? "I know." Know what? "I thank you." For what? "[He] fears his father." Whose father, and why is he afraid of him? And so forth, and so forth.

A system of verse translation based on the method of chopping speech out of a text makes Shakespeare vague because it destroys his vital and natural intonations one after another. It ends with a strange paradox: for me, a Russian reader, the English text is often more accessible and intelligible than the Russian translation. I read these two lines of the translation, for example: "He who laughs after the thief with contempt, / Lessens the burden of newly rising woes." What does "burden" mean here? What are those "newly rising woes"? And why is the burden of these newly rising woes lessened simply because someone laughs contemptuously after an escaping thief? The solution to this rebus is to be found in the original. There it is clearly stated that it is not simply a matter of someone in general, but of a particular man who has just been robbed—"the robb'd." According to Shakespeare: "The robb'd that smiles steals something from the thief; / He robs himself that spends a bootless grief" (I, iii). Shakespeare speaks here about "the robb'd," that is, about Senator Brabantio, whose favorite daughter has been stolen by the Moor. Throwing out the phrase "the robb'd" deprived the sentence of all meaning.

It is worth noting here that whenever I come across some unintelligible sentence in Radlova's translation and then look up the same sentence in the old translation by Pyotr Veynberg, I inevitably find that his translation is far more intelligible. I do not at all mean to say that Veynberg's translation is superior. To the contrary, it is watered down and prolix. But with all its shortcomings the translation is more precise and intelligible than Radlova's.

Let's take as an example two of the lines already mentioned:

"To say who I am, nothing weakening, / Not adding maliciously." To begin with, this is simply not Russian. No one speaks Russian like this. In Veynberg's translation the same lines read as follows: "Present me / As I am, not lessening the guilt, / Not adding with intent."[9] This translation is not beyond reproach, but all the same it is more faithful and grammatical and intelligible than Radlova's version. Compare both to the original: "I pray you, in your letters, / When you shall these unlucky deeds relate, / Speak of me as I am; nothing extenuate, / Nor set down aught in malice . . ." (V, ii). With Veynberg's help, it is quite easy to decipher still another of the vague lines we strove so valiantly to make sense of in Radlova's translation: "Though I will swear I saw it myself. It is excessive!" That incomprehensible utterance, "It is excessive!" is exclaimed in the play by the nobleman Lodovico when Othello strikes Desdemona. As Veynberg has it, Lodovico says that no one will believe him: " . . .though I'd swear / I saw it myself. . . . My lord, it is too much!" This is a natural Russian sentence. Its intonations are perfectly audible. But that phrase of Radlova's, "It is excessive!" No one ever speaks Russian like this. One can almost imagine one man striking and a bystander shouting reproachfully, "It is excessive!" And still another equally undecipherable line of Radlova's translation: "Hope took form—our ruler." Veynberg's translation, fully correspondent to the original, again sounds more comprehensible and natural: "Presentiment tells me, it is / Our ruler."

Several of Veynberg's lines have long ago become common usage. Who, for example, does not know the magnificent lines from the first act of *Othello* which have come to be quoted as widely in Russia as in England: "She loved me for the dangers I had passed, / And I loved her that she did pity them" (I, iii)? The translation of these two lines is among Veynberg's most brilliant achievements. But Radlova translated it as: "She loved for my martial labors, / And I loved her for her pity." Whom did she love? Pity for whom? Pity for what? In the first of these two lines in the original the word "me" is very perceptible. "She loved me." And the translator had to cast out just this word! As Shakespeare has it, the words of the two lines are parallel: "She loved me . . . / And I loved her. . . ." But by casting out the word "me" and pushing the word "her" toward the end of the second sentence, the translator completely destroyed the structure of the syntax. Besides this, she inflicted a new distortion of meaning on the second line. Othello loved Desdemona not because she was generally disposed to pity, but because she pitied him in particular. Othello says it himself: the dangers he passed aroused a tender sympathy in her, "And I loved her that she did pity them." By casting out the word "them" Radlova imposed an aimless, out-of-character pity on Desdemona.

Involved here is not simply the obscuring of meaning, but also the destruction of vital intonations. After all, if an actor is obliged to speak like an asthmatic, what sort of free diction will there be in his gasping, compulsive, broken shouting? It is one thing when Desdemona beseeches Othello to forgive Cassio by asking, "But shall't be shortly?" (III, iii). It is quite another if she barks jerkily, "But the time?" There can be no correct intonations in such an abrupt utterance as, "But the time?" In her pursuit of senseless brevity the translator ultimately destroyed the broad, free, whimsical flow of speech that is inherent to Shakespearian diction. By forcing Shakespeare's heroes to shout at random such broken, disconnected phrases as "But the time?" "But here's a defect!" "Are you decent?" "I'll be bloody," "Half your soul lost," "here—general," "Did you recognize her? How terribly she deceived . . ." "What did she tell you?" "Of the lamps . . ." "Call . . ." Anna Radlova has thereby vulgarized their vital, multicolored speech, rich in its spiritual tones, and imparted a drumbeat character to it.

When Emilia tells the unjustly suffering Cassio that Othello loves him as before, "And needs no other suitor to his likings" (III, i), we can sense her deep compassion. But when Radlova forces Emilia to say straight out, "There is no need for intercession!" we feel the callous vulgarity that underlies the entire translation. This vulgarity is not so much in individual words as in the syntax, the intonations, in the way the words sound. This insensitivity to all that is in Shakespeare refined, lyrical, pensive, fine, tender, has resulted in distortions the like of which have not occurred in our translation practice for decades. The reviewers for some reason noticed only the vulgarity of the translator's vocabulary. But truly, this vulgarity is nothing in comparison with the vulgarity of her intonations. The old translations of Shakespeare's *Othello* were are times naive and anemic, but the Shakespearian diction was preserved with great piety, and this allowed for the recital of Shakespearian lines of verse as lines of verse. But where is the sound of poetry in such stumps of odd phrases as, "Not love—guilt," "You say—robbery?" or "They point out—a hundred and seven galleys"? None of these verbal stumps can be recited as poetry. They can only be reported military fashion, like "Aye–aye, sir!" or "No excuse, sir!"

3 In mulling over the question of how the translator achieved such results, I have become convinced that in most instances it stems from the destruction of seemingly third-rate worldlets such as "this," "my," "she," "her," "it," "if," "though," "why," "really," "when," and so on. It never occurred to me before how much of the burden of vital human speech is borne by little words and verbalisms like these. Only now, when this miserable translator has cast out no less than 70 percent of the verbal small fry, have I realized what a naked, broken, colorless, gaunt, soulless thing this can make of a Shakespearian text! It becomes apparent that precisely these verbalisms play an immense role in the creation of intonations. It would seem to be all the same whether Cassio turned to Bianca and said, "Take out this work!" or, "Take me this work out" (III, iv). But "Take this work out!" is soulless, dead, while "Take me this work out" is a vital human sentence containing a multitude of intonational possibilities.

That it is precisely these verbal small fry—these supposedly empty words and verbalisms which can be so easily dispensed with—which function as the chief bearers of vital intonations, can be very easily proved by a simple experiment. Take any Russian poem, let's say a poem by Nekrasov, and try to deform it à la Radlova method. Cast out all the "unnecessary" words and verbalisms in the same way they have been cast out of her translations of Shakespeare, and then take a look at what is left of its intonations. Take, for example, these two lines: "Yet truly a storm there was! / Ere haven we found!" In accordance with the Radlova method, these lines would of course have to be translated into another language as: "There was a storm, / Haven was found!" Only such unobtrusive words as "yet," "truly," "we," and "ere" have been cast out or changed here. The meaning has not been touched. But nevertheless, all of the emotive expressiveness of the lines has vanished. When someone says, "Yet truly a storm there was!" he expresses a profoundly emotive attitude toward a storm which turned out to be more frenzied than expected. But when he says simply that there was a storm, he has made nothing but an indifferent protocol statement of fact. When someone says, "Ere haven we found!" the line is imbued with recently experienced terror. The speaker expresses amazement that the storm has not destroyed him and others. But if he simply states that haven was found, there can be no emotive coloration in such an amputation—not wonder, nor terror, nor joy.

This is why none of Shakespeare's inspiration, temperament, emotiveness can be conveyed in translations done by such a faulty method. Shakespeare's heroes always experience the simple facts of their utterances with great passion, and this passion is not to be expressed in such bare stumps of sentences as, "I fear," "But the time?" "But here's a defect!" "It is excessive!" Not only the expressiveness of Shakespeare's speech is lost in such broken sentence constructions, but also the logical connections. Shakespeare's characters are likely to speak in far-flung sentences which unfold in series of syllogisms. The Radlova method is impotent here too. Just compare the First Senator's long speech at the start of the first act, second scene, with the version given in her translation. According to Shakespeare, the speech is a single long sentence composed of clauses which unfold one after the other. As Radlova has it, it is broken into abrupt utterances. It is especially in the translation of logically constructed series of clauses such as these that this type of translator is weakest, because such translations are founded on the destruction of syntax, and what sort of clause construction is possible if the syntactic constructions of the original are not sustained?

The extent of Radlova's indifference to Shakespeare's intonations can be seen in the fact that she changes many of his statements into questions. This dubious device is used more than once or twice in her translation. In once instance Desdemona asks Iago for no apparent reason about his spouse Emilia, "Is she a chatterbox?" The question is inappropriate, to say the least. In the original, Desdemona does not ask Iago a question, but rebuts him, argues with him. Iago, who wishes to offend Emilia, complains to Desdemona that she has wearied him with her chatter. Desdemona comes to her friend and servant's defense by retorting, "Alas, she has no speech" (II, i). And from this positive assertion Anna Radlova has contrived the puzzling question, "Is she a chatterbox?" I need not even mention the touch of good manners here. In the original, Desdemona expresses regret that Emilia is so reticent, and thus emphasizes how pleased she would be if she could converse more often with her. But Radlova does not stand on ceremony with nuances. Instead of a well-mannered retort, she offers the almost contemptuous question, "Is she a chatterbox?"

The turning of a single sentence into three, the turning of smoothly flowing narrative speech into convulsions of shouting, the turning of answers into questions, the chopping of retorts down to bare verbal stumps, the forcing of Desdemona to express herself in a broken, teeth-gnashing style—these are possible only for someone totally deaf to Shakespeare's intonations. Even if Radlova's translation were an irreproachably precise copy of the original in all other respects, we would have to consider it totally inaccurate, because intonations play a leading role in works of verse. Only those translations in which the intonational distinctiveness of the original is conveyed along with meaning, style, phonetics, and rhythm can be called precise. If the intonational distinctiveness is lost, the translation is hopeless. Other errors of translation can be somehow corrected, but this one is not amenable to correction.

4 A debate over these stale, tongue-tied, antiartistic translations flared up in 1935. By some strange means Anna Radlova organized a loud chorus of reviewers and critics on her behalf in the press. Her translations of Shakespeare's plays were declared the highest achievement of art. The talented critic Yu. Yuzovsky rose up against this false appreciation by coming out at the end of 1935 in *Literary Gazette* (No. 69) with a negative comment on Radlova's translation of *Othello*. The critic L. Borovoy supported his opinion. The "influential" journalists of the time pounced on them. Yuzovsky was called an "oaf," a "catcaller," and an "ignoramus" in the press. Borovoy was subjected to the same attacks. The attacks were mixed with threats: "These catcallers and lovers of easy victory should be brought to order!" The result was the appearance of an article by the young Shakespearian scholar Vlas Kozhevnikov, who fearlessly sided with Yuzovsky and Borovoy.

At that time I had nothing to do with the polemic. But several years later, after studying methods of translating Shakespeare from the works of Druzhinin, Veynberg, Lozinsky, Shchepkina-Kupernik, and others, I carefully studied Anna Radlova's translations line by line for the first time and quickly became convinced that they were appallingly bad, worse than the others said they were. In the winter of 1939 I ventured to substantiate my opinion in a lengthy report at the Shakespeare Conference at the All-Union Theater Society. I think there might still be a few old Muscovites around who have not forgotten the frantic discussion provoked by my detailed and impartial report. My co-reader was Vlas Kozhevnikov, whose talk had immediate repercussions.[10] Since Radlova had succeeded in having every theater in the Soviet Union stage Shakespeare only in her translations, she mobilized every possible means of suppressing our criticism. My article on her translations was cut out of the leading journal *Red Virgin Soil* (to the chagrin of its editor Alexander Fadeyev). I considered it necessary to ask the following questions, among others, at the conference:

> Why is it that other writers who have labored to translate Shakespeare—Nikolay Polevoy, Andrey Kroneberg, Apollon Grigorev, Alexander Druzhinin, and others—have not enjoyed such extraordinary signal success over the course of a century as has fallen to the lot of Anna Radlova? Why is it that a special article devoted to a characteristic of the work of Anna Radlova in the *Literary Encyclopedia* has it in black and white that her translations are masterpieces?[11] Why is it that after the low estimation of her translations offered by authoritative critics, her translations are still called "classically precise," "the best translations of Shakespeare"? Why is it that publishers use only her translations to acquaint our new intelligentsia with these great works—the intelligentsia of plants, factories, collective farms, the Red Army, universities, institutes, and schools?

One well-known actor of the time (who did not know a word of English, incidentally) who had come to Radlova's defense in the press declared that since Shakespeare wrote his plays for the stage, it was impossible to judge them as works of poetry. No matter what literary criteria are applied to them, they are totally irrelevant. "Shakespeare thinks for the stage," the actor declared in his article. "Shakespeare's text must always be viewed as an 'element of the performance,' subject to the laws of the stage, to the laws of live action on the stage." This assertion exasperated me, and I felt I had to rebut my opponent in this new dispute.

Woe to the theater, I said, that comes to believe, if only for a short time, that the stage is one thing and literature another. The only authentic foundation of the theater is a combination of the stage with the highest qualities of literature, with poetry, with the purely verbal art. Shakespeare is the greatest of all dramatists because he is first of all a poet. Almost all his dramas are in verse, and it is only because his verse is superior that they have been staged the world over for four centuries. To turn Shakespeare into a mere "element of the performance" is to demean both Shakespeare and the Soviet theater. Like every poet of genius, Shakespeare possessed a marvelous power over sound patterns, over the instrumentation of the line, over every means of poetic expression. It is not without relevance here that a highly refined, too elegant cultivation can be discerned in his sonnets or in *Venus and Adonis*. The sonnet is the most difficult of all literary forms, and even in his youth, while he was still developing the form, Shakespeare showed that he could be a virtuoso of poetic elocution.

Generally, the age of Shakespeare was an age of almost unattainably high literary culture. Must we really obliterate, destroy, forget this literary culture simply because it suits some actor to do without it? This literary culture was so high that Shakespeare's contemporary Sir Walter Raleigh (1552–1618), the great explorer, military hero, "Shepherd of the ocean," one of the ancestors of English colonial politics, even while in prison, knowing he was to be beheaded in the morning, wrote verses which are as polished artistically as if he were a professional verse craftsman. Even pirates of the time were able to cultivate superior verse forms. And Edmund Spenser, "the poet of poets," "the poets for poets," a poet who typified his age, a legislator of literary taste, was hailed with rapture by his contemporaries because his highly refined poetic technique enabled him to achieve beautiful sounds that were not even supposed possible at the time. It is not without reason that his renowned "stanza," that is, the line structure he invented, was borrowed over two centuries later by such great lyric poets as Byron, Shelley, and Keats. Other giants of the age—Francis Beaumont, John Fletcher, Christopher Marlowe, Ben Jonson—belong, like Shakespeare, to the history of poetry as well as to the history of the theater. Of course, there was a certain vulgarity in their verse too, and they often displayed it—when they needed to—but their literary art is so refined that a complex, elegant music can sometimes be heard in their verses.

Shakespeare belongs among these poets; it was precisely this culture that engendered him. Later Shakespeare foreswore an excessive polish, but nevertheless, traces of his adherence to this school can be felt in his later poetry, and there is a certain refinement to his simplicity. There are scores of books about the prosody of his verses, their melody and rhythms, the secrets of their magnificent sound patterns. (The most popular of them belongs to Professor George Saintsbury.)[12] For, I repeat, it is only because Shakespeare's verse is of such high quality that the power of his stage images is so colossal. When we translate Shakespeare into Russian, we must not forget that we are translating a master of poetic elocution equal to Ovid, Virgil, and Dante, a genius capable of the same phonetic expressiveness as they.

When I read the lines of one of Macbeth's most stirring monologues in Anna Radlova's translation—the original reads, "If it were done when 'tis done, then 'twere well / It were done quickly" (I, vii)—I immediately note the horrible consonantal cluster *bsdelal* for " 'twere done," and it grates on my ears. And I am sure I am not alone in this. And then there are her versions of such lines as: "Your bedded hair, like life in excrements, / Start up, and stand on end" (*Hamlet,* III, iv), and: "O heaven, that such companions thou'ldst unfold, / And put in every honest hand a whip" (*Othello,* IV, i). In her Russian translation these lines have such awkward consonant clusters as *braschesannye, bdybom, bnebo, bplet'*. Should phonetics like this really be foisted on Shakespeare? In Radlova's translation of *Macbeth* there are unpronounceable lines like, *Smert' dnia i omoven'e iazv truda.* The tongue-twisting cluster *iazvtruda* at the end of the line is as bad as *bsdelal.* And almost as if by intent, she chose to do this to one of the most musical lines of the original: "The death of each day's life, sore labour's bath" (II, ii). In a later edition of *Macbeth* the translator cast out *iazvtruda,* but she preserved her sacred *bsdelal* in the 1935, 1937, and 1939 editions!

The phrase from the same tragedy, "Vaulting ambition" (I, vii), remained untouched too. In Shakespeare's original the phrase imparts the image of an overly enthusiastic horseman vaulting too forcefully into the saddle and tumbling pell-mell to the ground on the other side. As Anna Radlova has it—*podpry-givaiushchee chestoliub'e*, 'leaping ambition'—the image is of a horse running and jumping. The image is totally contradictory to what Macbeth really says. "Leaping ambition" distorts Shakespeare's prosody and his meaning too.

But I am not concerned so much here with distortions of language or meaning as I am with the outright war against all that is poetic in Shakespeare, which seems to be the motivating force of Radlova's translations. It is as if the translator set out to deliberately ensure that the greatest genius of poetry sounded as coarse and vulgar as possible. Can it really be imagined that Shakespeare cultivated coarse phonetics in his best creations? In *Richard III*, in the line, "Thy Clarence he is dead that kill'd my Edward" (IV, iv), the translator has the awkward consonant cluster *miortvtvoi* in Russian. The line, "Now, by the world—'Tis full of thy foul wrongs" (IV, iv), has the awkward cluster *polntvoikh* in the translation. Such coarse phonetics as *mat'vliubvi* are offered in the Russian version of the line, "Their aunt I am in law, in love their mother" (IV, i).

I do not at all mean to assert that Radlova translates every line this way. Not just a few of her lines are of higher quality. But nevertheless, this disregard for the sound patterns of Shakespeare's lines is very typical of her translations. As if to openly demonstrate her total indifference to sound patterns, Radlova tolerates such unnatural sound groupings in her translations as *sovestlivyvy, nebobol', neneliubov', vorotaadada, miortvtvoi,* and *kakkassio*—which is to say, such monstrosities as *vyvy, bobo, nene, tvtv, kakka,* the like of which are difficult to achieve even when translating a third-rate writer. For the phrase in *Macbeth*, "He chid the sisters" (III, i), she has the awkward cluster *ved'msprosil,* and for the phrase from the same tragedy, "Goes Fleance with you?" (III, i), the cluster *flinssvami.* Her version of the line in *Othello*, "My friend is dead; 'tis done at your request" (III, iii), has the awkward cluster *miortvdrug,* while her translation of the line from the same play, "Thou teachest me. Minion, your dear lies dead" (V, i), has *miortvvash.* To say that these bad lines are good for the theater is to show disrespect not only for poetry, but for the theater as well. The Soviet stage and Soviet audiences need the original Shakespeare, the Shakespeare who is a poet, Shakespeare the magnificent master of the word, and not a tongue-tied asthmatic or a scribbler of cacophonic doggerel!

5   With two or three lonely exceptions, the critics consistently refrained from noting the above-listed shortcomings of Radlova's translations, and inevitably pointed out one particular shortcoming, a shortcoming of secondary importance and completely harmless, namely the vulgarity of several of her words and figures of speech. They considered this vulgarity the surest guarantee of fidelity and precision of translation. For after all, anyone who reproduces even these extreme words so diligently must have reproduced everything else with the same precision! It never even occurred to any of these critics that Anna Radlova was painstaking in this respect alone. Whenever the characters are polite, kind, affectionate, she reproduced their speech without enthusiasm, casting out whole handfuls of salutatory words. But let the same characters begin pouring abuse on one another, under the influence of guilt or passion, and Radlova becomes as accurate as a chronometer. At times she is far more vulgar than Shakespeare. For example, Iago says in the first scene of the fourth act of *Othello,* "Ply Desdemona well." But according to Radlova he expresses this by saying, "Lie onto Desdemona!" This seems more Shakespearian to her. The same Iago says, according to Shakespeare, "She was a wight, if ever such a wight were" (II, i). But the translator obliges him to say, "If ever there were such a wench, she should be taken." Take a wench? What surprises me about concoctions like these is not so much their coarseness as their show-off style. Instead of, "Put money in thy purse" (I, iii), Radlova repeats three times, "Chase after money." And when a Shakespearian character says in her translation that someone cut off his nose, it never occurs to a single Russian reader of this dashing phrase that Shakespeare says nothing about a nose in *Othello*.

The critics were not very helpful when they fixed attention exclusively on this aspect of Radlova's translations. By pushing this aspect to the forefront, they obscured the most important and vital question—what is the most nearly correct method of translating the heritage of classics of verse into Russian? After all, it is not simply a matter of the specific errors in Radlova's translations of *Othello,* but of the theoretical apparatus and general principles that led the translator to make such errors. How did it happen that Anna Radlova, the author of translations of Guy de Maupassant's prose which are not at all bad, turned out to be so impotent when it came to translating Shakespeare?

Of course, even this translation has individual lines which speak of an adeptness with words and resourcefulness. But unfortunately, individual successes do not make an entire translation artistic. Not badly done is Radlova's translation of such lines as, "To mourn a mischief that is past and gone / Is the next way to draw new mischief on" (I, iii). Iago's monologue at the end of the first act concludes with a beautiful translation of two lines from the original: "I have 't. It is engender'd. Hell and night / Must bring this monstrous birth to the world's light" (I, iii). Very close to the original in both meaning and intonation is her version of two lines from the second act: "Come, Desdemona: 'tis the soldier's life / To have their balmy slumbers waked with strife" (II, iii). But these are exceptions to the general rule, chance successes which emphasize all the more strongly the fallacious basis of the theoretical principles that guided the author.

The theoretical principles which are the basis of Anna Radlova's translations of Shakespeare were fully defined in the twenties. It was just then that it became clear the old translations of Shakespeare, even the best of them, could no longer satisfy the readers of our time, and it was necessary to translate them anew, in a different way, on a different foundation. It became clear that the older translations, even the best of them, were done in a dilettante fashion, amateurishly, without scientific regard for the specific qualities of the artistic form of an original text.

In this regard, the same Pyotr Veynberg turned a single Shakespearian line into two whenever he felt like it, and sometimes even three, not a bit troubled by the fact that the famous dialogue between Iago and Othello in the third act takes only 167 lines in the original and a full 240 in his translation. He was just as heedless with rhymes, considering it fully permissible not to reproduce the rhymes consistently even in those rare instances where Shakespeare has rhymes. This was the translators' canon of the time. The translators of that time were concerned not so much with re-creating the form of an original text as with its ideas and images. But in the thirties and forties a new generation revolted against this "amateurism" and proclaimed a new slogan—scientific translation. According to their convictions, a scientific translation consisted of an objective regard for all the formal elements of an original text, which the translator is obliged to reproduce with pedantic precision. The victory of this allegedly scientific method over the arbitrariness of the long-cherished amateur translators was soon proclaimed in many articles which took on the character of manifestoes. It was believed that a new era was dawning in translation practice, because henceforth translations of verse would be guaranteed seemingly maximal precision through scientific analysis of the formal structure of a given poetic work. Henceforth translators would have to keep firmly in mind the demand that they reproduce the rhythms of the original, and the number of its lines, and its rhyme patterns, and its instrumentation, and so forth, and so forth, and so forth.

It was in response to this "scientific" era that Anna Radlova first came out with her translations of Sheakespeare. They were acclaimed so loudly because it seemed to everyone they marked the advent of a new era of scientifically exact reproductions of the classics. It seemed that at last, in place of the amateurish rehashing of Shakespeare in which there were so many empty-sounding concoctions, translations would be offered which would be fully adequate to the original as regards meaning, and as regards metrics, and as regards the number of lines. "Shakespeare has been born anew in the Russian language," exulted the Shakespearian scholar A. A. Smirnov. "This is the original Shakespeare which we have not known until now." Praising the "new method," which he claimed was first applied by Radlova in her translations of *Macbeth* and *Othello,* Smirnov asserted that only this method of translation could convey Shakespeare faithfully and bring him close to us. "Only through translations such as these can the reader who does not have a command of English understand and critically absorb the heritage of Shakespeare."[13] How could our journalists and critics not welcome in Anna Radlova the militant innovator marching straight to Shakespeare along an untrodden but singularly correct path?

Alas, as we now see, these fine-sounding declarations turned out in practice to be mere puffs. Radlova's translations did not and could not bring the reader any closer to Shakespeare. The loss of a multitude of semantic units, the complete destruction of vital intonations in almost every monologue, in almost every cue— this does not bring us closer to Shakespeare. On the contrary, it moves us many thousands of miles away from him.

But is it really the "scientific" devices and methods which are at fault here? Not at all. Scientific devices and methods can perform miracles in the capacity of ruling tendencies—*if they are linked with talent, inspiration, instinct.* But without this indispensable condition, science becomes a hindrance. A mechanical, uninspired application to art of ready recipes—be they even archscientific—leads inescapably to bankruptcy. It is impossible to make a fetish of official theories and principles, it is impossible to sacrifice taste and talent to such fetishes.

Anna Radlova once declared with no little boasting that—in the interests of precision—she translated Shakespeare *line for line,* without adding a single line, so that her translation of *Othello* has exactly the same number of lines as the original. A translation with exact line-for-line equivalency is greatly to be desired, of course, but it is not possible to say, "Long live exact line-for-line equivalency and may Shakespeare go to the dogs!" And this is exactly the slogan that underlies Radlova's translations. For the sake of line-for-line equivalancy she cast out dozens of epithets, mercilessly hacked away at Shakespeare's syntax, turned almost every sentence into a disorderly heap of verbal stumps. And when she has a choice—either line-for-line equivalency or Shakespeare's ideas and images—she inevitably prefers line-for-line equivalency. We can see examples of this formalistic fetishism on every page of her translations.

In translating the straightforward line from *Othello,* "She never yet was foolish that was fair" (II, i), Radlova preferred to completely distort the meaning of the original, if only to maintain line-for-line equivalency. The result is a line that has not the least resemblance to the original: "Whether foolish and fair, this is a delicate matter." Radlova's chief problem is thus not that she upholds "scientific" principles for the artistic translation of poetry, but that she upholds these principles at the cost of stifling taste and artistic instinct, temperament and the delight of poetic form, and taste for poetry and beauty. Formal requirements became for her an end in themselves, and in art this is an unforgivable sin.

The poet A.A. Fet was a giant, but in his translations of Shakespeare even he was a total failure precisely because he adhered automatically to the narrow codex of formal tasks, sacrificing both the beauty and the inspiration of the original. In his translation of *Julius Caesar* he is a forefunner of Radlova in that he was the first—as early as 1859—to apply (so far as Shakespeare's tragedies are concerned) the principle of line-for-line equivalency, which for some reason many have considered Radlova's invention. And just what remains of this translation, the highest triumph of formalism? Only two parodistic lines by Turgenev. Turgenev's parody strikes at the roots of all these pseudo-precise translations, which are comprised of the destruction of intonations and the cultivation of verbal stumps. As a translator of Shakespeare, Radlova belongs fully to the Fet school which mechanically reproduces three or four of the features of an original text to the detriment of its charm.

6   Studying the translations of Shakespeare done in the twenties and thirties gives us an opportunity to observe how formalistic methods were gradually overcome by methods which are vital and creative. But even the best of our translators paid homage to formalism in its time. It was precisely then that the fetishistic attitude toward so-called line-for-line equivalency and rhythm-for-rhythm equivalency was instituted for translations of poetry. A strict demand was put forth that every poem in translation—be it a tragedy or a love story—had to be comprised of exactly the same number of lines as the original, and that the rhythm of every line of the translation had to correspond exactly to the rhythm of the same line of the original. In and of itself this demand was quite useful. It signified the end of the unrestrained willfulness that reigned without check in the translations of the previous age. It meant the end for all time of dilettante attitudes toward Shakespeare, when a landowner like the lazy Nikolay Mikhaylovich Satin could do with Shakespeare's lines what he would in his translation of the comedy *A Midsummer Night's Dream,* stretching and straining them in accord with his own whims so that one line became a line and a half or two, and sometimes even three. As a result of such whims, Satin's translation ended up with 230 extra lines! And no one even protested, because at that time this was in the order of things, and right up until a short time ago his translation was considered the best because other translations of *A Midsummer Night's Dream* departed even further from the original. And when the talented Ukrainian translator M. Starytsky translated *Hamlet* throughout in trochees instead of iambs, he not only got away with this vandalism, but was hotly defended.[14]

The thirties put an end to this kind of arbitrariness. We were given the opportunity to rejoice that in a new translation of *King Lear* there was not a single line's difference from the original text. There are 2,170 lines in the original text, and there are 2,170 lines in the translation.[15] The critics were in raptures, of course. For the first time a Russian poet had managed to translate this world-famous tragedy line for line, reconstituting all the metric peculiarities of the English text with maximal scientific precision. The same thing can be noted in Mikhail Lozinsky's translation of *Hamlet*. This translation can be read alongside the original as a perfect interlinear model. In the original there are 2,718 lines and in the translation there are 2,718 lines, in addition to which the rhythm equivalency is sustained to an amazing degree. If in the original one line is a fifth of a beat shorter than the other, the line in the translation is exactly as short. If the original has four lines interposed among the others, with an ancient ballad rhythm and with internal rhyme in the odd lines, you can be sure that the translation has reproduced exactly the same rhythms and exactly the same rhymes.[16]

7 It would seem that we, the readers, ought to have welcomed with all our hearts these new methods of translation which guarantee that all translations of verse enjoy maximum approximation to the original. But it soon became apparent that many translators were applying the method too directly and blindly, even when it led to distortions of the original. As inevitably happens, the formalistic attitude toward practice proved ruinous here too. The formalists, as always, did not count on the unfavorable consequences which so often result from a too direct and unquestioning application of a useful principle. As a matter of fact, there are scores, even hundreds, of cases where such concern for precision led, strange as it may seem, to imprecision, and where concern for a strict correspondence in the number of lines drastically lowered their quality: in a word, where translators—even the best translators—made such huge sacrifices for this principle that they inflicted incalculable losses on Soviet readers. Nor is there any reason to think that these losses have been endured only by readers of Goethe and Shakespeare. There are dozens of other translations, from Georgian, Armenian, Yiddish, Ukrainian, Polish, which are characterized by the illusory pseudo-scientific "precision" that, as we will see, masks what is in fact a maximal departure from the original.

Let's take just one example—*Hamlet* in the translation of Mikhail Lozinsky. Lozinsky is a master translator. His translations of Dante, Cervantes, Fletcher, Lope de Vega, and Boccaccio are magnificent in their virtuosity. This is one of the very best Soviet translators. A scientific immersion in the text is combined in his translations with the authentic inspiration of a major poet. The range of his creativity is boundless, and at times his translations stand in their artistic perfection on the same high level as their originals. It is instructive to note how cleverly and resourcefully he solves the stylistic and semantic problems facing him in every line, and how inevitably the materials surrender to his translator's will. The very sound of his lines is like steel, classically clear, with the enchantment of antiquity. He has created excellent Russian versions of such lines from *Hamlet* as: ". . . diseases desperate grown / By desperate appliance are relieved" (IV, iii), and "The bark is ready, and the wind at help, / The associates tend, and everything is bent / For England" (IV, iii). Nevertheless, Lozinsky's translation of *Hamlet* is marked by errors caused almost exclusively by his commitment to the fetish of linear equivalency with excessive, I would even say fanatic, zeal. Take, for example, these fine-sounding lines in Lozinsky's translation: "To Hamlet the king does raise his cup / And dissolves a pearl in wine, / More priceless than that which crowned / Four kings. . . ." Even at first glance these lines seem a bit strange. First of all, how can a pearl be used to crown kings? Can it really have taken the place of the crowns covered with priceless gems that are usually used to crown kings? And how does a single pearl crown so many kings at the same time? Is it so large that it can cover four heads simultaneously like a huge cap? The original is quite different: "The king shall drink to Hamlet's better breath; / And in the cup an union shall he throw, / Richer than that which four successive kings in Denmark's crown have worn . . ." (V, ii). As it turns out, the translator has cast several of the most important semantic units out of the text: the crown, Denmark, Hamlet's better breath, and the fact that four kings did not have the jewel simultaneously, but in order of succession. In addition, contrary to the translator's version, the king did not dissolve the pearl (union) in wine; he merely threw it into the cup. How great the Soviet reader's losses in only three and a half lines of translation! Five absolutely essential words have been cast out of three and a half lines, and the loss not only deprives Shakespeare's text of all color, but even harms its meaning. And all this simply because the translator made it his unyielding goal to sustain the number of Shakesperae's lines intact.

In the original, to take another example, the queen interrupts Hamlet's speech with the portentous exclamation: "Thou turn'st mine eyes into my very soul; / And there I see such black and grained spots / As will not leave their tinct!" (III, iv). What, it may be asked, would this exclamation be worth if the red (grained) spots were cast out? After all, the queen here betrays the evidence of her bloody crime. And yet it is precisely the red spots that are missing from the translation: "Thou turnest eyes into the soul; / And there I see such black spots." The first line has also suffered considerable damage from an excessive economy of words. By casting out the possessive pronoun "mine" before "eyes," the translator leaves us wondering whether the queen refers to her own eyes or Hamlet's.

A memorable line spoken by Ophelia, one which has long since become a popular English proverb, sounds forth boldly in Lozinsky's translation: "Rich gifts wax poor when givers prove unkind." But the reader suffers a not insignificant loss here because the translator, in his pursuit of brevity, cast out the remark that such an attitude toward gifts is peculiar only "to the noble mind" (III, i). In the fourth act a grieving Hamlet, devastated by his inability to avenge his father, refers with characteristic contempt of self to "my dull revenge" (IV, v). This epithet as if sums up Hamlet's entire tragedy, and yet it is precisely this epithet the translator chose to cast out. At his death Hamlet turns to his just-poisoned mother with an epithet which signifies "pitiful" and "despicable" at once—"wretched." This epithet defines Hamlet's real attitude to the woman responsible for his moral torments: "Wretched queen, adieu!" (V, ii). The translator gives it simply as, "Mother, adieu," which once again is a loss to Soviet readers of *Hamlet*. When she is told that Hamlet is insane, Ophelia grieves especially that madness has destroyed "that noble and most sovereign reason" and clouded "that unmatch'd form" (III, i). These three epithets are of no little value in the text, but they are absent from Lozinsky's translation.[17] Sometimes Shakespeare's epithets perform an ornamental, rather than a semantic function. Such for example is the word "gentle" in the successive cues of the king and queen in the second act: "Thanks Rosencranz and *gentle* Guildenstern!" and: "Thanks Guildenstern and *gentle* Rosencranz!" (II, ii). And yet even this word has been cast out of the translation.

If such a skillful master of translation as Mikhail Lozinsky was obliged to pay so dearly for his zealous service to the principle of linear equivalency, what can be said about other translators! Several have preferred that whole pages of their translations of Shakespeare become totally garbled, if only 2,170 lines of an original text do not become—God save us!—2,175.

In a word, the principle of linear equivalency, which has great value in and of itself, becomes a hindrance and a burden if it is applied indiscriminately, always and under any circumstances—even to the detriment of the meaning and style of great works of poetry.

EIGHT

Today: From My Literary Notebook

MARSHAK   *A book on the art of translation
would have no right to exist if it did not include
a chapter on Marshak. Marshak is the first name that comes to mind
when we speak about the Soviet period of this great art. Unfortunately, no
study yet exists that offers anything like a detailed analysis of even the
most important of his translations. I include here the transcript of the
salutatory address I delivered in honor of S. Ya. Marshak on the occasion
of his seventieth birthday.*

In the early twenties when Samuil Marshak used to visit me, I
always recognized him by his knock—abrupt, impatient, precise, relentlessly militant—as if he were pounding out the two
syllables of his name. "Mar–shak." In the very sound of his name,
quick and sharp as a pistol, I could sense something belligerent
and aggressive. "Mar–shak!"

He was lean and spare in those days, and it could not be said he
was in very good health, but when we used to walk down the
street I had the curious feeling that if a truck were suddenly to
hurl down on him it would be smashed to smithereens and he
would go his way as if nothing had happened—straight down the
street, chest out, stopping for nothing. What his way would be
we did not really know at the time, but we felt that no matter
what obstacles he might encounter along the way, Marshak

would overcome them one and all, because even then, in those distant days, we could sense the strength of the man. The virtues of long-suffering, humility, and meekness were alien to his temperament. In his whole being there could be felt a readiness to repulse all opposition. He had just returned from the south, and I remember that stories were being told of how he slapped some scoundrel silly for mistreating children.

He valued an imperious, demanding, resolute spirit above all other things—especially in children's folk poetry. "How marvelous," he used to say, "that in Russian folklore a little child feels that he is the ruler of nature and issues haughty commands to the elements: 'Rainbow–bow, rainbow–bow, / Don't let the wind blow!' 'Sunglow, sunglow, / Look in my window,' 'Rain, rain, go away!' 'Shine hot, shine bright, / Chase away the night.' " When he recited these sayings, Marshak would pronounce all the "don'ts," and "looks," and "go aways" in such an imperious tone that it seemed to me that a child who addressed such verses to nature must really be a ruler of rainbows, winds, and rains. One other such priceless quality in Marshak also struck me, even before I got to know him well: I was immediately drawn to him, as if to a magnet, by his passionate enthusiasm, I would even say obsession, for great folk poetry—Russian, German, Irish, Scottish, English. Folk poetry—especially folk songs—was his selfless, all-consuming love. And since his tenacious memory held a vast multitude of songs, lyric poems, and ballads, he often recited them, and sometimes even sang them, forcefully communicating his enthusiasm to us, and it was apparent that he was drawn above all to heroic, martial themes glorifying man's powerful will to victory over nature, over pain, over passion, over the elements, over death.

Little wonder, then, that Marshak completely won me over at our first meetings, and we began wandering through the empty streets of the White Nights of Petrograd—this was at the very start of the twenties—not paying attention to where we were going, reciting the verses of Shevchenko, Nekrasov, Robert Browning, Kipling, Keats, and pitying the rest of mankind because they were asleep and did not know what beauty exists in this world. I remember to this very day the corner of Manege Lane and Old Nadezhdin Street where on the stone step leading down to a boarded-up, half-basement petty tradesman's shop Samuil Yakovlevich first recited Blake's ecstatic poem "Tiger! Tiger! burning bright," accompanying it with his youthful translation, his voice deep with emotion and urgent, clenching his fists with each line; and it became clear to me that his translation was essentially a duel with Blake, a skirmish, hand-to-hand combat, and that no matter how Blake might try to slip from his grasp, Marshak would sooner or later bind him to Russian poetry and force him to sing his songs in Russian. Marshak's translations of Burns are essentially the same act of aggression. Burns, who is protected from translators by a strong warrant against trespass, had eluded their grasp for more than a hundred years, seeming to tease them by drawing near—"Here I am! Catch me!"—and then darting away. But Marshak has a death grip and he somehow conquered the invincible genius and forced him to sing his songs in the language of Derzhavin and Blok.

Somehow, it seems strange to call Marshak a translator. He is more like a conquistador, a conqueror of foreign poets who makes loyal Russians of them by the sheer force of his talent. He has said as much himself, in his lines on translating Shakespeare:

> I've mastered Shakespeare's sonnet,
> Taken the bard from ancient abode,
> Forced him to speak a different mode,
> In other times, across our far-flung planet.

Above all else in Shakespeare and Blake and Burns, he values the fact they they are all three warriors, that they all came into this world of evil and oppression to combat it: "Not without reason does the glorious name Shakespeare mean to shake the spear." Marshak succeeded in his translations of these "shakers of spears" because he shared their anger and hatred deep in his heart, and, having fallen in love with them in his youth he was unable not to want us to love them too—in our other, our Soviet, times, on our side of our far-flung planet.

Here is the source, it seems to me, of an inviolable law for masters of translation: undertake to translate not just any foreign author you happen to read or who is foisted on you by some editor in a hurry, but only the one you love passionately, who is close to your own heart, whom you want your compatriots to love too. Marshak has tirelessly reiterated this law himself. "If you study the best of our translations," he has said in *Learning from the Word*, "you will discover that they are all children of love, not of a marriage of convenience."[1] It is solely because he fell in love with the genius of Omar Khayyam that Fitzgerald won a place for him among the greatest English poets. And could Zhukovsky ever have made Schiller's ballad *Der Taucher* an attainment of our Russian poetry as deserving of place as, say, a poem by Lermontov, if he had not been captivated by the original? Could Kurochkin have made Béranger into one of our most beloved Russian authors without the same feeling for the poetry in the original?

But enthusiasm is not enough by itself for the performance of miracles such as these. On top of everything else one needs to possess the most refined writing technique, to be the most skillful polisher of words, a virtuoso of poetic form and a master of the craft of words, a ruler over rhymes and rhythms—which is to say that one must possess precisely the literary qualities Marshak possesses to a superior degree. What is needed here is an iron discipline over the line which will under no circumstances tolerate careless, slovenly, muddled, vague, awkward, empty, or stiff lines. Take a look at any of Marshak's translations. You will find not so much as a single line that is slack, flabby, sluggish—every last one of them has powerful tendons and muscles. Each line has a distinct design, geometrically precise and strict. And seemingly done without the slightest effort. The rhymes are so unforced and simple that they seem to have been created of their own volition, completely subject to the meaning of the original. It seems impossible to say in any other way what is said in his simple—naturally breathing—lines.

"True skill is when you never notice the skill." This is why Marshak's translations never read like translations. Their execution is of such high quality, they have such rich sound patterns, such free and light diction of the type that is natural only to authentic original poetry, that often and in fact the reader experiences the illusion that Burns wrote his poetry in Russian.

Take for example, this stanza from Burns's *The Jolly Beggars*:

> I am a son of *Mars,* who have been in many
> *wars,*
> And show my cuts and *scars* wherever I
> *come*:
> This here was for a *wench,* and that other
> in a *trench*
> When welcoming the *French* at the
> sound of the *drum.*   (102)

In all its rhyme and all its scheme, the translation is exactly like the original—precisely what Marshak strives for in his translations:

> . . . . . stroiú // . . . . . boiú
> . . . . moiú // . . . . . rán
> . . . . . . dráke // . . . . . atáke
> . . . . mráke // . . . barabán.[2]

This is why I can say—and mean it as far more than a mere anniversary phrase—that Marshak stakes everything on his ability to force foreign writers to sing their songs in Russian. In order to achieve this, a translation of many of Burns's creations requires, in addition to everything else, the conveyance of their musicality, their vital lyricism, the buoyancy of their artfully artless speech:

> What can a young lassie,
> What shall a young lassie,
> What can a young lassie
> Do wi' an auld man?   (233)

Marshak has caught the refrain of these lines perfectly—the syntactic structure is identical, and so is the rhythmic structure:

Chto délat' devchónke?
Kak být' mne, devchónke?
Kak zhít' mne, devchónke,
S moim muzhen'kóm?   (I, 219)

When I say that in his best translations Marshak performs the miracle of making them read not like translations, but of making them sound as if Burns, or Petöfi, or Ovanes Tumanyan had written their poems in Russian, I have in mind the sound of his translation of a poem like Burns's "O, Whistle an' I'll Come to Ye, My Lad":

O, whistle an' I'll come to ye, my lad!
O, whistle an' I'll come to ye, my lad!
Tho' father an' mother an' a' should gae
        mad,
O, whistle an' I'll come to ye, my lad!   (202)

The sound pattern of his translation of the chorus is identical to the original:

Ty svistni,—tebia ne zastavliu ia zhdat',
Ty svistni,—tebia ne zastavliu ia zhdat'. (II, 5)

In fact, the sound patterns are amazingly identical in their musical structures:

Yet look as ye were na' lookin to me,
Yet look as ye were na' lookin to me!   (202)

A ból'she—smotrí!—na meniá ne smotrí,
A ból'she—smotrí!—na meniá ne smotrí! (II, 5)

Even the rhyme schemes of the stanzas are the same: *zhdat'—zhdat'—mat'—zhdat'* and *smotri—govori—podari—smotri — smotri —* AABA, CDDCC.

And how especially remarkable for its classically severe construction and its youthful, mischievous, exultant tones is his translation of "Wha is That at My Bower Door?":

"Wha is that at my bower door?"
"O, wha is it but Findlay!"
"Then gae your gate, ye'se nae be here."
"Indeed maun I!" quo' Findlay.   (236)

—Kto tam stuchitsia v pozdnii chas?"
"Konechno, ia—Findlei!"
—Stupai domoi. vse spiat u nas!"
"Ne vse!"—skazal Findlei.   (I, 136)

Need one say that Marshak's translation of these lines is a maxi-mally precise reproduction not only of their meaning, but even of their form—the rhythms, the sound patterns, the emotative coloration? Here is the epitome of the style of Soviet translation technique toward which our literature has been striving for more than just a few years. Marshak is one of the founders of this difficult style.

In addition to lyric poems, Burns wrote a great many im-promptu verses, epigrams, and epitaphs which presented Mar-shak with the problem of translating not a lyric line, but its opposite—a lapidary, laconic, trenchant line such as that which characterizes his epigram "On Andrew Turner":

In Se'enteen Hunder 'n Forty-Nine
The Deil gat stuff to mak a swine,
     An' coost it in a corner;
But wilily he chang'd his plan,
An shap'd it something like a man,
     An' ca'd it Andrew Turner.   (191)

Marshak's translation of this epigram eliminates the personal associations, thereby reducing it to pungent iambic-tetrameter lines which convey the insult with a sharp sting:

The Devil got stuff to make a swine,
But wilily he changed his plan
And shaped it something like a man,
He shaped it like you, milord!   (II, 155)

Ensuring that the verses of great poets retain their national character while also sounding like Russian verses, with the same unforced vital intonations, is no easy task, of course, and I remember that what delighted me most about Marshak in those long ago days was his furious love of work, to the last drop of blood. Filling page after page with his impatient, energetic handwriting until four lines distinguished for their absolute finish crystallized on the thirty-fifth page or so—lines à la Marshak, muscular, resilient, taut—this was the daily regime of his masterful labor with words in those days. I remember the time when he read an early variant of his *Mister Twister* for me—at that time it was still *Mister Blister*—and I thought the poem was finished to perfection. But it turned out that Marshak considered it a mere castoff, the first draft of a draft, and another dozen variants were required before he finally achieved the design that now defines the style of these smartly resounding lines:

> Mister
> Twister,
> Famed magister,
> Mister
> Twister,
> Millionaire.

And even after these verses were published he returned to them again and again, striving to achieve the sharpest possible epithets, the most energetic rhymes and rhythms.

One of Marshak's earliest literary triumphs was his conquest of a remarkable book which had stubbornly resisted the efforts of more than one translator before him. This book was created by the English people during the time of the greatest flowering of their cultural spirit, a book of songs and verses for children called *Nursery Rhymes* in England and *Mother Goose* in America, which has existed in its essential parts for many centuries. It is a multi-styled, indefatigably hearty, immortally happy book with thousands of whimsies and fancies, but it came out so puny, tongue-tied, and, above all, lackluster in previous Russian translations that it was embarassing to read it. So you can imagine

what joy I experienced when Marshak first read me his translations of these seemingly untranslatable masterpieces. His translations miraculously preserve all the dynamism and power of the
originals:

> Ei, kuznéts,
> Molodéts,
> Zakhromál moi zherebéts.

"Three Jovial Welshmen," "Humpty-Dumpty," "The Three
Little Kittens"—thanks to Marshak these rhymes have become
attainments of Russian poetry, for here as in all his other translations nothing in them reads like a translation. The lines retain
their clarity and resilience as if straight out of Russian folklore.
And I understood that Marshak had carried the day so brilliantly
over English folklore because his trusty weapon in this seemingly
uneven struggle was—as strange as this may seem—our own,
our Tula, Ryazan, Moscow folklore. While preserving the colors
of the original Marshak, so to speak, projected our Russian
number games, riddles, surprises, amusements, and teasers into
this translation. This is why the *Nursery Rhymes* in his translation
have entered into the everyday life of our children and taken their
place in our children's culture so freely and easily alongside our
native Soviet "pat-a-cakes." Our Soviet Natashas and Vovas have
come to love them with the same love they have enjoyed from
time immemorial by the Jennys and Johns across the sea. In order
to sew these two folklores together with such artistry that the
seams are completely invisible, there was need for great tact and
taste and a most refined verbal culture.

Generally speaking, Russian folklore had begun even in those
distant days to serve as the fulcrum, compass, and regulator of
Marshak's creativity. If he had not from his earliest youth been a
devotee, connoisseur, and admirer of Russian oral literature, he
would never have been able, despite all his virtuosity, to create
the remarkable children's verses that have brought him lasting
glory among tens of millions of Soviet children, as well as their
children and grandchildren. Such children's pieces as "The
Towering Tower" and "The Cat's Home" are particularly dear to

me because they are not a moribund stylization in the vein of children's folklore, not a mechanistic application of available models—they are a distinctive, free creativity in an authentic folk style with which Marshak feels as comfortable as a fish in water and which remains folkloristic even when he introduces such words as "kilometer," "piano," and "brigade." It would be quite easy to prove that such other children's verses as "The Tale of the Foolish Mouse," "Baggage," and "What an Absent-Minded Boy"—verses whose vocabulary is devoid of so-called folk colors—also have their origin in folklore: this is indicated by the symmetry of their individual parts and by many other distinctive features of their accumulate structures.

I remember every one of Marshak's children's verses by heart to this very day, because Marshak created them literally before my eyes and I experienced each new thing he wrote as it was being written. It could not have been otherwise in those early years of the establishment of the new Soviet culture. For with two or three exceptions, the children's literature of previous periods was offensively vulgar and pitiful. It was done for the most part by talentless people, or by shameless cynics, and it seemed to be aimed intentionally at corrupting and ruining children. In the prerevolutionary period I spent ten years shouting my head off on this subject in newspaper articles, and all my shouting signified, as I know now—"We Need Marshak!" How could I not be overjoyed by the young poet who made my long-time dream come true? I remember to this day the feeling of deep gratitude with which I met his books—*Post Office,* and *The Circus,* and *Kids in a Cage,* and *Yesterday and Today.* His books were diverse—diverse in subject and style—but they all displayed the most important theme of his creativity: the devilishly difficult but vastly entertaining struggle of man with nature, the triumphant theme that is so clearly expressed in his famous verses. That indominitable, militant, imperious something that is in Marshak found its reflection in his proud verses. Every act and action, every process of making things—"How the Planer Made a Plane," "How Your Book Was Printed," how the joiner, the watchmaker, the printer work, how the woods are planted, how the Dnieper dam was built, how deserts are turned into gardens—all these things are intimately close to the creative, dynamic soul of Marshak. The very word "build" is the most noticeable word in his vocabulary. But all of this will be written about much better by others. I, on the other hand, remembering those distant years when we stood shoulder to shoulder, struggling each in the measure of his own strengths and capabilities for the honor and dignity of the newly born literature for Soviet children, can only repeat for Marshak the words of his beloved Burns:

> And there's a hand, my trusty fiere,
>   And gie's a hand o' thine;
> And we'll tak a right guid-willie waught
>   For auld lang syne.
>
> For auld lang syne, my dear,
>   For auld lang syne,
> We'll tak a cup o' kindness yet
>   For auld lang syne.

At the end of 1963 I received from S.Ya. Marshak a long letter devoted to the art of translation. I would like to offer a few excerpts from it here.

"Every once in a while," Samuil Yakovlevich wrote, "I receive letters asking me to explain to some ignoramus or another that translation is an art, and a very difficult and complex art. There are so many versifiers, idle and lazy, barely in command of line and word, who bear the name of poet while masters and devotes of translation are considered unworthy even to belong to the Writer's Union. In my own personal experience I have seen that of all the genres in which I have worked, the translation of poetry is perhaps the most difficult. . . .

"Unfortunately, to this very day Heine, Mickiewicz, Byron, and other great poets continue to appear in hack-work translations. We have to accumulate good—authentically poetic—translations and not include a foreign poet in the plan until such translations have been accumulated. . . .

"The chief failing of translators of Shakespeare's plays is that they do not feel the musical structure of the original. Just as in his sonnets a musical notation can be placed over almost every line—allegro, andante, etc.—so also in his plays the style, character, and internal rhythm change now and again in accordance with the content. Remember Othello's words after murdering Desdemona—'Tell the Senate . . .' and so on. This is an address not to the Senate, after all, but to the ages. And how magnificently tragic the address is. The translator must feel the rhythm of the original like a pulse. And in Shakespeare's comedies, as in an opera, every personage has his own voice—bass, baritone, tenor (the lover), and so on.

"Verlaine's words 'above all music' ought to be applied to translations. To me personally it was always important—above all—to feel the musical structure of Burns, Shakespeare, Wordsworth, Keats, Kipling, Blake, English Nursery Rhymes. . . ."

IN Defense of Burns   As if just to make the high quality of Marshak's translations of Burns clear to the reader, in 1963 a smart little book came out under the imprint of the Soviet Russia Publishing House: *Robert Burns, Songs and Verses in the Translation of Viktor Fedotov*.[3]

I open the book at random. The poem *Christmas Night*. But please, could this really have been written by Burns? I read it and can scarcely believe my eyes! The Scottish farmers that Burns always celebrated so tenderly are presented here as all but dolts—at the harshest time of winter, when the frosts are crackling and blizzards raging, these idiots set off in a crowd for the snow-covered fields and, as if nothing were out of the ordinary, begin gathering their harvest. Dumbfounded, I read in this *Christmas Night*: "On Christmas Night / They gathered rye, / And then made merry" (179). But after all, Christmas night is at the end of December, and winters in Scotland are not all that mild. They must be lunatics to go out in a cold December frost—one week before New Year's—straight out to gather rye in the empty fields. And, as if that were not enough, the silly fools even go out in the garden to pick cabbages:

> Some friendly country folks
> Together did convene,
> To burn their nuts, and pound their cabbage
> On Christmas Night. (172)

Luckily, I remember the poem in the original. Need I say that it has nothing to do with Christmas? It is titled *Halloween*—this is the name of one of the national holidays in Scotland, and it is celebrated not in winter but in autumn. At the end of October. *Autumn.* This is the source of all the muddle. It turns out that the translator insulted those Scottish farmers for no reason. They were not at all as dumb as he made them out to be in his translation. The original lines read like this:

> Some merry, friendly, country-folks
> Together did convene,
> To burn their nits, an' pu their stocks,
> An' haud their Halloween
> Fu' blythe that night. (23)

For that matter, can they even be called Scotsmen? Judging by this translation—hardly. Above all because they are loyal subjects of the Russian Tsar-Autocrat and in their native Caledonia, they sing the Russian patriotic hurrah, "God Save the Tsar!" That's just what the translator writes in his book: "He who won't sing 'God Save the Tsar!' / They sorely punish" (129). And on the next page the tsar again figures twice. And as if that were not enough, when a Calvinist preacher makes an appearance in one of Burns's poems the translator calls him *batiushka* (124), and right away we get the image of a Russian village priest, braid and all.

But even this is not enough. The translator dethrones the English King George III and establishes the Orthodox Church in Protestant Scotland by forcing Burns's Scotsmen to express themselves in such dialect words as *dolia-doliushka* (159), *sud'binushka*

(159), *nochen'ka* (159), *parnishka* (142), *tiaten'ka* (103), and *devchata* (172), and he even introduces our Russian coins into Scotland—right here in his translation he has a *piatak* (157), and a *kopeika* (116), and a *kopeiechka* (116), and even a ruble note (62), so that you are taken by surprise when you meet (right here in his translation) a miller who accepts an English shilling for his work instead of a two-griva piece (45). He measures Scottish roads with Russian versts (132).

It would have been all right if he had simply turned Scotland into Ryazan or Pskov gubernia. At least there would have been a common principle here, there would have been a system. But the fact is that just as he mixes shillings with five-copeck pieces and one-griva coins, he mixes realia of the Russian native environment with realia of the Scottish environment throughout the whole book. Right next to his *parnishka* and *tiaten'ka* he has bagpipes, and plaids, and fairies, and Stuarts. In general, the most rude stylistic discord does not bother him a bit, and he can always be counted on to juxtapose a high style with a vulgar one, as when referring to a "wench's orbs" (189).

The original poem *Halloween* is fitted with precise, clear-cut rhymes: dance–prance, beams–streams, and so forth. These rhymes have the same sharp mint as the rhymes of, say, *The Bronze Horseman* or *Eugene Onegin.* But the translator considers it possible in the very first lines of his version of *Halloween* to rhyme the word *Kasílz,* 'Cassilis,' with *prekrásnym* (171). At first it seems that this might be a misprint, but no, in the second stanza he rhymes *kocherýzhki* with *blízhnikh* (171)! And elsewhere: *ustremlén'ia–deń'gi* (173), *kolós'ia–kradiótsia* (174), and so on, and so on. If you take a look at other pages you will find even more effete rhymes: *zachát'sia–zardiás' vsia* (189), *bárd moi–blagoródnyi* (195), *vot ón–golodión* (188), *sméla b–séroi* (190). His effrontery in this regard knows no bounds. The translator boldly rhymes the word *Nénni* with *serdtsebiénie* (151) and *rúch'ia* with *liubímaia* (149). Of course, these devices make the task of translation much easier for him. But they do not make it easier on Burns, because they oblige him to stand up in front of his Russian readers like some unruly slattern of the word who scribbles his lopsided doggerel with his sleeves up, any old way, for a hurrah, for a foo–foo. Just think what the results would be if Pushkin's poem "Anchar" were done in the Fedotov style. I think Pushkin's admirers would not thank a savage who would dare ascribe such monstrously blasphemous words to him. And this is exactly how Fedotov treats such poems by Burns as *Halloween,* "The Vision," and "Epistle to a Young Friend." What some translator would do to Pushkin's poem would seem too precise and strict for the rhymes of someone who rhymes *ótrochka* and *góroda* (35), *stóit* and *muzhskóe* (148).[4]

So as to make his work even easier Viktor Fedotov resorts to an even more astute device: if a word does not fit the correct rhythm scheme he mangles it with inept stress positioning. Thanks to this reckless unruliness many of Burns' crystal clear ideas and images become so vague in the translation that it is impossible to get to their meaning. No matter how hard you try, you will never get to the meaning of a couplet like, "Exchanging with a silly woman / The dignity of a man" (148). Sometimes this vagueness of thought reaches major proportions. In the original text of the famous poem "The Volunteers of Dumfries" (which is in fact titled "Does Haughty Gaul Invasion Threat?") Burns calls his compatriots to fraternal unity with *England* in the face of ominous national danger, but in the translation he calls upon Scotsmen to join with *Scotsmen,* even though Burns repeats the words "British" and "Britain" four times. This is the poem where, to cap off the ridiculousness, the Russian tsar usurps the English king.

And then, "with all this and all that," such immense lack of taste cries out from every page. For example, in the poem, "The Lads from Gael Botey" (which is actually titled "Sae Fair Her Hair") he forces Burns to rhyme *krushíny,* 'thornbushes,' with *krushílas',* 'she was ruined.' The lass forgets her laces in the thornbushes and is ruined for it. This is a play on words which would put even Dostoyevsky's Lebyadkin to shame. The same thing happens in "The Vision." A Scottish lass's robe flowed down to boldly show her leg, and such a leg, "my Jean could only peer it." The bad pun here is on the rhymes *smélo,* 'boldly,' and *sméla b,* 'could peer it'—that is, be as bold or as daring. And then just try to recite or sing such a clumsy combination of words as *Dzhin lish' smela b*—a tongue-twisting vowel cluster that fails to impart to the line the mellifluousness inherent to Burns's euphonious poetry: "My bonnie Jean could only peer it" (20). This is the translation which has those clumsy bits of verbiage *zardias' vsia, nerv natianut, bard moi,* and so on.

I write these words with deep sadness, because I sincerely pity the translator. It is impossible to say he is devoid of talent: now and then a semblance of vital intonations creeps into this translation, here and there an epithet is not too jarring. I am sure he has far more strength and capability than one would think from reading his wretched little book. Not everything is lost, he can still save himself. Right after an unsettling, rough set of lines, one catches the sound of a finely melodic voice—a bit banal, it is true, as in the translation of "O, Stay, Sweet Warbling Wood-Lark":

> O, stay, sweet tender nightingale,
> Nor quit for me the trembling vale,
> And soothe my soul's travail
> With lays of tender plaints.   (137)

The translation compares very well to the original:

> O, stay, sweet warbling wood-lark, stay,
> Nor quit for me the trembling spray!
> A hapless lover courts thy lay,
> Thy soothing, fond complaining.   (275)

In general, it is impossible to say that the songs translated by Fedotov are totally devoid of musicality. There are flashes of authentic lyricism in his translation of some of the frivolous, erotic verses—in such verses as "Meg o' the Mill" ("O, ken ye how Meg o' the mill was bedded?"), "Ah, Woe Is Me, My Mother Dear," and "I'm O'er Young to Marry Yet" ("I am my mammie's ae bairn"), and a few others, although what with Burns comes across as smiling, graceful, playful sounds for some reason sounds bawdy and vulgar in the translation. Whatever the case, here (but not in the translations of the long poems) he could have been successful. Sometimes, right in the midst of limp and lax lines, one suddenly encounters firmly put together, smooth, solid lines. And in "The Tree of Liberty" there are a few places which, if they do not quite sound poetic, are fully convincing.

But these rare gleams are in piles of verbal dross which no shovel will ever dig out. Couldn't the translator have found a friend who might have restrained him from reveling in slovenliness? Is the translator so cut off from educated, knowledgeable, truly cultured people? Why did he have to so recklessly ruin his work and his good name? If only he had turned to some enlightened person for help and advice, I am positive he would have been very easily convinced that translations such as these would not bring him laurels, and he would have been advised in a friendly way to refrain from publishing them. "It is impossible to translate any old way, without even understanding the words," a well-intentioned friend would have told him. "After all, it means you will make yourself a laughing stock—especially in our country where the art of translation has reached such a high level." And here his authoritative and well-intentioned friend would have taken the pages of his manuscript reproduced in the book on pages 170 and 171 and begun counting the mistakes which crowd a space of twenty or so lines of his translation. "Here," he would have said, "judge for yourself from your own sources. . . . In his preface to the poem *Halloween,* Burns uses the ethnographic terms 'charms and spells,' and you have understood the term as an emotional expression of rapture and translated it with the words 'the charm and fascination of this night,' which is to say you have perceived a metaphor where there is not even a hint of one, and you have thereby distorted Burns's ideological stance. It was not 'charm and fascination' that Burns saw in these superstitious rituals, but evidence of backwardness and the dark side of his Scottish farmers. He even said so in his preface: they are 'in a rude state.' But you, because you did not understand this mournful thought, replaced 'backwardness' with the diffuse, hazy, abstract word 'primeval,' which means essentially nothing. It would be as if some Englishman or Frenchman translated Tolstoy's drama *The Power of Darkness* as *The Power of the Primeval*. And here, right in the same place, there is still another mistake. Burns says:

> Upon that night, when fairies light
> On Cassilis Downans dance,
> Or owre the lays, in splendid blaze,
> On sprightly coursers prance;   (23)

In the translation there is nothing left of the 'coursers,' and for some reason it is said of the fairies:

> And every lay, in splendid blaze,
> The fairies' light is lovely.   (171)

The original has 'coursers,' the translation has 'light,' as if the place were lighted by automobile headlights. You were obviously misled by the line where the poet says that the riders pranced 'in splendid blaze.' But after all, 'blaze' is a metaphor here and you are not supposed to take it literally. There are at least half a dozen other mistakes in these twenty or so lines, but I think these will suffice to convince you it is a bit too soon to publish your translations."

This is what any well-intentioned friend would have told Fedotov.

It is possible that in other times Fedotov's violence against Burns would not seem to be so bothersome, but now, when the art of translation has reached unprecedented heights with us, when even the strongest of our poets—Anna Akhmatova, Tvardovsky, Pasternak, Marshak, Zabolotsky, Antokolsky, and their worthy successors Martynov, Samoylov, Mezhirov—have devoted so much creative force to translation, the hack work of a dilettante seems especially embarrassing. As if a stutterer with a bad voice were to suddenly start singing in a choir of magnificent singers. We would not be so hostile toward his stuttering if the new generation of masters of translation who are continuing the lofty tradition of their successors did not include such powerful talents as Konstantin Bogatyrev (his translations of R.M. Rilke),

Boris Zakhoder (his translations of A. Milne, Capek, and—recently—Goethe), and others. Or let's recall the collection of *German Folk Ballads* in the translation of Lev Ginzburg.[5] Thanks to his classically sharp, transparent, and melodious verses, many of these masterpieces of folklore will undoubtedly enter (I take full responsibility for saying this) the treasure house of Soviet poetry. Lev Ginzburg has boldly won for himself one of the first places among Soviet masters, and they serve as a sharp reproach to overly presumptuous literary stutterers. One has to read his *Lay of Lament and Comfort* to appreciate this.[6]

LOFTY STARS   The lines of a poem have stuck in my mind today. Whatever I do, wherever I go, I keep repeating them again and again:

> Dorogáia moiá, mne v dorógu porá,
> Ia s sobóiu dobrá ne berú.

They are from an old-fashioned love song, so that, of course, for obvious reasons, the theme could not but find response in an old man's heart. But I think they would never have pursued me so relentlessly were they not so musical. If you were to read them aloud you would feel vitally how enticing these musical lines are, for despite their mournful theme they sound forth boldly and triumphantly. "DoROgaia moia, mne v doROgu poRA, / Ia s soboiu dobRA ne beRU." Read them aloud and you will understand why I repeat them again and again, in my room, in the garden, and on the street. "DoROgaia moia, mne v doROgu poRA, / Ia so soboiu dobRA ne beRU." The broad, elegant anapest, organically merged with the triumphant theme of the lines, those trumpetlike clarion sounds RA–RO–RA–RU which resound so artfully through the lines give rise immediately to a desire to sing. Is it any wonder that this refrain has not left me all day today? "DoROgaia moia, mne v doROgu poRA."

Whose lines are they? I simply cannot remember. An old poem or a modern one? It cannot be a translation: there is such a breath of fresh air in them, they are so natural in each intonation, they are so firmly tied to traditional Russian melodies.

This is why I was so surprised when someone in the house who heard me mumbling the words all day informed me that they are the lines of the distinguished Daghestan poet Rasul Gamzatov translated from Avarian into Russian by the poet N. Grebnev. And I immediately recalled that I really had read them in Rasul Gamzatov's book *Lofty Stars,* but from the bad habit of many readers I did not trouble myself to look to see who had translated these marvelous lines. People have started talking about Grebnev only recently, after the version of *Lofty Stars* in his translation (with Ya. Kozlovsky) won the Lenin Prize. But in fact, despite his youth, Grebnev is by no means a novice in literature, and I think it is time our critics took a closer look at him.

He has done a great service for the Soviet reader: by dint of long stubborn work he has created two by no means insignificant books in quick succession—two anthologies of folk verse: *Songs of Anonymous Singers: Lyric Folk Poetry of the Northern Caucasus* and *Songs of Bygone Times: Lyric Poetry of the Peoples of Central Asia.* [7] The first contains hundreds (not dozens, but hundreds) of his translations of songs of various Caucasian peoples; the second offers an equally rich collection, again in his translation, of Central Asian folklore—songs of the Uzbeks, Tadzhiks, Kirghiz, Turkmens, Uygurs, and Karakalpaks. The compilation of such vast collections of the monuments of oral folk works and their reproduction in another language are usually things that can be done only by a large collective of poets. The collections Grebnev has compiled are the fruit of his single-handed labor. He is not just the translator of all these songs, but also their indefatigable collector, and he is not just a poet, but a research scholar. He approached his translations of Gamzatov's lyrics fully armed with this vast experience, a mature and dependable talent who has firmly assimilated the traditional forms of oral folk poetry.

Were Rasul Gamzatov not a folk poet, Grebnev, I think, would not even have attempted to translate his songs. He loves and knows how to re-create chiefly popular—folk—poetry. Or poetry that is akin to it. Other poetry, so far as I am aware, has never attracted him. One of the most prominent forms in the work of Rasul Gamzatov is of course the song. And this is completely natural: all authentic folk poets have loved to pour out their feelings in the canonical song forms given them by their people—Burns, Shevchenko, Petöfi, Koltsov, Nekrasov. Grebnev has long had a command of these forms. In his musical translations we continually encounter all the signs of the song structure: parallel arrangement of the lines, symmetrical disposition of semantic units. Note here Gamzatov's songs in Grebnev's translation of *Lofty Stars,* such as "My Heart's in the Mountains," "How do You Manage to Live, You Braves?" "There by the Window," "It's Time I Was on My Way," and so on.[8]

But songs do not exhaust the creativity of this bard of Daghestan. He has other poems too—his philosophical poems. This is also a folk genre: every folklore, especially Eastern folklore, has an incalculable multitude of verse-aphorisms, verse-sayings, which embody the wisdom of their people. In his last years Gamzatov was drawn more and more often to these verses. This is the second of his beloved genres. Here he appears before us not as a poet-singer, but as a searching sage in quest of the true meaning of things. These verse-aphorisms, verse-sayings, verse-exhortations have become the so to speak exclusive specialty of Grebnev. This is where he has achieved his greatest successes. Rasul Gamzatov's song poems have been successfully translated by other poets too: Ya. Kozlovsky, Vera Zvyagintseva, I. Snegina, E. Nikolayevskaya. But only Grebnev has devoted his powers to translating the verse-aphorisms.

Gamzatov wrote a multitude of these verses. The first among them are his famed *Inscriptions*: "Inscriptions on Doors and Gates," "Inscriptions on Daggers," "Inscriptions on Gravestones," "Inscriptions on Hearthstones and Fireplaces," "Inscriptions on Wine Goblets." Many profound maxims are also to be found in Gamzatov's *Octaves,* which are included in the collection *Lofty Stars* along with *Inscriptions.* It is by no means easy to translate them. Engendered by philosophical meditation, they are considerably removed in their rhyming and timing from the canonical song. Because they stake everything on laconicism, on pungency, they demand the purest mint. Their entire content has to be lodged in a minimum number of lines. Not a single superfluous word can be permitted here, not so much as one flabby line. Many translators keep a full supply of parasite words on hand to fill in their metric schemes. This is fully permissible with the song form. But the style of verse-sayings loathes such words and always soundly rejects them. Here every letter is on the scale, on the count. Typical of this genre is one of Gamzatov's inscriptions on a gravestone:

> He fought injustice with a will,
> This noble brave;
> Injustice walks among us still;
> He's in his grave. (255)

This is an immense idea, but Gamzatov lodged it in four short lines. It would be impossible to express it more laconically. Only those words it is impossible to do without are mobilized.

Grebnev underwent a long schooling in this demanding style. He showed himself an able striker of the pure coin of aphoristic lines long before, in his translations of Caucasian poetry. Especially fine is the mint he struck from a pungent saying of the Balkaro-Karachai people in his anthology of Caucasian songs (113). And he did marvelously with a bitterly ironic saying of the Laks:

> Any man can say,
> He'll live a thousand years;
> No matter:
> There's always one more day. (242)

And with a profoundly thoughtful precept of the same people:

> Take no pride in thy dress,
> Nor the gait of thy horse;
> A man is made a man
> By woman's will alone. (248)

Each of these verse aphorisms has an "abyss of space" (as Gogol would put it). Each could easily be developed into a long, prolix parable. Just as powerful and finely minted are Grebnev's translations of Rasul Gamzatov's *Octaves*. Sometimes Gamzatov's verse-aphorisms depart so far from musical rhyming and timing that they come close to prose:

> Any man can drink,
> He need only think,
> With whom and where,
> To what, and when, how much?   (246)

It does not follow from all this that Grebnev is an irreproachable master, of course. He is given to flops and failures, a sad consequence of overly hasty work. In one of the poet's translations, for example, the final line of one quatrain ends with the awkward phrasing, "Father, keep it in mind," so that the translator can rhyme *imei v vidú,* 'keep it in mind,' with *kak na bedú,* 'to my sorrow,' (357). The conversational construct *imei v vidu* is obviously out of keeping with the style of lines about a daughter who will perish if not allowed to marry her lover. Moreover, the first line is not too solid. It awkwardly mixes two prepositions—"*Into* the mirror I look, *to* my sorrow"—and the meter was disrupted for the sake of making a rhyme.

The translation was done in the late fifties. Such failures are not typical of Grebnev now: he has perfected his craft in the intervening years, and the discipline of his lines is much tighter. One often has to listen to his verse-aphorisms as if they were the fruit of a "coldly observing mind and a sorrowfully marked heart." But if these lines are applied to Rasul Gamzatov, they should be paraphrased as "an ardently observing mind and a joyfully marked heart," because although his *Octaves* and *Inscriptions* are often likely to be colored by the notion of the fleeting quality of all that exists, the notion consistently leads him to optimism. We all die, Gamzatov says, there are no immortal men—this is known to all and there is nothing new about it. But we all live to leave our mark—a house or a road, a tree or a word. Generally, despondency has no place in this life-loving soul which can even show joy through tears, bless, exalt, take delight. It is not irrelevant here that there are multitudes of eulogies, dithyrambs, and hymns in Gamzatov's books. He has an ode in praise of the city of Baku ("Baku, Baku, I bow to thee"), and an ode in praise of his native Daghestan ("How dear you are to me"), and an ode to the city of Makhachkala ("Dear city on the Caspian Sea"). And an ode to Mount Ararat ("I gaze at distant Ararat"). And to the city of Sofia ("Sofia, I love thee"). And to a Russian comrade: "In labor my teacher, my shield in battle." Rasul Gamzatov would not have been a true Caucasian if his most triumphant majestic odes were not capped by an unexpected witticism, as if he were a regular toastmaster sage making a banquet toast. In this he is an inimitable master, a master of hearty toasts and salutations which come straight from the heart and are accompanied by unexpected witticisms. Even many of his most inspired eulogies come truly close to toasts in their style. Very typical of him is the toast in praise of Georgian girls which he ended with an eccentric exclamation: "But keep what I have told you from my wife, dear things."[9]

This paradoxical mixture of pathos and humor, triumphant hymns with a smile, is one of Rasul Gamzatov's most profoundly national distinctive features. In his hymn to the beauties of the world, for example, he expresses rapture with another unexpected witticism: I have loved the girls all my life, which is why I am out of my mind with jealousy over my rivals, who are millions (42). Every time he introduces his brilliant wit into his tenderly impetuous confessions of love, which resound so ardently and hotly, I think with deep gratitude of his other translator, Ya. Kozlovsky, who knows how to re-create this distinctive feature of Gamzatov's creativity in translation. It is obvious that the translator himself is in command of this wealth of spiritual tonalities which are so typical of Gamzatov's poetry. Generally, there is much in Kozlovsky's talent that draws him close to this poetry. He is a born vocalist-poet: his resounding, flowing, musical speech is inseparable from his translations. It seems that he could not write a single unmusical, rough, inarticulate line, even if he wanted to.[10] In his translations the words seem to create a musical refrain by themselves. In a word, when we congratulate Rasul and offer him a fraternal acknowledgment of his great services, we must also congratulate him that among the friends of his poetry there were masters who so lovingly, with such fine and powerful art, made his verses an attainment of Russian poetry.

MORE on Imprecise Precision   There is a lyric poem by Fet which for some reason has gone unnoticed by critics. It has always delighted me for its bold whimsicality of composition, for the classical clarity of its every image and every line. If the author were not known, no one would guess it was Fet. It is so unlike the rest of his poems, whose chief charm is in their diffuse halftones and nuances. It is so monolithic in its syntactic structure that it cannot be broken into parts: sixteen of its seventeen lines form a single sentence. The poem describes in unrelenting detail how a hunter tosses a live pigeon into the air to a hawk which dives swiftly down to pierce it with its vicious beak and lift it exultantly to the sky where it tears its pulsating flesh to bits and pieces and greedily devours them, the narrator then likening his addressee to the hunter for tossing him bits and pieces of Caucasian songs in which the blood we call poetry pulses and throbs. The poem concludes with the sentence: "Thanks, you've given this old hunter a treat!"[11] The songs which were torn to "bits and pieces" and "tossed" to the "old hunter" Fet were sent to him by his old friend Lev Tolstoy. The poem is the poet's thank you to Tolstoy for his precious gift. The songs to which he refers are Chechen-Ingush. Tolstoy found them in a Russian ethnographic *Collection of Accounts about Caucasian Mountaineers*.[12] "Verse treasures like these are rare," Tolstoy said of these songs in a letter to Fet.[13]

The songs were printed in prose form. They are not really translations, but literal interlinear models. Fet tried to turn them into verse, but he was never given to the art of translation. He translated them fairly well, but they entered literature without notice (see Fet, 62). Many years later Tolstoy remembered one of these Chechen-Ingush songs—a song about the grave of a *djigit*—and incorporated it into chapter twenty of his tale *Khadzhi Murat*. He did not use Fet's translation, but a prose version: "The grass will grow over my grave, and you will forget me, my mother! The cemetery will be overgrown with grass, and you will forget me, my mother!" These lines coincide almost perfectly with the lines of the version printed in the collection.

Ninety years after the first translation of the song appeared in print it was translated again by N. Grebnev in his *Songs of Anonymous Singers* (208). His translation coincides almost perfectly in meaning with both the first translation and Fet's. But it has one word, a single little word but a very important one, which changes the meaning totally. The version in the original collection and in *Khadzhi Murat* and in Fet's translation says that the hero will be forgotten by his "mother," but Grebnev's translation gives it as his "wife."

The question here is: did Grebnev have the right to ignore Fet, and Tolstoy, and the original text, and recarve the song to his own liking by introducing content not to be found in the original? Can translators be permitted unchecked freedom like this? "What guarantee do we have," readers will ask, "that this translator who permitted himself to replace the word 'mother' with 'wife' has not introduced similar concoctions into his other translations?" This situation is a matter of general curiosity, but it is also important because it involves a matter of principle, and I would therefore like to look into it a bit more deeply.

Grebnev has translated not just this song, but no less than three hundred others—the songs of the Avarians, Circassians, Kumyks, Kabardinians, Adygevs, and Ossetians. Thoroughly erudite in Caucasian folklore, he was obviously convinced that this song about the grave of a *djigit* violates one of the most important canons of folklore—the law that demands that a mother never, under any circumstances, forget her dead son. A knowledge of the *entire* body of the monuments of Caucasian folk poetry obviously gave the translator the idea that the image of the mother contained in the original contradicts the *Weltanschauung* of the people who created the song. He comprehended an individual song as a specific part of a great whole. It is quite likely that this explains his departure from the original text.

Did he act properly? To tell the truth, I do not know. For me the question remains open. Generally speaking, a translator has not the slightest right to dispute an original text and introduce his own amendations. But in a specifically given instance such disputation is perhaps fully permissible, because the basis of Grebnev's transformation is not a translator's caprice, but a fully legitimate striving toward the most accurate re-creation of the original. All the more so in that the original of this song from Chechen folklore is extant in a large number of variants.

It is scarcely necessary to say that a method like this cannot be applied as a general principle. So far as I am aware, Grebnev does not apply it anywhere else. But translators of previous times have applied it quite often. The Ukrainian translator M.P. Starytsky, whom we have already met on foregoing pages, resorted to this method of translation literally at every step of his work. For example, in translating *Serbian Folk Meditations* and encountering the story of a beauty who in the original "hissed like a furious serpent," he replaced the simile with a "cuckoo's plaint." Starytsky explained this transformation of a serpent into a cuckoo by saying that although a simile between a piteous plaint and a serpent's hissing is fully in keeping with Serbian folklore, a literal reproduction of this image evokes associations in the mind of a Ukrainian reader (and a Russian reader as well) which are totally unlike those the image evokes in a Serb. In order that the impression produced by a given metaphor of the original be at least similar to the impression it produces in the original, Starytsky believed he had the right to replace a "furious serpent" with a "cuckoo," which is more familiar in the traditions of Ukrainian folklore.

I took this example from an instructive article by V. V. Koptylov, "The Transformation of Artistic Images in Translation of Poetry" in *Theory and Criticism of Translation* (39–40), where, incidentally, it is noted that the later translator of *Serbian Songs* Leonid Pervomaysky reproduced the same Serbian metaphor literally, without resorting to transformation. Leonid Pervomaysky, as we see, was not the least bothered that the metaphor is "contraindicative" to Ukrainian folk poetry. Here, as in all other areas of literary creativity, there can be no universal recipes.

DON JUAN   If I were challenged to name a translation that has put the ruinous theory of literalism to shame, finally, once and for all, I would naturally name the translation of Byron's *Don Juan* by Tatyana Gnedich.[14]

The immortal poem has been translated more than once into Russian. I can remember from childhood the translation done by P.A. Kozlov (not to be confused with Ivan Kozlov, Byron's great translator in the Romantic period). It was a fully proper translation, but it was so anemic that Russians who read it got an unintended picture of Byron as an untalented writer of tedious doggerel. Later, in the Soviet period, *Don Juan* appeared in the translation of Georgy Shengeli. Shengeli was a diligent drudge, but his conscientious work of many years on Byron's work of genius turned out to be a fool's errand because of the erroneous principles which formed its basis. If his translation of *Don Juan* is ever mentioned in the literature, it is only as a sad example for other translators: how a poetic text should never, under any circumstances, be translated. In his pursuit of mechanical, sham precision Shengeli attempted to reproduce each stanza word for word, line for line, without concern for communicating its sparkling style.

It is thus with great joy—truly unexpected joy!—that we have found *Don Juan* in the translation of Tatyana Gnedich. Reading this translation after being immersed in the previous translations is like emerging onto a broad, sunlit expanse after deep grieving in a dark tomb. To the amazement of Russian readers, *Don Juan* turns out not to be a pile of countless rhymed rebuses which no one cares to decipher, but an inspired—and crystal clear—work of art fully worthy of the delight with which it was hailed by Pushkin, and Goethe, and Shelley, and Walter Scott, and Mickiewicz. Tatyana Gnedich must have said to herself, let the individual images and the individual colors of the original be lost, just so long as the reader is given the poem's crystal clarity, the vital naturalness of its intonations, the unforced lightness of its simple and distinct diction. This was her only concern. Any given stanza of her translation has lost almost half the semantic units of the original: the translator readily threw out dozens of details for the sake of guaranteeing her translation the sharp verbal expressiveness inherent to the original. Away with verbal ambiguity and inarticulate mumbling!

Listen, for example, to the sound of the hypocritical howls of offended innnocence cast at her jealous husband by Donna Julia, who has just betrayed him, at the very moment Don Juan is hiding beneath her mattress:

CXLV

During this inquisition Julia's tongue
    Was not asleep—"Yes, search and search,"
        she cried,
"Insult on insult heap, and wrong on wrong!
    It was for this that I became a bride!
For this in silence I have suffered long!
    A husband like Alfonso at my side;
But now I'll bear no more, nor here remain,
If there be law or lawyers in all Spain.

CXLVI

"Yes, Don Alfonso! husband now no more,
    If ever you indeed deserved the name,
Is't worthy of your years?—you have threescore—
    Fifty, or sixty, it is all the same—
Is't wise or fitting, causeless to explore
    For facts against a virtuous woman's fame?
Ungrateful, perjured, barbarous Don Alfonso,
How dare you think your lady would go on so?

CXLVII

"Is it for this I have disdain'd to hold
The common privileges of my sex?
That I have chosen a confessor so old
And deaf, that any other it would vex,
And never once he has had cause to scold,
But found my very innocence perplex
So much, he always doubted I was married—
How sorry you will be when I've miscarried![15]

The reader, I am sure, will not be upset that I have offered such a long quotation. It is necessary to provide a concrete example, so that it can be appreciated what vital intonations of human speech Tatyana Gnedich had to convey—and did convey with irreproachable fidelity and unerring artistry. This rushing, stormy torrent of shameless self-praise, false reproaches, and complaints is re-created with such skill in Gnedich's translation that one hears—one actually hears—all the modulations of a feignedly outraged woman which are heard in the original.

And of course, we do not in the least regret the many sacrifices she had to make in order to achieve what she did. These sacrifices are insignificant in comparison with the benefit they bring us. Where Byron says: ". . . her soft lips lie apart, / And louder than her breathing beats her heart" (CLVIII), we read in Gnedich's translation: "She was lovely as an angel" (47). With Byron it is: "God grant you feel not then the bitterest grief!" (CLVII); with Gnedich: "How stupid, and wretched, and cruel he was" (47). Literalists will generally find a rich mine here. No one will prevent them from the mean pleasure of caviling at the supposedly impermissible "imprecisions" that can be easily discovered in Gnedich's translation. "In this translation," they will say, "it says that Julia was 'majestically pale' (47), that she has 'silken shoulders' (46), and that she exclaims ironically, 'The sofa is perfect for a dwarf to hide!' (46), while Byron's text says nothing of dwarfs, or silken shoulders, or majesty." And again: "In the translation of octavo CXLIX Cazzani is titled count, while in the original he is a simple musician. The count is actually his 'countryman' Count Corniani (and not his 'friend,' as the translator has it). The count does not call Donna Julia a 'virtuous Spanish woman,' as it says in the translation (44), but 'the only virtuous wife in Spain.' And again, in the translation of octavo CXLIX it says, 'Were not many English at my feet?' while in the original it says, 'Were there not also Russians, English, many?' The final three lines of the octavo can be shown to be even further from the original. Byron says:

> The Count Strongstroganoff I put in pain,
> And Lord Mount Coffeehouse, the Irish peer,
> Who killed himself for love (with wine) last year.

But the translator composes the rhyme *poshcháda—dosáda,* thereby adding the words 'mercy' and 'vexation' to the work." This is what literalists will point out with mean pleasure. Literalists who demand that translations of poetry be done verbatim—even though the implementation of this demand turns the text of a translation into cacophonic nonsense—will be happy to cavil even that the number of bishops at Donna Julia's feet is also given incorrectly in the translation—the original has two, and the translation one. And so on. And so on.

But essentially, what does it matter to us whether there are two bishops or one? Or whether Corniani or Cazzani was the count? Or that it was Irish blood flowing in the veins of Lord Mount Coffeehouse? These are all third-rate details whose sacrifice in the cause of re-creating the vital, emotative intonations of the original with maximal precision is not to be in the least regretted.

Tatyana Gnedich would never been able to achieve this if she did not have such great linguistic resources at her command. Her lexicon has a handsome supply of fine words, rich in nuance, facilitating the liveliness of the poem's speech with great strength. She writes of Suvorov that he was "a bit eccentric and frivolous" (*Chudakovatyi i vertliavyi,* 268), which is just fine for "a little—odd—old man." Every single page is characterized by this lively, animated, never translation-like speech.

True, there is one quality of the original that remains almost untouched in Gnedich's translation: the whimsical rhyme system. *Don Juan* has an incalculable multitude of mischievous, punning, unexpected, distracting rhymes which impart a special character of grotesquely virtuoso play to the text. On me they make an impression of a fireworks display. But instead of demanding that the translator re-create these brilliant whimsies, we will instead express our gratitude to her for her great gift to Russian readers—her intelligent, loving, talented translation of one of the greatest works of world poetry. When one realizes that every octavo demands two sets of triple rhymes, to say nothing of the resounding concordances at the end of each and every line, and that there are a total of 1,763 octaves in *Don Juan*—the only words we have a right to speak about Tatyana Gnedich's self-sacrificing labor are the words "heroic deed."

These lines were already written when a report appeared in the newspapers about the extraordinary conditions under which Tatyana Gnedich performed her heroic creative deed. She was arrested in 1944 and, as it says in the newspapers, "shared the tragic fate suffered by so many in the period of the cult of personality." In her solitary cell there were no books, no paper, no pen, no ink. But happily, she knew the fifth, the ninth, and part of the first canto of Byron's poem by heart. "Tatyana Gnedich was obliged to carry out her immense work on the translation of *Don Juan* in her head."[16] An amazing memory, a magnificent force of intellect, heroically overcame these almost insurmountable obstacles.

GOOD and Bad   To be frank, I was a bit worried when I first saw an English translation of Pushkin's *Eugene Onegin*. It was painful to think that in place of Pushkin's lines I would be obliged to read bland and lackluster doggerel worked up by the limp hand of a hack. I have

observed more than once in my life that Pushkin sounds in French
and English translations like a routine second-rate poet, a composer of hackneyed verse tales and empty romances.

It is no wonder, I used to say, that when foreigners read him in
these translations they simply shrug their shoulders if we try to
convince them Pushkin is a great poet.

It was therefore with a heavy feeling that I sat down to read
Eugene Onegin in English, sure that I would be driven to a rage of
indignant curses. But the feeling vanished after the very first
lines. The translator turned out to be a remarkable master. He
excellently reproduced the versatile diction of the original in his
own language, and the steel-like resiliency of its manner of verbal
execution, and its rich and varied stylistic nuances. The very
sound of Pushkin's iamb is conveyed so accurately that even those
who do not know English will recognize *Eugene Onegin* from the
sound of the translation the minute they read the first lines:

> My uncle, rich and well respected,
> When his old bones began to ache,
> Determined not to be neglected
> (A proper line for him to take).
> The moral's hardly worth exploring,
> But, Oh my God! how deadly boring
> There by the bedside night and day
> And never walk a step away!
> The meanness and the degradation
> To smile and keep his spirits up,
> Then lay the pillows in their station
> And sadly tilt a medicine cup,
> To sigh and think at every cough
> When will the devil take him off?

As can be seen, the translation is of very good quality. Despite
all the unavoidable departures from the original, it tries to preserve its spirit. Every stanza has the requisite fourteen lines.
Every first quatrain of every stanza has, like the original, an
alternating rhyme scheme (aBaB), the second a contiguous
scheme (aaBB), the concluding couplet is once again contiguous

(AA), and only the third quatrain has an alternating instead of an enclosing scheme (which, of course, introduces a note of dissonance into the musical structure of the Onegin stanza). But the first eight lines of every single stanza preserve the rhythmic structure fully. Of course, only the beginning of the novel in verse is translated—fifteen stanzas in all—but every one of these fifteen stanzas is a perfect model for imitation. I do not by any means wish to say that the English poet has dispelled our conviction regarding Pushkin's untranslatability. Not at all. But still, he was fortunate enough to surpass all other translators in the complex work of translating *Eugene Onegin, Mozart and Salieri,* and such lyric poems as "I Loved You" and "When for Mortals the Noisy Day Subsides." Among the most notable of his other translations are Fyodor Tyutchev's "Silentium" and Alexander Blok's "Dance of Death." Throughout his translations there can be felt an exacting, sensitive artist with a refined authentic taste.

It is of course possible to argue over a few details. Why, for example, did he add four lines to Blok's "Dance of Death"? Why did he willfully change the meter in his translations of Vladimir Solovyov, Anna Akhmatova, and Sergey Esenin? But still, he has achieved the most important thing. He has preserved the charm of the poetry almost throughout.

The translator's name is Reginald Hewitt. Naturally, it was with deep distress that I learned that this powerful master is deceased. His biography is given in considerable detail in a small, rare book devoted to his memory by a group of friends.[17] From this biography I learned that Hewitt was a broadly educated professor, a pedagogue by calling who could read fluently in seemingly almost all languages—including Russian, Persian, Ancient Hebrew, Latin, and Greek. Toward Russian literature, as is clear from the letters published in the book, he felt a particular sympathy. Reading Chekhov, Tolstoy, Leskov, Turgenev, and Blok in the original was for him a pleasure.

Hewitt's biography is written by his friend Professor Vivian de Sola Pinto, who studied Russian under him and lovingly translated Lermontov, Tyutchev, Fet, and several other more modern poets into English. To the same pleiad of enthusiast translators belongs the well-known Hellenist Professor Bowra, who has translated poems of Pushkin, Koltsov, Nekrasov, Baratynsky, Alexey Tolstoy, Polonsky, Blok, Esenin, and Mayakovsky, and compiled two anthologies of selected poems in very modern translation.[18] In the preface to the first of these, in which he expresses warm delight with the wealth and beauty of Russian speech, he informs his readers with particular satisfaction that the majority of translations contained in his book reproduce not only the content of the poems, but their forms and rhythms as well. And as a matter of fact, even Lermontov's "Ethereal Clouds," written in a meter not inherent to English prosody, preserves its dactylic rhythms here, and even Koltsov's "Do Thou Not Whisper, Rye" is conveyed with maximum approximation to the original.

But after all, any other kind of translation is unthinkable: fidelity is the minimum we should expect from a translator. This is the method, for example, of one of the best masters of translation, the poet and critic Maurice Baring, any one of whose translations is distinguished for its amazing closeness to the original.[19] One of the most successful of these is his translation of Lermontov's "Testament." Here is the last stanza of "Testament" in his translation:

> We had a neighbour, as you know,
> And you remember I
> And she. . . . How very long ago
> It is we said goodbye!
> She won't ask after me, nor care,
> But tell her ev'rything, don't spare
> Her empty heart; and let her cry;
> To her it doesn't signify.[20]

In comparison with the interest in Russian literature being shown nowadays in England, the shoddy time would seem to be gone when Leonard A. Magnus (also at Oxford) cited Nekrasov's lines "Contemplating the horrors of war . . ." in the commentaries to his clumsy translation of *The Song of Igor's Campaign* and boldly signed them—M. Lermontov![21] It was acceptable to know nothing about Russian poetry in those days, and such blunders bothered no one. It is perhaps indicative that when the distinguished *Encyclopaedia Britannica* came out in 1911—which is to say seven years after Chekhov's death—it did not deign to honor him with so much as a single short entry.[22] And another, even earlier fact: when Maurice Baring advised a London firm in 1903 to publish the novels of Dostoyevsky, who enjoys solid success in England these days, the firm declined on the grounds that "readers can't be found for novels of this sort."[23] Not that it can be said such scorn for Russian culture is never encountered even now at times. I have before me at the moment a weighty tome—the third edition of a literary guide compiled by Sir Paul Harvey. The guide has 930 pages. It is a solid, imposing work, widely respected for its thoroughness, But from sheer force of inveterate English traditions long since rejected by life itself, it says only a few unreliable words in all about Russian writers: fifteen short lines on Pushkin, twelve on Turgenev, ten on Chekhov. And that is all. Not a word about Lermontov, or Herzen, or Blok, or—God save us—Mayakovsky. And then as if to compensate for this annoying omission, a rogue who never published so much as a single line is numbered among Russian writers. Grigory Rasputin (654)! Rasputin instead of Herzen and Lermontov! And to cap it off, the information given about him is more accurate than that given the writers who were so honored as to be included in the book. About Chekhov, for example, it is said that he is the author of *novels*! And about Pushkin that he was a very unoriginal writer who imitated Shakespeare and Byron and was called Alexander Sergivitch.[24] It might not have been so bad if such mistakes adorned some shabby publication, but Paul Harvey's monumental labor enjoys the reputation of a dependable reference unprecedented for the wealth and accuracy of the information if offers its readers. It deserves its reputation. And its attitude toward Russian literature is, I repeat, a relic of bygone times.

And of course, it is most reassuring that there also exist the translations of Herzen's *My Past and Thoughts* and Aksakov's *Family Chronicle* done with such love and sensitive artistry by the

Latinist Professor James Duff. There is also a charming translation of Turgenev's *First Love*. It is gratifying to think that the business of re-creating the poetic heritage of Alexander Blok has been blessed in the very same England by the outstanding powers of such poets as Robin Kemball (who was so successful with "Scythians"), Alex Miller, O. Elton, Francis Crownford, Sir Cecil Kisch, and others. (See article by A. Pyman in *International Links of Russian Literature*, 417–33.) But unfortunately, along with these artisitcally valuable creative translations, dozens of translations are being published which have no relation to art. The diverse levels of the translator's craft are striking: there is an immense abyss between the upper and lower levels of quality. Above, a noble enthusiasm and stubborn toil, below, the indifference of hasty hacks who meet deadlines any way they can. And these hacks are far too many. These are the translators who dominate attention. Art of any sort is beyond their reach, and they could not care less anyway. To translate the story—more than this they do not demand of themselves. The heavy losses suffered from this by the Anglo-American reader are what I tried to demonstrate on the foregoing pages on the translations of *The Inspector General* and *Ivan Denisovich*.

Such translations can appear only in the total absence of the strict, principled, and acute criticism that can exercise the unremitting control needed to protect the interests of readers and at the same time defend Russian authors from the cruel violence inflicted on them by translations such as these.

Despite all my esteem for the memory of the distinguished propagandist of Russian literature Constance Garnett (1862– 1946), who has translated *seventy* volumes of classical Russian prose into English, I cannot dismiss the thought that these translations would have been far more nearly perfect if in the early years of her selfless, titanically immense work there could have been found authoritative critics who might have taken a vital interest in a higher quality of her translations. By making strict, sharp demands on her, they would have saved her from many mistakes and helped her to express the individual styles of writers more powerfully and clearly in translation. At the present time in our literature great interest is being shown in Constance Garnett. The leading Soviet linguist A. Tove has devoted herself to a noble task—the task of resurrecting the image of this remarkable toiler in our memory. An ardent article by A. Tove, "Constance Garnett—Translator and Propagandist of Russian Literature," has been published in the journal *Russian Literature,*[25] and her study of "Translations of Chekhov in England and the United States" has been published in the collection *Scholarly Reports of the Higher School.* In the latter work she proves convincingly that "the first place among translators of Chekhov belongs by right to Constance Garnett, who has done a great deal on behalf of acquainting the readers of England and the United States with Chekhov." Constance Garnett's "truly creative translations," A. Tove says, "were a literary-historical event of immense significance."[26]

I recently ran across a biographical essay on Constance Garnett in *The Garnett Family.* The essay cites a letter from A. Tove in which she reports that after doing a stylistic and linguistic analysis of seven English translations of *Dead Souls,* she proved in one of her scholarly works that Mrs. Garnett's translation was superior (194).[27] We cannot doubt this superiority—if only because the other six translations are of very low quality. Both here and in England memoirs on Constance Garnett have been recently appearing. In one voice they affirm that she was a great person: she was friends with Russian revolutionary émigrés in London, was warmly sympathetic to them—and in her old age, blind, sick, deathly tired, she did not give up her work for so much as a single day. The press called her more than once a Columbus who discovered for millions of Anglo-American readers a new unexplored continent—Russian literature. But she worked in an empty desert, in solitude, surrounded by an immense silence. She translated seventeen volumes of Turgenev, thirteen volumes of Dostoyevsky, six of Gogol, four of Tolstoy, six of Herzen, seventeen of Chekhov—and, in addition, books by Goncharov and Ostrovsky. If only someone could have helped deliver her from her chief sin: the leveling of writers' styles, as a result of which Dostoyevsky comes in some strange way to resemble Turgenev. True, journals and newspapers published not a few articles about the writers she brought to the acquaintance of Englishmen, but almost nothing was said about her methods of translation. It was believed they were irreproachable.

Arnold Bennett, and Katherine Mansfield, and John Galsworthy, and Hemingway, all of whom expressed delight over her translations in print and in correspondence, knew not a word of Russian. But if they had read, for example, the original text of Dostoyevsky's *Notes from the Underground,* and compared it with her translation, they would have seen how great is the abyss between the style of the translation and the style of the original. In reading the original, who does not feel the convulsions, the nervous trembling of Dostoyevsky's style? It is expressed in convulsions of syntax, in a frenzied and somehow piercing diction where malicious irony is mixed with sorrow and despair. But with Constance Garnett it becomes a safe blandscript: not a volcano, but a smooth lawn mowed in the English manner—which is to say a complete distortion of the original. The same thing can be said about her translation of Tolstoy's *The Death of Ivan Ilich,* for the same tendency toward blandscript can be found here too. It is not without reason that, at the end of an apologetic essay devoted to her, the author of the English book I just mentioned considered it necessary to say: "Of course, it is quite likely that sooner or later in the course of time other more perfect translations will appear. In examining the most recent translations [of Russian dramas, tales and novels—K. Ch.], it is impossible not to conclude, even in the absence of complete familiarity with the original texts, that the opportunity exists to re-create them far better in the English language" (195).

Of course, nothing said here in any way diminishes Constance Garnett's great historical services. No matter what the shortcomings of her translations, they will always remain models of conscientiousness. Much of her work even now retains its high artistic value—for example, her translations of Turgenev. I collated two translations with the originals—*Smoke* and *Virgin Soil*—and I believe I have the right to confirm that they fully correspond to the originals in their tonality. But her translations of the works of Gogol, Dostoyevsky, and Chekhov have to be done over. All of her translations seem insipid, pale, and—worst of all—trivial. I repeat: her translations would have been considerably better if they had been submitted at the time of their publication to the intense scrutiny of critics. This would have facilitated the development of her talent: by recognizing the shortcomings of one of her translations, she could have avoided their repeat in another—and in so doing she would have perfected her craft. But there was no criticism. And this lack of responsibility on the part of translators as regards public opinion led to the complete disorientation of readers.

At the present time an end to all this muddle, however, seems to have come. Here, for example, is a passage by the American writer Sidney Monas which appeared not long ago in a curious book, *The Craft and Context of Translation,* published by the University of Texas Press:

> Gogol has been massacred. Needed: a new translation of *Dead Souls,* the plays (see below), and a dozen or so of his best stories, including the interesting fragment *Rome,* and the amazingly modern yet all but forgotten *Notes of a Madman.*
>
> Theater. Here the record is dismal. There is scarcely a single major Russian play that has been adequately rendered into speakable English. New translations of Chekhov are in the offing, but although Chekhov is the greatest Russian playwright, he did not write the greatest Russian play. Gogol did. It is called *Revizor.* . . . Griboedov's *Woe from Wit* . . . should be translated by Richard Wilbur, . . *A Month in the Country* is a masterpiece that has fared badly; and it is *not* the only play Turgenev wrote. Ostrovsky is essentially a repertory playwright, and at least six of his plays deserve longer shrift than they have received; *The Storm* is a masterpiece. Mayakovsky has written at least two funny plays, definitely dated and by no means on a level with the best, but interesting, and there: *The Bath-House* and *The Bedbug.*

After pointing out how abominably matters stand as regard the matter of translations of Russian poets in England and the United

States, Monas addresses himself to American writers: "Learn Russian, Arrowsmith, Lattimore, Wilbur, Hecht." And naming a whole succession of past and present translators of Russian poetry, he writes with indignation: "Nie—e—e—e—e—t!" And he lists the poets who ought to be translated anew into English: "Pushkin, Lermontov, Tiutchev, Fet, Nekrasov, Blok, Esenin, Mayakovsky, Pasternak, Akhmatova, Tsvetaeva, Zabolotsky, Evtushenko." In addition, Garshin's short stories, Leskov's *Rabbit Park,* Bunin, the *byliny* or epic songs, a good book of Russian proverbs are waiting for translators. "Memoirs, journals, reminiscences: a great form in Russian. A form to which much of Russian fiction aspires. . . . Why not the diary and letters of Peter the Great? . . . Bolotov, the Russian Pepys. . . . Annenkov's *A Remarkable Decade* and Panaev's *Literary Reminiscences.* . . ."[28] And so on.

Sidney Monas is an authoritative person: a historian, novelist, translator. His article reflects the new demands beginning to be made more and more often by the younger generation of Anglo-American readers on translations of Russian writers old and new. We must hope the anarchy in this area will soon be overcome once and for all, and Russian writers will at last see the time when they will be translated into English in England and the United States with the same conscientiousness, the same artistry, with which our masters of translation have been re-creating the works of English and American letters for Soviet readers.

NOTES of a Long-Suffering Author

■   Some time ago I wrote "The Cockroach" —a children's story. Among other things in the story, it is said that the poor crocodile swallowed a toad:

> Bédnyi krokodíl
> Zhábu proglotíl.

Now the story has been translated into English. The translation
says nary a word about the toad. The couplet reads like this in the
translation:

> The poor crocodile
> Forgets how to smile.[29]

As you can see, it was not the crocodile who had to swallow a
toad, but me. And not just one toad, but five or six of them.

The plain fact is that the translators have herded animals into
my story that were not there and could not have been there: a
couple of skunks, some raccoons, turtles, unicorns, snails. . . .
These uninvited guests began behaving any way they pleased in
my story, without paying the least bit of attention to me. The
hippopotamus, for example, takes to shouting at the elephants,
"Be careful—don't crush the ants!" even though according to me
he shouts:

> Ei, býki i nosorógi,
> Vykhodíte iz berlógi
>   I vragá
>   Na rogá
> Podymíte-ka!

"Be careful—don't crush the ants!" is a long way from asking the
bulls and rhinoceroses to leave their dens and toss someone's foes
on their horns. The lion addresses other beasts the same way in
the translation, even adding behind my back:

> I don't blame the little snails,
> Everyone knows they don't have nails.

Of course, I understand that no translation of verse can get by
without concoctions. But to begin with, only the strictest dosage
should be prescribed here, and in the second place, only concoctions that do not run contrary to the spirit of the original should
be introduced. In the original the tale ends by saying that the
only thing left to do is to dig the moon out of the bog and pin it to
the sky with snails. The translation, however, has this ending:

The moon again sheds silver light;
The world is peaceful, friendly, bright.

As you can see, the author's style has been mercilessly distorted.

But can one even speak of style when the translation has not even observed the rhythm? I have always considered diverse rhythms which shift in response to each change of subject to be one of the devices that have the most powerful effect on little readers, because children are particularly sensitive to the musical bases of poetry. I have always thought that each episode, and sometimes even each image, should be fitted with an appropriate rhythm, an appropriate phonetic pattern. But the translators paid not the least heed to this. Where I have anapests, they have the same old spiritless iamb, and where I have a ditch, and a nettle, and shrubs, and hillocks, and crocodiles, and elephants in four anapestic lines, they have nothing, not one single image, nothing but bare, purely abstract phrases:

But everyone's tongue is tied with fright,
What a melancholy sight!

And they use the same old hackneyed, moldy rhymes that make even our *morózy—rózy* seem like a model of fresh innovation: light—bright, donkeys—monkeys, kittens—mittens, crocodile—smile.

In a word, the text of "The Cockroach" which has been ascribed to me has nothing in common with my original text—a fact I hasten to expose not so much in my own interest as in the interests of our common cause: the mutual trade of high-quality literary products.

I feel that I am not being very polite here, because one of these translators, Mrs. Miriam Morton, has treated me and my work with the highest degree of kindness and affection. The translation of "The Cockroach" she has done with Mrs. Nina Wiren was included in an article in which my children's and non-children's books are offered to readers in a most attractive light. And, of course, I am grateful to the bottom of my heart to Mrs. Morton for her kindness, but I cannot keep silent about the deep sorrow I experienced in reading her translation.

After all, there are some skillful translators of Russian prose and poetry in the United States and England. Franklin Reeve has done a marvelous translation of Mayakovsky's *Bedbug* and Shvart's *The Shadow*.[30] A few years ago in the magazine *Esquire* I came across talented translations of the stories of the all but untranslatable Zoshchenko. This testifies to the fact that the English language is wonderfully suited for artistic translations of Russian prose. But when it comes down to children's verses the language immediately becomes weak and impoverished under the pens of unskilled dillettantes. I cannot recall a single translation of Soviet verses for children that could not be considered an unintentional slander of the original.

Poems for children are far more difficult to translate than poems for adults. This is to be explained first of all by the fact that writers for children take into account children's sensitivity to the phonetics of each word and therefore equip their verses with a maximum quantity of resoundingly dynamic rhymes. Moreover, the words which serve the rhymes in children's verses are the chief bearers of meaning. The heaviest burden of semantics is placed squarely on the rhyme words. Thus, the ending of my story "Telephone" would lose whatever expressiveness it has were it not supported by three cohesive accordances:

> Okh, nelegkaia eto rabóta—
> Iz bolóta
> Tashchit' begemóta.

Without these three accordances (and without the rhythm, which conveys the strain of the intense effort needed to drag a hippopotamus from a bog), these lines would never have come to life. But the English translator of "Telephone" was not a bit troubled by this. He deprived the lines of both rhythm and rhyme (which is to say, of everything that gives them the breath of life) and offered his readers these limping lines:

By golly, it's really a job
To pull hippo out of the bog![31]

One has to be a deaf mute to think that this translation, done by D. Rottenberg of the Foreign Languages Publishing House, has even the slightest resemblance to the original! And of course, these verses for deaf mutes have not the least attraction for children abroad. Far from propagandizing the work of a Soviet writer, a translation like this only creates aversion to him.

My story "Wash-'em-Clean" has been translated far more attractively in another translation for the Foreign Languages Publishing House, but even here one finds the same sort of verses for deaf mutes. One quatrain constructed of five accordances is cast in blank verse:

> Every morning, bright and early,
> All the little mice go washing,
> And the kittens and the ducklings,
> And the ants and spiders too.[32]

Is the English language—the language of Edward Lear, Lewis Carroll, and A.A. Milne—really so frightfully impoverished that it cannot provide the accordances for such unassuming, unpretentious rhymes as *rassvete—kotiata – utiata – myshata – zhuchki – pauchki?*

Another serious disorder incurably suffered by many translators of children's verses is garrulity, incontinence of speech. Whenever they find a solitary, modest word in the original, they pile on scores of overly free and unruly words which completely bury the original. One story of mine that has suffered terribly from this cruel method is "Crocodile." In the original the story begins like this:

> Zhil da býl
> Krokodíl.
> On po ulítsam khodíl,
> Papirósy kuríl,
> Po—turétski govoríl.

What could be more simple than these lines? There once was a crocodile, he walked down the street, smoked cigarettes, spoke Turkish. But in the English translation, these very few lines are heaped over with myriads of parasite words:

> Once a haughty Crocodile left his home upon
> the Nile,
> To go strolling off in style on the Av–e–nue.
> He could smoke and he could speak Turkish
> in a perfect streak.
> (And he did it once a week),–
> The most haughty, green and warty, very sporty
> Crocodile.[33]

Little children, as is well known, are not in the least interested in epithets—they demand not qualities, but actions. I would betray my very self were it to even occur to me to burden my story with good-for-nothing stuff-and-nonsense to the effect that my crocodile was, first, green, second, warty, third, haughty, fourth, sporty. And to this burdening of the text with parasitic words are added the translator's stage directions to the effect that the crocodile did not speak Turkish every day, but only "once a week," and that he could speak Turkish "in a perfect streak," and that he did not simply walk, but went "strolling off in style," and that he "left his home upon the Nile." Where I have thirteen words, the translator has forty-three! More than three times as many! A 250 percent rate of concoctions! As if the translator's sole aim were to mouth as many trifles as she could in order to amuse herself with her own cheap rhymes: Crocodile–Nile–style, speak–streak–week, warty–sporty.

There is another translation of "Crocodile," done by Mr. Richard Coe. "Crocodile" sounds like this in his translation:

> Once there was a Crocodile.
> Croc!
> Croc!
> Crocodile!
> A Crocodile in taste and style.
> And elegant attire!

> He strolled down Piccadilly,
>   Singing carols in Swahili,
> Wearing spat he'd bought in Chile.
>   And a–puffing at a briar.
> Crocodile!
>   Crocodile!
>   Croc!
>   Croc!
>   Crocodile!
> Alexander Crocodile, Esquire.[34]

In place of the cheap, frayed rhymes of the previous translation, this one piles on rare and exotic rhymes — Chile – Swahili – Piccadilly — but the basis is the same: an illegitimate striving to pile on as many vacuous words as possible, the result being that the author is made to look like a tireless windbag who parades around with feigned playfulness and simulated frisking.

So that the reader can better appreciate what heavy damage is inflicted on children's verses by this system of translation, I would like to offer here a farfetched example. Imagine to yourself that a Soviet translator were to reproduce for Russian readers the verses of the talented Dr. Seuss, the favorite of American children. He has a happy story called *The Cat in the Hat,* in which little children say of the rain:

> So all we could do was to
> Sit!
>   Sit!
>   Sit!
> And we did not like it,
> Not one little bit.[35]

And now picture to yourself what would happen to these simple and laconic lines if the Children's State Publishing House were to publish them in a translation like this:

> We were sitting on a divan,
> Chattering about Mdivan,
>   And a fountain
>   In Hindustan,
> About the beauty Zeinab,

> And all the while, as if in a bath,
> As if in a washtub,
> The little rain dripped,
> Drip!
>   Drip!
>   Drip!
> Dripped on our pickup.

If one of our translators were to come out with a translation like this, our critics would take up arms and Dr. Seuss's honor would be saved. But I have never heard of anyone in the United States or England standing up for the honor of our Russian verses for children that have been reproduced with this sort of disregard for the original.

The fact is that when we translate the children's verse of Kipling, Milne, Lear, Ogden Nash, or Vazha Pshavela, we dutifully rack our brains to translate the style, and the rhythms, and the images of the original text as faithfully as possible—and this bespeaks our appreciation for them. But there can be no talk of appreciation when our own texts are mangled any which way some translator likes, and when the arbitrariness of translators verges on fisticuffs. We are totally defenseless here. Perhaps it is time to begin negotiations with the friends of our children's literature abroad about the princples they ought to bring to bear to ensure that their subjective intentions do not result in such scandalous variance with the originals.

To begin with, the musical sound script of the original text must be re-created. Second, the percentage of concoctions must be reduced to an absolute minimum. When you translate poetry for adults (whether a lyric poem or a heroic epic), you have at your command a large variety of imperceptible, neutral words and word constructions that perform a function in a translation similar to a catalyst. But when you work on a translation of children's verses, you have no right to resort to these liberties, because their swift pace precludes the burdening of a text with such heavy ballast. It would be generally beneficial to our common cause if foreign translators of our children's verses studied as carefully as possible the methods of Samuil Marshak in his translations of

English *Nursery Rhymes* (for example, "The Three Little Kittens"), A. Milne's "Ballad of the Royal Slice of Bread," Kipling's "How the Camel Got His Hump," "I've never sailed the Amazon," and "When the cabin port-holes are dark and green"—and the multitude of other foreign masterpieces created for the joy of the world of children.

The first translation of "Crocodile" mentioned here came out some time ago in a publication by Lippincott in New York. It was translated by the well-known poetess Babette Deutsch. It is very painful for me to express my objections to her translation, because I know the translation was done with a sincere heart. Babette Deutsch is a serious writer of broad diapason, of great and diverse culture. Lying right now on my table is a book of her critical essays, *Poetry of Our Time,* which gives literary portraits of the most prominent Anglo-American poets of the twentieth century.[36] It is an interesting and attractive book. The year before, the same writer was published in *An Anthology of Russian Verse,* which presents her translations of Pushkin, and Blok, and Mayakovsky, and Margarita Aliger, Robert Rozhdestvensky, and others.[37] Much in this *Anthology* is unacceptable to me (for example, the systematic impoverishment of the rhymes), but it is nevertheless a very respectful and diligent work. "Crocodile" is beautifully printed in her translation. A beautiful cover, elegant print. The edition so charmed me that at first I was naively joyful over its appearance. I would even now remain silent about its shortcomings if I were not just now concerned with the question of how Russian verses written for children in the contemporary dynamic style should be translated.

THE Power of Love I have recently become aware of a certain most curious distinctive feature of Soviet poet-translators. They have so enthusiastically re-created the songs, legends, epics, and lyrics of different peoples that they have little by little reached out to those peoples with a live sympathy; they have devoted not only their talents to them, but their hearts too. In translating the Georgian poets, for example, Boris Pasternak and Nikolay Zabolotsky have fallen completely in love with Georgia. And when Samuil Marshak was captivated by the poetry of Robert Burns, he began to experience the most tender feelings for his favorite bard's homeland.

Now the same thing has happened to Vera Zvyagintseva, the translator of the Armenian poets. "It is difficult to name an Armenian poet whose verses have not sounded forth at least once in a Russian translation by V. Zvyagintseva," says the critic Mkrtchian in the foreword to Zvyagintseva's latest book.[38]

Long association with Armenian poetry has finally given the Russian poetess a "crush" on Armenia. At first she wondered at the fervor of this new, unaccustomed feeling. She even wrote a poem expressing her refusal to divine the reasons why she, who was raised in and loves the Russian frost, has been captivated by the blazing opulence of the Armenian south. She is simply unable to understand the unfathomed joy of "this late, uneasy love." Her collection of selected translations from Armenian was published in 1964. The book was even titled *My Armenia*. The translations were preceded by a cycle of Vera Zvyagintseva's own poems which can be called hymns to the country, its songs, its Ararat, its Isaakyan, its Saryan. In her poems devoted to Armenia, Zvyagintseva has demonstrated the intensity that can be reached by the feeling whose embryo is in a captivation by Armenian poetry.

The phenomenon is indicative. It would not be a bit strange if Semyon Lipkin had prefaced his translations from Kirghiz with a similar cycle of poems under the title *My Kirghiz* or if Grebnev had sung the praises of the country of his translations from the Kabardino-Balkars in a verse tale *My Kabardino–Balkaria*. There is no poet-translator who could remain indifferent to a people whose spiritual life has spread itself before him so broadly and fully over long years of constant association with it. And he would never succeed in realizing his great mission—conciliation, unity, and mutual understanding among peoples—if the country whose poetry he re-creates in his native language remained an alien land to him.

And I do not even need to mention here that when a translator becomes involved over a long period of time with an author whose works he re-creates in his own language, he develops such a sympathy for his subject's personality, mannerisms, thoughts, and feelings that he cannot tolerate any negative judgments of him. I remember how back in the days of World Literature Anna Vasilevna Ganzen, the talented translator of Ibsen, was aggrieved and offended when Gumilyov declared that from his youth he felt antipathy to the works of the distinguished Norwegian. And Grigory Lozinsky, who translated the Portuguese novelist Eça de Queiroz for "Worldlit," felt personally flattered when Gorky said that Queiroz's novels were to his liking. This often happens to us even today. The very process of translation brings the translator so close to his subject that he becomes the poet's friend, his apologist, his defender. Let's recall here how I. A. Kashkin taught us to love Hemingway. And the same thing happened to V. Levik, who recently translated Baudelaire. Just how typically he is carried away by the poets he translates is apparent in his recent article on Baudelaire in which his love prompts him to bring to the forefront the best features of his subject's personality and skip over—and in passing besides—his dark side.[39] If someone were to mention Charles Baudelaire without proper respect, Levik would feel deathly insulted. It is only because he is inspired by this ardent love that he is able to re-create Baudelaire's poetry in Russian with such painstaking care. Levik's translation of Baudelaire's distinguished poem "Albatros" sounds forth with resilient metal lines. There are so many translations of "Albatros" in Russian! But next to Levik's translation they all seem hopelessly inaccurate because they lack that beating of the heart of love that can be heard in every line of Levik's translation and without which art is not art.

I have no doubt that among the foreign masters of translation who are re-creating our tales, novels, and poetry in their own languages, there are many who cannot but feel a similarly ardent sympathy for their writers—Gorky, Mayakovsky, Ilf and Petrov,

Bulgakov, Bagritsky, Pasternak. I would like to meet these translators in Italian, French, and English literature.

RUSSIAN Literature Abroad   But among these masters of translation there are whole regiments of ignorant and hasty hacks who are offering our literature to their compatriots in such disfigured form that one wants to shout help. On the preceding pages I have presented enough examples of the intolerable slovenliness with which our writers are being translated in the United States. I have established that because of these poor translations the reader across the ocean has not the slightest idea what Gogol, Chekhov, Leskov, or our contemporary Solzhenitsyn is really like. I have received two indicative letters on this subject—one from Professor Ernest Simmons, the other from Professor Sidney Monas. I would like to present a few excerpts from these letters.

Professor Simmons writes:

> You are perfectly right, translations of Russian literature into English both here and in England are for the most part awfully bad— especially translations of poetry. Hack work is the rule. . . . We have never had a "school of the art of translation" similar to the wonderful school that exists in the Soviet Union. With very few exceptions, the work of a translator has never been considered a "high art" here. By the same token we have very few masters of translation who at the same time would be familiar with the basic principles of their craft. This can be explained by a number of reasons, the most important of which is monetary, inasmuch as our publishers want to make a maximum profit from their books. . . . True, in recent times there have been a few propitious signs of improvement: an interest has grown in the qualitative side of translation.

And from Professor Monas's letter:

Until now neither our critics nor our publishers have generally paid attention to the quality of translation. But now the situation is a bit better. It has been decided to give an annual incentive (and quite respectable) prize for the best artistic translation. Among the critics and even publishers there have appeared a few who have begun to make more serious demands of translators. But basically the situation remains as you know it from your own bitter experience. . . . Many of us have joined together in order to initiate a broad national consideration of the problem of translation—not only from Russian but from several other languages. We intend to start a journal devoted to the critical evaluation of modern translations and organize at several universities special courses where young people could learn the art of literary translation. We have other projects too. At the present time our main task is to arm the most gifted translators—those for whom translation is not a craft but an art— with theoretical equipment and general principles of the skill.

Later on in his letter Professor Monas points out the unfavorable circumstances hindering the normal development of the translator's art in the United States. He defines the chief obstacle in these words:

The pursuit of commercial profit. If a book has a good market, the publisher could not care less about the quality of the translation. No small role is played here, of course, by the fact that translators are badly paid. It is very hard for a professional translator to make a living. The majority of our best translators have to have some other work to go with their translation work. And "professionals" have to work at a pace which makes it practically impossible to reach a high standard even when they have the strength to do so.

This is all very sad. But we will not add to the picture—it is depressing enough as it is. And I also discern a few rays in this gloomy picture. Right now on my table there is a copy of *Eugene Onegin* in the verse translation of Mr. Eugene Kayden.[40] No matter what can be said of this translation, we have no right to call it hack work. It is impossible not to esteem the translator's conscientious efforts to reproduce this work of the Russian genius in his own language with the greatest possible care. These efforts are far from always crowned with success, but this is hardly due to Mr. Kayden's carelessness or haste. In the foreword it is said that the translator worked on *Eugene Onegin* some twenty years— almost twice as long as Pushkin himself. One can well believe this, because each and every line of the original presents the translator with almost insurmountable obstacles.

A few months later still another translator of *Eugene Onegin* appeared in the translation of Miss Babette Deutsch.[41] Although many other translations by this productive writer bear the imprint of unforgivable haste, her translation of *Eugene Onegin,* which has just come out in the popular Penguin series, is executed with great diligence and a high sense of responsibility. Miss Deutsch first attempted *Eugene Onegin* a long time ago—some thirty years—but now she has thoroughly reworked her previous version. This new version is even now not devoid of many sins, but not even the most captious critic would consign it to the category of hack work.

There are seven verse translations of *Eugene Onegin* in English, and one literal prose translation published in 1964. Of these I have carefully studied five, including Dorothy Prall Radin's translation published in 1937 and Oliver Elton's in the same year. These translations have convinced me that the beauty and distinctiveness of the immortal original are simply impossible to reproduce in another language. Fairness obliges me to say that the translations are done with the greatest care, and that the demands made on these translators in this instance are very high. Yes, and some other translations I have seen speak of the same aspiration to a high level of achievement. But these are all surprises, accidents. Hack work still remains the basic rule. Can it be that we Soviet authors must silently and passively endure this insufferable lack of care for our labors? True, once in a while (very rarely) we are defended in countries where Russian books have been mutilated by irresponsible and inept translators. This happened, for example, with a collection of A. Voznesensky's poems. I learned this from the following notice in the journal *Foreign Literature*:

American admirers of Russian Soviet poetry were deeply disillusioned a short time ago when they were offered a collection of Andrey Voznesensky's poems in the translations of a certain Anselm Hollo. The translations were so incompetent that they provoked indignation among specialists and even angry rebukes in the press.

The reviewer for The *New York Times Book Review* had this to say:

> Sometimes poetry is translated by totally illiterate and ignorant people who not only do not know Russian, but do not even know English. The result is catastrophic: the American reader is being acquainted with a monstrous distortion of the contemporary new poetry of Russia.[42]

But such "angry rebukes" are, unfortunately, not frequent. About a year ago a very weak translation of my book *From Two to Five* was published in the United States and England. Of the ten reviewers and critics who commented on the book, only one mentioned in passing the translator's mistakes and blunders, while the other nine expressed confidence in it—and did not even think to compare it with the original. No one defended my poor little book. It is painful to think that every day many works of our writers are distorted in this way. And, of course, we have a right to want the tales and stories of Viktor Nekrasov, I. Grekova, Vladimir Tendryakov, Yury Kazakov, Vasily Aksyonov, and Yury Nagibin translated with the same skill and the same love as Volzhina, Kalashnikova, Viktor Khinkis, Nora Gal, Litvinova, and Oblonskaya translate Steinbeck, Updike, Graham Greene, and John Cheever.

The letters of the American scholars I just cited contain the sad confession that modern Anglo-American literature has not worked out orderly and somehow stable methods of the translator's art. This is confirmed by a significant number of facts. Not long ago, for example, the London journal *Encounter* published an article in defense of false, outmoded theories long since discredited by literary scholarship, and so far as I am aware no one has rebutted it. The English writer Robert Graves boasts in this recent article that in his translation of *The Iliad* he corrected (!) Homer by reconstructing in his own way the marvelous enumeration of the ships (in the second song) and willfully excising all the repetitive epithets of the gods and heroes. For me, as for anyone who loves poetry, the unchanging repetition of epithets is what gives the epic its particular charm. Even in my childhood, when I first read *The Iliad* in Gnedich's translation, I was always enthralled that Thebes was consistently called "Thebes Silver-Bow," and the ruler of the gods, "Zeus Cloud-Chaser," and Hector, "Hector Shining-Helmet." The same feeling of joy was evoked by the many times repeated epithets applied to various objects: "long-shadowed spear," "winged speech," "seafaring ships." Without these charming features so characteristic of the ancient epic, Homer's songs lose their inherent antique coloration. And it is just these that Robert Graves presumed to excise from the text because to him they seem totally superfluous. He is hostile to the marvelous translation of *The Iliad* done a short time ago by the American scholar Richard Lattimore. Robert Graves pronounces translations such as this worthless, and he proposes to accommodate *The Iliad* to the tastes of the most tasteless reading public. In his article he introduces a small fragment of the sixth song in his translation as a model: it comes out something like a libretto or a playbill briefly paraphrasing the content of an opera.[43]

By what right has the translator thrown out the epithet "rosy-fingered Io" and replaced it with the word "dawn," and why does he kill the rhythm and destroy the style, and above all, why does he recommend such a depraved method to other translators?

And why has a serious English journal published his article without a rebuttal?

NINE

Translations Past and Present

> Every age deserves the translations it tolerates or
> admires. —Ivan Kashkin

1 *The Song of Igor's Campaign* has been translated into Russian forty-four or forty-five
times, each time in a different way. And each of these forty-four
or forty-five translations has reflected both the personality of the
translator with all his individual qualities and the age in which
the translation was done, because each translator introduces into
his version precisely those elements which constitute the aesthetics operative in his time.

Every translation is therefore a new distortion of the original
conditioned by the taste of the social stratum to which the translator addresses himself. That is, in other words, every age pre-
scribes its own recipes for departures from the original, and
translators follow this recipe to the letter because they realize it is
precisely the departures their contemporaries will consider the
translation's chief merits.

The age of pseudo-Classicism dictated to its poets translations
of "Yaroslavna's Lament" in majestic couplets: "To the mighty
river a turtledove I shall wing, / My beaver sleeve in the soft
Kaiala to wring."[1] As a result *The Song of Igor's Campaign* was

given in opulent alexandrine lines obviously intended to be declaimed on the stage. This is the same line in which the "thundering" tragedies of Ozerov, Knyazhnin, and Sumarokov were written. Yaroslavna came to resemble Queen Osnelda, who declaimed the same sort of lines in Sumarokov's tragedy *Khorev*. The Romantic period demanded that its translators turn "Yaroslavna's Lament" into a love song. The result was a sensual love song with harpsichord accompaniment. V. Zagorsky's 1825 translation was even titled just to suit: "Yaroslavna: A Love Song." It was written in iambic tetrameter quatrains with alternating rhyme scheme and filled with phrases such as "O, where art thou, my beloved friend? / Where is thy Yaroslavna's bright-shining light?" In that day of the Romantic cult of ancient Slavdom and rapturous restorations of works of folklore, N. Grammatin's 1823 translation of "Yaroslavna's Lament" was written in long trochaic lines and endowed with an archaic style typified by the usual old forms—*grad* for *gorod,* 'city,' *glas* for *golos,* 'voice,' and so on. During the period of enthusiasm for Homer (right after the appearance of Gnedich's translation of *The Iliad*), M. De La-Pyu obliged Yaroslavna to do her lamenting in hexameters (1839).

In the period following the collapse of the high poetic culture which distinguished the first third of the nineteenth century, "Yaroslavna's Lament" sounded forth in a still different way in the 1854 translation by M. Gerbel—in a resilient and ringing but empty line devoid of lyricism, with plain trochaic tetrameter lines and alternating rhymes, with predictably common metaphors.[2] As always happens with the verses of epigones, the mechanical rhythms were not even slightly related to the theme—they came out like a dance instead of a lament. In the same period of epigones, about eight years before at the very height of dilettantism, another "Lament" appeared in the translation of D. Minayev (the elder) which was similarly resilient yet empty, and was sweetened besides with concoctions in a sentimental style. Yaroslavna was made to "bow her little head" on her "snow-white bosom," and she even had to sing rhymes like *polechu–omochu–zalechu. Chu–chu–chu*—these three rollicking, dancing sounds are not even faintly expressive of sorrows and sobs.[3] And since a moribund exoticism peculiar to the ornamentalist style was flourishing at that time in fashionable journal verses (for example, in *Library for Reading*), this too could not but be reflected in the "Yaroslavna's Lament" of the day: "Wind, wind, why dost thou howl, / Why plowest thou thy broad road / With widespread wing?" Flowery concoctions such as "the slave of Avarian hosts" seem especially intolerable disfigurations here because this is one of the simplest, most sincere sections of the lament, hardly in need of ornamentation. In the Modernist period "Yaroslavna's Lament" sounded forth in G. Volsky's 1908 version with cheap pseudo-Decadent rhythms. The dreamlike somnolence into which the translator steeped the lamenting Yaroslavna is blatantly typical of Decadent poetics.

An end was put to such distortions only in our age, when the art of translation was closely linked to science. "When we examine the translations and adaptations of the Soviet period," says a modern scholar,

> we note a generally higher level of artistic culture in comparison with prerevolutionary translations. Almost every translation represents serious work in an artistic, and often even in a scientific regard; they do not bear the imprint of provincialism and hack work which characterizes many prerevolutionary translations, especially those of the years just prior to the revolution (1908–16). There was a significant growth of interest on the part of the broad masses of our people in *The Song of Igor's Campaign*. Theory and culture of translation reached a high level in our country. To these favorable conditions must be added the appreciably more profound study to which *The Song of Igor's Campaign* has been subjected by modern science. All of this has helped Soviet translators perfect their translations.[4]

In the thirties "Yaroslavna's Lament" was translated by Georgy Shtorm. His translation is not a rehash, not a paraphrase, not a variation on a theme, but an interlinear model maximally approximate to the original. The translator's personality does not thrust itself upon the attention, as was the case with the translations just cited. Georgy Shtorm treated the text with the objectivity of a scientist—his translation is a contribution to both belles-lettres and science. It is in the style of the translator's art established in the thirties and forties. Concurrently with Georgy Shtorm, *Song* was translated by Sergey Shervinsky, who was guided by the same aspiration toward scientific precision, but nevertheless produced a quite different translation, one sharply distinct from Georgy Shtorm's: more feminine, more lyrical, and, I would say, more musical.[5] Where Shtorm offers a drily rationalistic, effaced phrase such as, "The banners flutter," Shervinsky preserves the priceless metaphor of the original, "The banners speak forth." Shtorm's translation is more solidly based on principles, more firm, more confident, but also more prosaic and coarse. What is important, however, is that both translators tried equally hard to avoid introducing subjective moments into their translations. Neither translator employs concoctions, of course, neither attempts in any way to "improve" the original, to "beautify" or "adorn" it as was typically done by the translators of previous times. And yet their translations are as different as their personalities.

The same scientific-artistic principles can be found in the translation of *The Song of Igor's Campaign* done by Ivan Novikov.[6] This translation is also perfectly typical of the period just past: no embellishments or concoctions, a perfect combination of poetry with strictly scientific analysis of the text! The translator's chief aim was to re-create the ancient *Song* by means of a maximum approximation to the original—its rhythms, styles, vocabulary, poetic images. Next to this modern translation the majority of translations done in the nineteenth century seem like dilettante work, capricious paraphrases of the great literary monument. Ivan Novikov does not "adorn" it with loud, impertinent rhymes, as was done by Gerbel, Minayev, and Mey. He attempts to restore the stylistics of the original, to renew the movement of the line inherent to the original. And although his commentaries testify that his translation is based on extensive research on the text, this work not only did not destroy the poetic charm of *Song,* but on the contrary, allowed it to manifest itself in all its full-ness: "It is not spears that sing on the river,— / It is the voice of Yaroslavna I hear. . . ." The translation not only preserves the requisite negative simile of the first line, but conveys each word and image of the original with great precision, carefully preserv-ing its linear and syntactic structure.

Of course, even here the translation only seems to be objective. (Is it not poetic caprice, for example, that some lines are amphi-brachic, others anapestic, and still others a mixture of oral narra-tive rhythms?) And yet it is impossible not to admit that objec-tively calculated departures from the original are far fewer than in any other translation of *The Song of Igor's Campaign*. Of all forty-five translations done of *Song* in the century and a half since the text was first published, Ivan Novikov's translation corresponds most closely to the literal meaning of the original and serves as an excellent interlinear model for anyone wishing to study the work.

Novikov's method of interpreting the text cannot be consid-ered the only one, of course. There is a great temptation for Soviet poets to adapt *Song* to the modern period, to phrase it in the "nowadays" style. This temptation overcame Mark Tarlovsky, and he created an extremely curious work of poetry which only with reservations can be called a translation. More than anything else, this is an adaptation of *Song* into the complex, multistyled language developed in modern poetry. The headings of the individual sections of the translation are deliberately vulgar— the headings of adventure films and novels: "Head on into the Eclipse," "Head on into Fate," "Trapped," "Lessons of the Past," "Svyatoslav's Dream," "The Dream Is Fulfilled," "No Warriors, Alone in the Field," "Glory to the Donets," "Gzak's Nemesis," and even "United Front." This translation of "Yaroslavna's La-ment" is in quatrains with mixed iambic-anapestic lines which are most definitely modern, as is the vocabulary.[7]

But of course, Tarlovsky's translation is not typical of the translation trends of the modern period. It stands detached, like a rarity which no one will ever imitate. The great majority of practicing translators of the thirties and forties set quite different tasks for themselves: objectivity, precision, an absence of concoctions and capricious embellishments, equirhythms, equilinearity, and so forth. These principles seemed completely inviolable when in 1946 there suddenly appeared the miraculous, authentically poetic translation of Nikolay Zabolotsky.[8] This translation does not satisfy the demands whose observation would seem to guarantee maximum precision in a translation, but it is actually more precise than the most precise of interlinear translations because it conveys the most important thing: the poetic uniqueness of the original, its fascination, its charm. Never before in a single translation have the uncoordinated images of *The Song of Igor's Campaign* been brought together with such powerful lyrical feeling. The line is strongly forged throughout. The brave prince's warriors fight from morning to night and through the night to morning again in a bold trochaic line, with swift, bold images, one following the other in quick succession: "mountains of bloody corpses," "sabers striking helmets." "In terms of a scientific understanding of the composition of *Song*," says V. Stelletsky,

> its exposition is divided into three parts and a prelude. Zabolotsky has divined the mosaic character of the composition of *Song,* and the entire exposition, with the exception of the prelude, is subdivided into forty-five structurally different complex or combined stanzas. . . . With great tact and taste Zabolotsky introduces into his exposition separate stanzas written in trochaic trimeter with dachtylic endings and in trochaic tetrameter. . . . It can thus be said with great pleasure that Zabolotsky has found a new way to the free poetic recreation of *The Song of Igor's Campaign.*[9]

Nikolay Zabolotsky's "Yaroslavna's Lament" is composed of trochaic pentameter lines, the majority of lines following the same strict pattern: $-- \, '- \, '- \, -- \, '-$. All the advantages of the authentic Soviet method are clearly evident here—the joining together of scientific knowledge with poetic feeling. Zabolotsky has called his translation an adaptation, but his adaptation conveys the original more accurately than many other translations, because it conveys its lyricism, its dynamism.

2   I have cited "Yaroslavna's Lament" here only in the interests of graphic demonstration. The methods of artistic translation in the reproduction of French, English, and German works of poetry changed in exactly the same way in the nineteenth and twentieth centuries—in complete dependence on the changing tastes of readers. Every period dictates its own special style, and this style is considered the most suitable for the interpretation of a given author.

A Classical period of embellished translations is the eighteenth century, when the unified, universal norms of the beautiful were considered to be fully established. The individual distinctiveness of the original did not even have value at the time: in translating foreign authors, the writer of the eighteenth century strove diligently to erase all the individual features of the original, anything of its national character that gave evidence of "barbaric taste." The French of the eighteenth century, who belonged to aristocratic court circles, imagined themselves the sole possessors of perfect taste, the direct descendants of the ancient Greeks and Romans, and when they recarved foreign works to their own liking and made them pleasing to the tastes of "the propertied and enlightened representatives of the nation," they were convinced that in so doing they were bringing these works closer to the ideal of perfection. The attitude of that time toward the art of translation was formulated excellently in an article on Russian Classicism by G.A. Gukovsky:

> One of the fundamentals of aesthetic thought in the mid-eighteenth century was the principle of the absolute value of art. This principle can perhaps be considered an unacknowledged but characteristic nuance of aesthetic consciousness, something on the order of *a feeling of absoluteness*. The principle of absoluteness rested in its turn on the nonhistorical character of the thought of the time. The habit of fixing every apprehended cultural fact in a specific place in a historical perspective—a habit developed predominantly in the nineteenth century—was nonexistent. Facts were apprehended predominantly through an appreciation founded on nonhistorical

criteria, rather than on the basis of evidence. In particular, artistic facts were not apprehended in terms of local color.

Directly dependent on principles and points of view for the appreciation of poetic phenomena, for example, were the specified techniques of translation so typical of eighteenth-century thought. It is especially necessary to link with the circumstance that the majority of translations were perceived in their approximation of absolute value—the notorious disrespect of translators for the original text. To the degree that an author of an original text did not attain his aim, but only approximated it, it was necessary to go beyond what he attained and make use of the achievements of poets who came after him to add new merits; it was necessary to go one step further along the way from the point where the author of the original work stopped, to adorn and improve the original text to the degree that it was in need of improvement. A translation which changes and corrects the text serves only to the benefit of its merit. It was important, after all, to offer the reader a good work which was as close to the ideal as possible, and questions as to what the primary author wished to offer in his work, or as to how many persons took part in the cumulative creation of the work and to what degree their creative efforts were in accord, could not have essential significance.

Translators of prose and poetry, fully cognizant of their responsibility for their actions and for the methods of their work, purged and corrected the original text in accordance with their own notions of what was aesthetically proper and beautiful, cut out what seemed to them to be superfluous, inartistic, or inept, introduced their own tidbits where they found imperfection, and so on. Conversely, if the text seemed to the translator to be absolutely perfect, fully attained to the only possible beautiful solution of a given aesthetic task—the translator treated it with the utmost care, even with something verging on slavish servility to the original. He strove diligently to translate it word for word or, if it was poetry, line for line.[10]

The highest development of this dogma was reached in France of that time, and thus no foreign writer could escape becoming in French translation as fashionable, elegant, and "pleasing" as a French writer. Even Cervantes and Shakespeare were titled "Marquis" by French translators. When Antoine Prévost translated one of Richardson's most famous novels in 1714, he even declared in his preface that a translator must exert all his efforts to bring what is "pleasing" to the reading public. Richardson describes a death in his novel. Prévost cast out this entire scene because, in his words, it was too vulgar and depressing. "True, it is perfectly suitable for Englishmen," he explained, "but its colors are so vivid and, unfortunately, so offensive to the tastes of our people that no revisions can make it tolerable to Frenchmen." The same Prévost willfully changed the last chapters of another of Richardson's novels, and in so doing boasted that he "imparted a universal European character to the mores which are too obviously English and would shock French readers." Sterne's French translator of the time went even further: he declared in his preface that inasmuch as he found the English humorist's jokes and witticisms unsuccessful, he replaced them with his own! Cervantes's translator disfigured *Don Quixote* in exactly the same way on the grounds that "Cervantes was not French, but Spanish, and he wrote for his own nation, whose tastes are not in keeping with our own." The French translator of Pushkin's *The Fountain at Bakhchisaray,* Jean-Marie Chopin, titled his translation *The Fountain of Tears.* Chopin did not even dare call the fountain made famous by Pushkin by its real name, fearing that "a Tatar word might offend the ears of some Frenchmen, who are accustomed to euphony."[11]

All this was exceeded by Diderot, who, by his own admission, never even looked at a book he translated, but instead, "read it through once or twice, penetrated to its essence, and then shut it and began translating." True, the book was a philosophical study, but the French treated artistic literature in the same way. And this arbitrary attitude toward the original emigrated to Russia. The young Zhukovsky, in translating *Don Quixote* from Florian's French translation, repeated the opinion that slavish fidelity to the original is a sin. "*Don Quixote* displays elements which are in poor taste—so why should they not be cast out? . . . When one translates a novel, the most pleasing translation is of course the most accurate."[12] And Zhukovsky repeats after Florian in the preface to his translation: "Cervantes has many shortcomings. Some jokes are frequently repeated, others are too strained; there are some unpleasant scenes. Cervantes's taste was not always refined. . . . I have made so bold as to change some things, and have softened certain overly strong expressions; I revised many of the verses, cast out repetitions. . . . Persons who are not so severe as to deny translators good sense and taste can credit my love for Cervantes; I cast out only what in translation is unworthy of him."[13]

This was the attitude in that period toward all writers, including even Shakespeare. Anthony, Earl of Shaftesbury, wrote this about Shakespeare in 1710, for example:

> Our old dramatick Poet, Shakespear . . . notwithstanding his natural Rudeness, his unpolish'd style . . . his Defiency in almost all the Graces and Ornaments of this kind of Writings; Yet by the Justness of his Moral . . . he pleases his Audience. . . .[14]

So that if the Earl of Shaftesbury had happened to translate Shakespeare into a foreign language, he would of course have polished his style for him and given him, insofar as it is possible, "the Graces and Ornaments of this kind of Writings."

For a method of translation stems in entirety from the outlook of a given period. A new literary school inevitably means a new approach to the practice of translation. Some time or another the opinion was expressed that there are essentially only two systems of translation which alternate with each other in the history of literature. The first is Classical, the second is Romantic. With each change from Classicism to Romanticism, methods of translation acquire seemingly diametrically opposed characters, for in the period ruled by Romanticism there is "no ideal of the beautiful whose realization must be strived after," but rather, there is a concrete work and a concrete author whose individuality must be preserved in translation even by reproducing his errors and lapses. According to this view, "we are presently standing on positions articulated by the men of the Romantic period and subsequently developed by the theory and practice of the nineteenth and twentieth centures."[15]

I do not think that schemes such as this are consistent. It seems to me that the demand being put forth for artistic translations by modern-day Soviet readers are conditioned by social factors other than those which gave rise to the demands made on the Romantics. But whatever the case, one thing is certain: the modern reader is uncompromisingly hostile to the translation traditions of Classicism. He no longer demands what is "pleasing" from literature. Every willful mistreatment of a text seems criminal to him. His ideal has become no less than the maximum precision which Russian literature is reaching only now, after a century of wandering in wrong directions. Some forty years ago Professor F.D. Batyushkov made a not uninteresting attempt to provide an interpretation of the various methods applied by translators in different periods. He wrote in the 1920 edition of *Principles of Artistic Translation*:

> The first method. In those cases where the translator belonged to a nationality which stood above or perceived itself as standing above the level of artistic development of the people from which a translation was adopted, *imprecision of translation was raised to the level of a principle.* The translations of Richardson, Shakespeare, Cervantes, and many other writers who exerted a great influence on eighteenth-century literature were all subjected to a demand for "accommodation to one's own taste" (*accomoder à son goût*). Without "corrections" which accorded with the prevailing notions of quality of style and form of expression, translation would not have been acceptable to readers, they would have made no impression.

The second method, in Batyushkov's opinion, was applied when the translator's nationality stood in a literary regard below that of the language from which the translation was made. In this case *a slavish dependence on the language of the original* could be observed:

> An example of this is furnished by our own literature of the eighteenth century. Our literary language was only just then being developed, we did not have "our own taste," our vocabulary was gaudy with foreign expressions, there were apt and inept turns of speech, stilted, trite, and completely unsuitable words all mixed together. I will take two or three examples from Abbé Prévost's *Les Mémoires d'un Homme de qualité*, retitled *The Adventures of a Marquis* when translated into Russian by Elagin. The translation was obvi-

ously appealing, since it sustained three printings over a short period of time at the end of the eighteenth century: "The house from which I was born produced many great men of society"—"Je sors d'une Maison illustre qui produit des grands hommes." That is, "I come from a glorious lineage which. . . ." Or: "Many years in service having spent, it occurred to him (French syntax permits such an expression, but it is impossible in Russian) that he must all alone produce a total lineage, for he alone remained. . . . The born out of this reflection as to the rebirthing-of-a-lineage love. . . ." The translator obviously sought words and expressions by copying the French original literally instead of finding his own words, because he did not know how to express himself properly in his own as yet not fully formed language.

The third method is, in Professor Batyushkov's words, predicated on an identical degree of the spiritual development of two peoples. This method presupposes sufficient education to understand the difference between what is one's own and what is foreign. The principle of artistic translation is then served by a striving to not only convey the precise sense of the original, but also to preserve as far as possible the original form by seeking an expression which both corresponds to it and meets the normal comprehension of one's own people. A translation done under these circumstances must be fully adequate to the original.

The practical experience of Soviet translators has introduced extensive amendments to Professor Batyushkov's formula.

3 Aspiration to translation adequacy is to be explained equally as well by the fact that in recent years the methods of the exact sciences could not fail to be reflected in the thought habits of the reading public. Precision, realism, scientific measurement have penetrated all spheres of our intellectual life. Literary scholarship has become in many of its areas a scientific discipline. In close connection with this development, voices among theorists and masters of translation have sounded forth ever more insistently about the necessity for building the translator's art on a strictly scientific foundation. Here is how convincingly the well-known contemporary scholar E. Etkind writes on this subject in his book *Poetry and Translation:*

The best masters of the translator's art combine the talents of remarkable artists with those of distinguished, independently working scholar-scientists. The verse master Maksim Rylsky has recreated masterpieces of Russian and world literature in Ukrainian, but to his pen also belong major studies in literary scholarship and poetics. Pavel Antokolsky is not only a poet-translator, but also a well-known Pushkinist, the author of interesting studies of *The Bronze Horseman* and Pushkin's lyric poetry, the author of the literary-research and critical book *Poets and Time.* S. Marshak has published the excellent collection of critical articles and essays on theory of literature, *Learning from the Word.* The leading translator of Shakespeare into Georgian, Givi Gachechiladze, is a doctor of philological science, author of major studies in the theory of artistic translation. The Lithuanian poet A. Venclova writes that in translating *Eugene Onegin* he utilized "a multitude of diverse studies and commentaries," and that these works and the academy edition of Pushkin's *Complete Collected Works,* which offer "all the draft variants of the works, permitting a glimpse into the author's laboratory," were his "constant help in the difficult work on the translation of the greatest of Russian poets." Scientific philological work is joined with poetic ingenuity by such acknowledged masters of translation of poetry as Anna Akhmatova, Tatyana Gnedich, Vera Markova, Lev Eydlin, Nadezhda Rykova, Adelina Adalis, Vsevolod Rozhdestvensky, and many others. At the source of this scientific-artistic movement in Soviet translation of poetry stand the two coryphaei of the Russian translator's art—V. Bryusov and M. Lozinsky. (67)

Before undertaking his translations of Armenian poetry, Valery Bryusov considered it his moral duty to study the country in all its aspects. "The desire to know Armenia became so strong," says the Armenian literary scholar Levon Mkrtchian, "that V. Ya. Bryusov, in a short period, in the course of seven months of unrelenting work, read a whole mountain of books about Armenia in Russian, French, German, English, Latin, and Italian, mastered its culture and history, became a splendid expert on Armenian literature. As Valery Bryusov himself reports, he capped his study with a trip to the Transcaucasus, to Armenia. Here he observed the life, culture, and mores of the Armenians, and became acquainted with the most major representatives of Armenian literature contemporary to him. Ovanes Tumanyan and Ioannes Ioannesyan."[16] Recounting in detail Valery Bryosov's scientific studies devoted to profound research in Armenian culture, E. Etkind says correctly:

> It is only along this road that we can expect success and triumph. It is naive to think any art could do without science. It is impossible to be a sculptor without mastering anatomy. It is impossible to be a painter without knowing the laws of optics. It is inconceivable that a composer would not possess a knowledge of the theory of music. A poet working in the field of verse translation—that is, in a field which is quite specific, a very complicated and demanding art— cannot do without the science of philology in the broadest sense of that concept, comprising linguistics, aesthetics, the history of literature and society, poetics. To renounce philology means for a poet-translator to doom himself to hopeless dilettantism. Without a command of both languages and their comparative stylistics, without an understanding of the laws according to which in both literatures genres, poetic and verbal styles developed, without a profound knowledge of the history of both literatures and their mutual influences, an authentic creative translation is impossible. (201)

Here, as everywhere, the Soviet reader has decisively rejected any favors from dilettantes and demanded that the mediator between himself and the art of another language be only those masters of translation who, when they reproduce a poetic text, can guarantee the reader scientific precision of interpretation. What value would Dante's *Inferno* have in Lozinsky's new translation if we did not feel in every terza rima what an immense work the translator carried out in the study of the age of Dante, its philosophy, theology, history, in the assimilation of an entire mountain of commentaries to *Inferno* built up over several centuries? It would seem that nothing could be further from modern-day Soviet people than the medieval, feudal-scholastic poetry of Dante. If Lozinsky succeeded in conveying this poetry in such an upright, richly saturated, full-blooded verse line, this occurred because he combines the erudition of a scholar with the giftedness of a poet. A scientific penetration into the original is a dependable guarantee of a precise reproduction of the original —with the indispensable condition, of course, that the translator has an inclination for science. And the Soviet translator has it to the highest degree.

When I wrote these lines I had no idea of the immensity of the preliminary work Mikhail Lozinsky did before he undertook his translation of Dante's *Divine Comedy*. Now, after the death of this first-class master, the same theorist of the translator's art just cited, E. Etkind, has studied Lozinsky's archive and found "dozens of folders containing various research, summaries, conspectuses, remarks, lists, diagrams, extracts, and photocopies related to Dante's creativity":

1) A folder marked "Bibliography of Dante":
   a) a card index with almost exhaustive "Danteana," each card indicating the libraries of the Soviet Union in which a given book, journal, or collection is kept—in the most important language and with the library call number;
   b) correspondence with scholars and researchers of the history of Italy and Italian literature;
   c) painstakingly coped and in many cases augmented commentaries on the statements of Marx and Engels on Dante and his poem.
2) Folders marked "Books about Dante" containing conspectuses of monographs on the Italian poet, general and specialized works on him, his age, the history of Italy, the culture of the Italian Middle Ages, and so on. Here we find vast excerpts from the three-volume *Commentary* to *The Divine Comedy* by Giovanni Boccaccio, conspectuses of Michele Barbi, *Vita, opere e Fortuna di Dante* (Florence, 1933), E. Parodi, *Poesia i storia nella "Divina Commedia"* (Naples, 1920), Gaetano Salvemini, *Florence in the Age of*

Dante (in English, 1936), Arni Ovetta, *Dante* (Paris, 1911). We have presented the titles of only a few works—in addition to these M.L. Lozinsky studied and made conspectuses of dozens of books on history, philosophy, and art scholarship. The materials in these folders indicate that in preparing for his translation Lozinsky studied "Danteana" in Russian, Italian, French, German, and Spanish; they encompass in addition to general works, even specialized research.

3) Folders marked "Materials on *The Divine Comedy*" containing a large number of references and research in a wide variety of fields.

4) Folders summarizing the special features of Dante's prosody.

5) A folder marked "Rhymes" giving lists of the end rhymes of the translation for all cantos of *The Divine Comedy*. These lists were compiled in order to establish whether the diversity of rhyme words of the translation approximates the original. (185–87)

It would be difficult to name any major work devoted to Shakespeare which had not been read by Boris Pasternak when he undertook his translations of *Othello* and *Hamlet*. German Shakespeariana, as well as French, to say nothing of English and Russian, were studied to exhaustion.

4 Russian literature did not work up to this ideal all at once. Beginning in the twenties of the nineteenth century, the business of translation came under the proprietorship of journals whose editors believed they had a right to mangle translations any way they wished. Foreign authors were treated especially savagely by the famous Baron Brambeus, editor of *Library for Reading*. He struck out pages by the dozens and replaced them with his own, adapting them to the social stratum for which his journal existed. Other journals avoided this scandalous barbarism, but to make up for it they created a pleiad of indifferent hackworkers who translated Anthony Trollope, and George Sand, and Bulwer-Lytton, and Balzac, and Eugène Sue in a slipshod manner and a single awkward style (anything to meet the deadline!). It was they who worked out the drab translation jargon that was the curse of our literature of the seventies, eighties, and nineties. The specialty of these journal translators was that the authors they translated came out looking just alike, Flaubert resembling Spielhagen, and Maupassant, Bret Harte. They took note of neither style nor rhythm, and translated only the story, without the least concern for the original author's personality. The vast majority of these hasty hack workers were needy women exploited by publishers in a most conscienceless manner. There were not a few with talent among them, but verbal culture had fallen so low by that time, the demands made on the art of translation by the reading public were so vague and paltry, that their work came to nothing, not one of their translations has remained worth saving for posterity, for an accurate conveyance of the story does not make a translation artistic. It is not without reason that we have had occasion to relentlessly condemn almost the entire production of translations of that unprincipled time: the translators of Shakespeare, and the translations of Molière, and the translations of Sterne, Defoe, Thackeray, Flaubert, Mark Twain, Maupassant, Balzac. These writers had to be translated again, for the previous translations were fallacious in their very basis.

Only after the revolution, when there appeared such publishing houses as State Literature, World Literature, and Academia, which set for themselves the task of providing precise translations of the finest foreign writers, did maximum precision become an immutable law. The modern reader is no longer willing to be satisfied with Don Quixotes, Robinson Crusoes, and Gullivers in the paraphrases of various and sundry irresponsible persons. He demands translations which can *replace the original*.

Take, for example, the translations of Gustave Flaubert published in the nineties: this trash was addressed patently to unexacting, idle readers who sought only empty diversion in a book. Who Flaubert was, when and where he was born, how he wrote his books, what were the basic features of his creativity, what was the age in which he happened to work like—of this you will find not so much as a word in the edition of that time. But leaf through the first Soviet *Complete Collected Works of Gustave Flaubert*: each volume has such an abundance of articles devoted to his life and works, such a multitude of all possible commentaries, explanatory notes, and so forth, that from the very first glance it is clear that these books are addressed to people who do not tolerate superficiality.[17] To them the works of Flaubert are above all a priceless cultural monument which they have to study. Alongside the translations of his works in this edition are printed the following elucidatory articles by the editor M.D. Eichenholz and his closest associates: "*Madame Bovary* as a Stylistic Phenomenon," "The Creative and Literary History of *Madame Bovary*," "Gustave Flaubert's Methods of Portraiture," "On the Satirical Novel *Bouvard et Pécuchet*," "On Flaubert's *Le dictionnaire des idées reçues*," "On Flaubert's *Trois contes*," "I.S. Turgenev as a Translator of Flaubert," "A Historical and Archeological Commentary to the Novel *Hérodias*," "Flaubert's Working Techniques," "Flaubert's Style and Poetics as a Unity," "A Description of Flaubert's Correspondents." In the minds of modern readers a purely artistic perception of the works of a foreign author is linked inescapably with a scholarly scientific interest in them. And this scholarly scientific interest, so characteristic of our modern-day attitude toward art, has been conducive to a radical change in the very nature of editions such as this.

Just what the editions of the past were like, the reader can picture to himself by acquainting himself with the old translations of Swift. Swift was one of the most monumental, laconic, and precise of all writers. The petty, brisk, vacant words with which we lard our flabby style today were barred from the pages of his works. All those expressions like "whereas," "nevertheless," "it is necessary to note," "it is impossible not to acknowledge," and "on the one hand, on the other hand," and so on, and so on, were organically alien to him. But the old translators transformed him into a graphomaniac suffering from verbal incontinence. Let's compare a few simple phrases of the original with the translation of *Gulliver's Travels* by M.A. Shishmareva.[18] Where Swift has, "He made no further answer than by telling me that I had not been long enough among them" (266), Shishmareva has, "Milord replied with several commonplaces on the theme that, he said, I had not lived long enough" (236). Where Swift has simply, "The other project was a scheme for entirely abolishing all words whatsoever" (212), Shishmareva has: "The other project—a project for the absolute abolishment of words—offered an even more radical measure in the sense of simplification of words. In the words of its inventor, it has above all greater advantages from the point of view of public health" (248). Sometimes Swift begins a chapter of *Gulliver's Travels* without introductory phrases. This brilliant directness was not to Shishmareva's liking, and she composed introductions like this for Swift: "Understanding how the reader is certain to be interested in the Lagado Academy of Projectors, I will enter without delay upon a description of everything that I saw there" (241). Above all, she fears that Swift's humor will seem too weak to the reader, and she tries to strengthen it with her own wit. Swift, for example, says, "This bolus is so nauseous that they generally steal aside and discharge it upwards before it can operate" (213). Shishmareva translates this as, "Every student who swallowed such a pill usually steals immediately to the side and by putting two fingers in his mouth causes it to hop right back out" (251). And there are inevitable additions to the text. Swift: ". . . rouse the stupid, and damp the pert" (215). Shishmareva: ". . . thus bringing all affairs to the swiftest possible conclusion" (255). Swift: ". . . in the school of political projectors I was but ill entertained" (214). Shishmareva: ". . . in my view it was distinguished by a total absence of common sense" (252). The result of all this is that a writer of monumental style begins to fuss around, gesticulate, and twitch like a spastic—which is to say that he once again loses the basic features of his own personality.

The cause of this loquacity in former times was, of course, the ruble. Upon receiving an assignment from a publisher, the translator strove to all but double the length of every line of the translation so that there would be as many pages as possible and the sum of the honorarium would thereby grow. A typical example of such a translation, which I call "commercial," is served by Mark Twain's well-known novel *The Prince and the Pauper* as translated by Lev Umants for the Moscow publisher Sytin.[19] The translator set a quite frank goal for himself: to make two lines of every one, and wherever possible, three. And he fully succeeded. If in the original someone shouts, "Long live Edward, King of England!" (94), in the translation he goes on shouting without stopping: "Long live the new King! Long live our beloved Monarch! Long live Edward, King of England! Long may he live!" (178). And if the author says in the original, "The reign of blood is ended" (94), the translator, considering such a short line unprofitable, loads it with dozens of synonyms or, as Dal expressed it, "identiwords": "The end came to the reign of blood, the reign of cruelty, violence, assassination, and hangings. There began a reign of meekness, mercy, love, compassion" (178). How fortunate that the Russian language has so many synonyms of all sorts! Profiteers like this were able to amass not inconsiderable fortunes from them. And when they ran out of synonyms they promptly found other resources that were perhaps even more profitable than tautologies. I speak here about the explicatory phrases which added loquacious commentaries to what needed no commentary. In the original, for example, Mark Twain says, "The prince is prince no more, but king" (101). In the translation he says, "He took the hand of a prince, or, more properly speaking, of a king, inasmuch as Edward had become king immediately upon the death of Henry VIII" (78). The reader could understand the original without this, but the translator had to squeeze out as many lines as he could! He devoured the entire fabric of the text, sucked all its juices out, and swelled it with monstrous excrescence. There is an amusing incident in *The Prince and the Pauper* where Tom Canty's nose itches terribly during dinner in the royal palace, and not knowing court etiquette for such situations, he scratches it with his fingers (65–66). But this was not enough for the parasitic translator, and he appended this outcome to the event: ". . . seizing a napkin, he calmly raised it to his nose and blew" (78). Tom Canty blows his nose in a napkin—such a vulgarity is completely alien to

Mark Twain—but for all that it gave the translator a few extra lines.

This method flourished with uncommon force in highly irresponsible translators' circles of prerevolutionary times. For example, *The Adventures of Tom Sawyer* in A.S. Suvorin's deluxe edition swelled a full third with such concoctions.[20] Mark Twain, for example, says, "bundles of candles were procured" (62), and the translator has it as, "they took from a basket a packet of candles supplied for just such a contingency by the thoughtful Mrs. Thatcher" (272). Where Mark Twain has, "The first thing Tom heard on Friday morning . . ." (59), the translator has, "Although it is said that Friday is a difficult day, on this morning Tom was awaited by a pleasant novelty" (275). By adding extra words like this, the translator covered every sentence with sticky tar, completely drowning the author's voice. These profiteers of the word are already extinct in Soviet literature, and I recall them here only for historical reasons.

5 I have had occasion on previous pages to speak of the high quality of the new thirty-volume edition of Dickens brought forth by the State Publishing House in 1957–63 with the close cooperation of such brilliant translators as M. Lorie, N. Daruzes, S. Bobrov, M. Bogoslovskaya, T. Litvinova, and others. The edition is distinguished by its scholarliness. Every last detail of the English cultural environment of the historical periods depicted by Dickens has been studied to exhaustion by these translators, and in general one can sense the thorough scholarly knowledge underlying every single word. This feeling becomes even stronger when one reads the authoritative commentaries at the end of each volume by A. Anikst, D. Shestakov, N. Dezen, and others. So that the reader can gain some appreciation for the character of the growth that has been going on before our very eyes, I consider it not superfluous to recall the translations of Dickens put into circulation at the end of the twenties by the same publishing house.

At that time the well-known journalist Ivan Zhilkin emerged as the editor of Dickens's best novels. I pick up one of the novels, *Dombey and Son,* and read: "I wish you to return as often as possible from the other world." From the other world? As often as possible? I check the English text and find that what Dickens really said was: "Hope that we shall meet again on this side of the grave"! The translator did not understand the English felicitation, "Many happy returns," and invented this fantastic, unheard-of rendition, and Zhilkin allowed this nonsense to get by without correction.[21] I turn the page and read, "She was chasing demons up the chimney" (450)—that is, she was seeing apparitions in the smoke. I compare this with the English text and find that what Dickens really said was: "How long it seemed . . . since she had felt the solemn yet soothing influence of the beloved dead. . . " (407). I pick up another book, *David Copperfield,* and read: "The pitiful woman . . . it was impossible for her to show her face on the street or in church." I again refer to the English text and find that what Dickens really said was that the graves in a churchyard could not contain more repulsive worms. The translator confused the colloquial English word "wurem" ("worm") with "woman" and the word "churchyard" ("cemetery") with "church."[22] Where Dickens has "rubbing her nose" (273), Zhilkin has "pushed it back" (304). Where Dickens has "after tea" (418), Zhilkin has "in the morning" (447). Where Dickens writes "days" (387), Zhilkin writes "nights" (417). Where Dickens has "at no time have I enjoyed . . . a higher degree of satisfaction" (258), the translator has "without satisfaction" (285). And where Dickens refers to people staggering beneath their burdens (421), the translator has "people resting in groups" (450). The translator permits himself such liberties that he ascribes completely contrary things to Dickens. Where Dickens has "on the margins of his books" in *Dombey and Son* (406), Zhilkin has "on the walls" (449). Where Dickens says "small arms" (35), the translator has "long arms" (69). Where

Dickens has "full of hope" (237), the translator gives it as "there is no hope" (279).

Obviously, we cannot expect much from Zhilkin. But the translator he has "edited" so cynically requires our utmost attention. The translator bears a most illustrious name—Irinarkh Vvedensky. In the mid-nineteenth century he was considered the very best translator. For many years Dickens was known to Russians chiefly "according to Irinarkh Vvedensky." And of course, no one would deny him his reputation for his great talent. But his talent was so slovenly and unruly (in the artistic sense) that many pages of his translations are an outright humiliation of Dickens. It is incredible that such violence (virtually mayhem) was allowed to be inflicted on the English writer without protest by educated Russian society. Where, for example, Dickens says simply that the darkest days are too fine for such a witch, Irinarkh Vvedensky translates it as: "And so far as that riff-raff of the seas is concerned, she, as is well known, swarms around in Peruvian mines, whither the first ship sailing under Bombazine flag ought to be sent after her." This intricate sentence was composed in its entirety by the translator himself and magnanimously presented as a great gift to the author.

For that matter, Vvedensky seems to consider himself the rightful author instead of Dickens. Why else would he have composed whole pages of concoctions which for over seventy years we have taken to be Dickens's work? In his translation of *David Copperfield* in the old Enlightenment Edition of *The Collected Works of Charles Dickens,* we find this tirade, for example:

> The mercantile house which acquired a resounding and solid fame on all the islands and continents of Europe, America, and Asia. . . . My true friend, the esteemed Robinson, will not, I hope, take offense at these truths, which are as clear as day to any thinking gentleman who has been enriched by a sufficient supply of experience in the affairs of the world.[23]

There is not a single word in this tirade which could possibly have been written by Charles Dickens. The entire passage, from start to finish, must have been composed by Vvedensky, because *Dom-*

bey and Son, David Copperfield, and *Pickwick Papers* do not have variants, and no later alterations were forthcoming from the author. Vvedensky composed for his translation of *David Copperfield* an ending of his own for the second chapter, an opening passage for the sixth chapter, and so forth. Even the chapter titles frequently turn out to be his own inventions. He generally assumed that it would have been better if he, not Dickens, had written *David Copperfield* and *Dombey and Son.* In *David Copperfield,* for example, Dickens describes how the cruel pedagogue Mr. Creakle removes an offensive sign from the back of the schoolboy David—on his own, without prompting from someone else. This was obviously not to the translator's liking. It seemed to him that it would be better to have someone come forth on David's behalf and defend him from Mr. Creakle, and so, without any heed for Dickens, he composed this sentence: "Steerforth, insofar as he was able, petitioned on my behalf before the person of Mr. Creakle, and thanks to this petition I was at last freed from the sign pinned to my back" (163). This is entirely Vvedensky's composition. As Dickens has it, Steerforth did not petition on David's behalf, because according to Dickens he was an egoist concerned only with himself. But according to Vvedensky he is far more kind.

Where Dickens's David says simply he does not want to see someone, Vvedensky has him say, "Oh, I want to see him!" (76), thereby radically changing the young hero's psychology. Where Dickens speaks of an abode of saintly martyrs, the translator has "the adventures of heroes of the acrobatic profession" (264). This seems much better to him. Some might say that the censorship, which forbade mention of martyrs in a novel, was to blame here, but it was not the censor who obliged Vvedensky to turn martyrs into clowns! Besides this, Vvedensky foists verbal adornments on Dickens on almost every page. Dickens refers to a fantasy, and Vvedensky could not refrain from saying, "call it a fantasy or a chimerical hypothesis" (251). Dickens mentions a kiss. This will not do for Vvedesnky, so he writes, "I planted a kiss on her cherry lips" (260). If Dickens says someone began crying, Vvedensky considers it his duty to say, "Tears appeared on the cheeks of my little darling" (270). His gallantry is so great that he turns all the parts of the female body into cute diminutives. In his opinion, women do not have heads, they have cute little heads, they do not have teeth, but cute little teeth, not cheeks, but cute little cheeks, not eyes, but cute little eyes. When he encounters the word "refuge," he inevitably writes, "the refuge where I enjoyed the peaceful joys of my childhood years." And if Dickens uses the word "abode," he translates it as, "our family residence, the concentration point of my impressions of childhood." (250, 260, 270)

To top it all off, Vvedensky did not understand the most ordinary English words and constantly fell into foolish traps. In one instance in his translation of *David Copperfield,* we read, "It stands near the porter's loge" (138). What is this porter's loge? Could the porter be a Freemason? Does the event take place in a theater? No, in the original the word is "lodge." It means a doorkeeper's room, a cottage, a hut. Vvedensky translates the word "speaker" as "the most loud-mouthed orator of the Lower House," when in fact, quite to the contrary, this is the quietest, most taciturn person in the entire Parliament, a person who almost never utters a word—the person who presides over the House of Commons. As for technical terms, Vvedensky always managed to misunderstand them. He changed a military vessel —"man-of-war"—into a military man! When I read *David Copperfield* in my youth, I remember that I was very upset because David was almost exiled to some Island of Coventry. I imagined that the Island of Coventry was like Sakhalin, a wretched place for convicts. I looked for the island on the map and have not found it to this day because Coventry is not an island but a pleasant town in central England which was bombed to the ground by the Fascists in the last war. The expression "to be sent to Coventry" is a figurative expression, and it means to ostracize or to subject to ostracism. Little David Copperfield was afraid his schoolmates would shun him, not wish to associate with him. Vvedensky, on the other hand, made this monstrous sentence out of it: "What if, by common agreement, I were to be exiled to the Island of Coventry"! Vvedensky not only did not know English, he did not even know Russian. He writes, for example: (she) did it with a patter of speech" (89), "I look a girl" (84), "cruel-hearted hearts" (230), "a sweetbriar briar hedge" (41). Ekh! no wonder Dickens once referred to Vvedensky as Wredenskii [Harmsky].[24] The page has not been written this translator could not harm.

And despite all this, Vvedensky's translations are dear to me. Perhaps he did make many mistakes but if it were not for him we would not have had Dickens. Of all the old translators, he alone brought us close to Dickens's works, imbued us in the aura of Dickens, infected us with Dickens's temperament. He might not have understood Dickens's words, but he understood Dickens himself. He did not give us Dickens's literal expressions, but he gave us his intonations, his gestures, his rich verbal mimicry. In Vvedensky's translations we heard Dickens's real voice—and fell in love with him. Vvedensky somehow made himself over into Dickens, mastered his movements, his gait. He did not convey Dickens's words, but he conveyed his manner, his style, his rhythms. He superbly translated the turbulent impetuousity of his unreined phrases coursing from page to page like magnificent steeds. To put it frankly, he was Dickens himself—a small, mumbling Dickens, but unmistakably Dickens. Concoctions are not permissible, of course, but every one of Vvedensky's concoctions is so perfectly in harmony with the original text that it would be a pity to excise them. And who knows? Dickens himself might not have excised them were they to have come under his pen! Everyone remembers, for example, the watchman with the wooden leg in David Copperfield's school. Vvedensky calls him Derevyashka from the Russian word for wood. "Derevyashka hit," "Derevyashka said." And this is so perfectly Dickensian that Dickens is more Dickensian in Vvedensky's translation than in the original. This is a delusion, of course, but we will always prefer the imprecise translations of Vvedensky to the "precise" translations of other translators. Despite his concoctions he is far closer to the original than the most diligent and conscientious labor of some Rantsov, or Voloshinova, or Auerbach—Dickens's more recent translators. The same thing must be said of the translations done under the editorship of M.A. Orlov. A writer rich for his verbal colors was translated here as if by some petty clerk who never wrote anything except office drudge work. According to Orlov, poor Dickens speaks in *Bleak House* in a language like this: "I was amazed that, if Mrs. Jellyby performs her chief and natural duties before directing her telescope on the distant horizon and not espying there any other objects for her cares, she had obviously received numerous warnings not to fall into absurdity. . . ." Or: "I endured a multitude of conceits with another multitude. . . ." Or: "He could not understand why it was that, even though, perhaps, it was even predestined by fate itself that one person must rush about and be admired for his silk stockings."[25] These wooden translations are textually precise, but who would not prefer the translations of Vvedensky in which, despite all their shortcomings, there is a breath of the original Dickens?

It is revealing that in the 1840s and 1850s Irinarkh Vvedensky's capricious treatment of original texts seemed quite normal to the reading public and aroused almost no protest. Right up to the revolution—which is to say, for a full seventy years, from one whole generation to another—they were published over and over again, in preference to all other translations, and only now, when the business of translation has been put on the right track, are we constrained to completely reject the enticing versions given us by Vvedensky and offer our own far closer to the original translations, without concoctions and lapses. If Vvedensky were working today, not a single publishing house would print his translations. And we realize now that the theory with which he attempted to justify his method of translation is an impermissible heresy.

Vvedensky promulgated his theory in an article "On Translations of Thackeray's *Vanity Fair*" in the journal *Notes of the Fatherland* in 1851 when a polemic developed regarding the liberties he permitted himself in translating Thackeray's *Vanity Fair*. His theory consists of the translator's right to lard his translations with concoctions if his pen is in the same "mood" as the pen of the novelist himself. As for his own pen, Vvedensky had not the slightest doubt, for he saw in his translations "the artistic re-creation of the writer." He wrote: ". . . in the artistic re-creation of the writer, a gifted translator (that is, Irinarkh Vvedensky himself—K. Ch.) directs his attention first and foremost to the writer's spirit, to the essence of his ideas, and then to the appropriate form for the expression of these ideas. When one undertakes to translate, one must grasp the writer's essence, understand his thinking, live his ideas, think with his mind, feel with his heart, and in so doing refrain from one's own personal manner of thinking."[26] Which is to say that, if we are to listen to Vvedensky, his concoctions are, in essence, not concoctions at all. In his "artistic re-creation" of Thackeray, he, according to his own statement, completely renounced his own personality, felt himself a second Thackeray, Thackeray's deputy in Russia, and it was to be naturally expected of him that under the influence of this feeling of self every line he wrote had the feeling of Thackeray's own lines. We must not censure him for writing whole pages he felt like foisting off on the English author. He did not write them in his capacity of Irinarkh Vvedensky, his pen was guided during the writing by the "spirit" of Thackeray himself. This is the splendid theory with which Vvedensky tried to justify the illegitimate liberties he took in his translation of *Vanity Fair*.

Moreover, when the critics pointed out that, for all his system for the "artistic re-creation" of foreign writers, he had, in addition to everything else, impermissibly Russified them, he proclaimed this Russification to be one of his chief tasks. "Transfer the writer you translate to the realm where you yourself reside," he advised translators, "and to the society in which you yourself have developed, transfer him and pose the question, in what form would he have conveyed his ideas if he had lived and acted under circumstances identical to your own" (70). This is why Dickens, and Thackeray, and Charlotte Brontë became Russian citizens, natives of Peski or Okhta—it was thanks to Vvedensky. Fully in agreement with his own theory, he resettled them beneath the skies of Petersburg, in the society of our collegiate assessors and titular councilors. So it is little wonder that they began "theeing—and—thouing" their lackeys, riding around in sledges, drinking vodka instead of rum, and drinking tea from samovars instead of teapots. In other words, English bourgeoisie became bureaucrats of the tsarist empire.

Irinarkh Vvedensky's manifesto emphasizes all the more strongly the unacceptability of his claims in our day. Nowadays the resettling of one environment as another is permissible only in operettas and farces. All his giftedness as a man of letters, all his ardent temperament, all the plasticity of his language could not give force and effect to his fallacious theory of the "artistic re-creation of a writer." Of course, Soviet masters of translation share an affinity with his passionate hatred of dullish literalism, slavishly formalistic precision, passive calques. But as we have seen, they demand in addition the strict intellectual discipline, the unconditional adherence to the original text that can be achieved only through a scientific-scholarly approach to their materials. "We must not forget," Ivan Kashkin has said, "that Vvedensky's flagrant deficiencies and outright merits are for the most part not accidental carelessness or incidental successes, they are an attribute of the time. Vvedensky's translations were not insignificant factors in the literary struggles of the 1840s, they are militant stages in the development of Russian literature and the Russian literary language. The soil for the appearance, and most important, the success of Vvedensky's translation was prepared in advance."[27] And the critic proceeds to sketch in fine lines the low tastes of the literary milieu that engendered Vvedensky. To his characteristics we need add only the small amendation that Vvedensky was an extreme radical, a friend of Chernyshevsky and ardent adherent of Gogol, and neither Benediktov nor Veltman, nor still less Senkovsky, whom Kashkin had in mind, aroused any sympathy in him. When one speaks of his translations, one cannot forget Gogol's powerful influence on him. But Kashkin's general conclusions are profoundly true. Precision is a concept that is historically variable; it is dialectical. Therefore, speaking for myself, no one can predict in any way what will be considered a precise translation in the year 1980 or 2000. Every age creates its own idea of what a precise translation is.[28]

Notes

Translator's Introduction

1. See Miriam Morton, "Kornei Chukovsky—the Pied Piper of Peredelkino," *The Horn Book Magazine,* Oct. 5, 1962, pp. 458–68.
2. The work is available in numerous editions and can be found in Chukovskii's *Sobranie sochinenii* (6 vols.; Moscow, 1965–67).
3. *From Two to Five,* tr. Miriam Morton (Berkeley and Los Angeles: Univ. of California, 1968).
4. "Confessions of an Old Story-Teller," tr. Lauren G. Leighton, *The Horn Book Magazine,* Dec. 6, 1970; Feb. 1, 1971.
5. *Chukokkala. Rukopisnyi al'manakh* [Chukokkala: A Manuscript Almanac] (Moscow, 1979).
6. As reported in an eulogy in Leningrad at Writer's House, Feb. 1970.

About This Book

1. *Katalog izdatel'stva "Vsemirnaia literatura"* (Petrograd, 1919).
2. *Problemy khudozhestvennogo perevoda* (Leningrad, 1931); *O khudozhestvennom perevode* (Moscow, 1941); *Vvedenie v teoriiu perevoda* (Leningrad, 1958); *Poeziia i perevod* (Leningrad, 1963); *Masterstvo perevoda* (Moscow, 1955, 1959, 1963, 1964); *Tetradi perevodchika* (Moscow, 1960, 1962, 1963, 1964); *Mezhdunarodnye sviazi russkoi literatury* (Leningrad, 1963); *Teoriia i kritika perevoda* (Moscow, 1962). [These and other scholarly studies of the art of translation are indebted to the early editions of Chukovsky's work, and his later editions of *A High Art* are in their turn heavily indebted to

269

these studies. Hereafter these primary sources will be identified not in the notes but in the text as part of Chukovsky's discussion, with appropriate references where necessary in parentheses to page number and date of publication—LGL.]

3. *Printsipy khudozhestvennogo perevoda* (Petrograd, 1919); 2d ed. (Petrograd, 1920). [Hereafter this primary source will also be cited in text rather than notes—LGL.]

4. *Segodnia i vchera* (Moscow, 1963), 49.

Chapter One: Slips of the Vocabulary

1. See, for example, *Izvestiia,* 25 Sept. 1932.

2. Rudyard Kipling, *Izbrannye stikhi,* tr. Mikhail Froman (Leningrad, 1936), 221; *Rudyard Kipling's Verse: Definitive Edition* (Garden City, N.Y.: Doubleday and Doran, 1943), 27.

3. *Polnoe sobranie sochinenii* (Petrograd, 1923), XX, 258.

4. *Selected Poems* (New York: Knopf, 1959), 118; *Izbrannye stikhi* (Moscow, 1960), 109. The error was first pointed out by E.G. Etkind in his *Poetry and Translation* (145–47).

5. *Saga o Forsaitakh* (Moscow, 1937), I, 706; *Awakening. To Let; The Forsyte Saga* (New York: Scribner's, 1934), 157.

6. K. Marx and F. Engels, *Sochineniia,* 2d ed. (Moscow, n.d.), XXI, 237–38. [Chukovskii has misunderstood the awkward motion called "fishing for crabs." The oars are pulled not too deeply, but rather not deeply enough, so that the rower falls backward.—LGL]

7. See, e.g., the text of *Notes from the Underground* in *A Treasury of Russian Literature,* ed. Bernard Gilbert Guerney (New York: Vanguard, 1943), 443.

8. *Modern Poems from Russia,* tr. Gerard Shelley (London: Allen and Unwin, 1942), 85.

9. *Plays of Chekhov,* 1st series. Tr. Marian Fell (New York: Scribner's, 1916), 105.

Chapter Two: The Translation—Self-Portrait of the Translator

1. *Literaturnaia gazeta,* 1933, No. 38.

2. *The Complete Writings of Walt Whitman* (New York-London: Putnam's, 1902), IX, 39. Written in 1855 or 1856.

3. *The Poetical Works of Percy Bysshe Shelley.* with Memoir, Explanatory Notes, etc. (London: James Finch, n.d.), 619; *Polnoe sobranie sochinenii v perevode K.D. Bal'monta* (3 vols.; St. Petersburg, 1903), I, 186.

4. *Leaves of Grass,* Inclusive Edition edited by Emory Holloway (Garden

City, N.Y.: Doubleday, 1926); *Pobegi travy,* tr. K. D. Bal'mont (Moscow, 1911), 133.

5. *Polnoe sobranie sochinenii* (16 vols. and suppl. vol.; Moscow-Leningrad: Academia, 1937–59), XIII, 38. [Pushkin's statement is actually a quotation of a line from a poem by Prince P.A. Viazemskii—LGL.]

6. *Sobranie sochinenii,* IV (Moscow-Leningrad, 1960), 223.

7. *Polnoe sobranie stikhotvorenii* (Leningrad, 1939), 222.

8. *Iz evropeishkikh poetov XVI–XIX vekov,* tr. V. Levik (Moscow, 1956), 67–68.

9. N. Cherniaev, "Kak tsenili perevod 'Odissei' Zhukovskogo" ["How Zhukovskii's Translation of *The Odyssey* Was Appreciated"], *Filologicheskie zapiski* [*Philological Notes*], 1902, No. 2–3, p. 158.

10. "Predatel' Koriolan" ["The Traitor Coriolanus"], *Literaturnaia gazeta,* 1934, No. 12.

11. *Pis'ma,* III (Moscow-Leningrad, 1961), 30.

12. See *Sbornik obshchestva dlia posobiia nuzhdaiushchimsia literatoram i uchenym* [*Collection of the Society for Grants to Needy Authors and Scholars*] (St. Petersburg, 1884), 498.

13. *Stikhotvoreniia Zhukovskogo* (St. Petersburg, 1849), VIII.

14. *Sobranie sochinenii O.I. Senkovskogo (Barona Brambeusa),* VII (St. Petersburg, 1859), 332. (Emphases are mine—K. Ch.)

15. *Polnoe sobranie sochinenii,* VIII (Moscow, 1952), 240. (Emphases are mine—K. Ch.)

16. *Sobranie sochinenii A. V. Druzhinina,* III (St. Petersburg, 1865), 40.

17. A.S. Bulgakov, "Rannee znakomstvo s Shekspirom v Rossii" ["Early Acquaintance with Shakespeare in Russia"], *Teatral'noe nasledstvo* (Leningrad, 1934), 73–75.

18. *Avetik Isaakian i russkaia literatura* (Erevan, 1963), 120, 126.

19. See F. Batiushkov, "Bodler i ego russkii perevodchik" ["Baudelaire and His Russian Translator"], *Mir Bozhii* [God's World], 1901, No. 8.

20. *Pis'ma V.Ia. Briusova k P.P. Pertsovu* (Moscow, 1926), 76.

21. *Gruzinskaia klassicheskaia poeziia v perevodakh N. Zabolotskogo* (Tiflis, 1958).

22. On Guramishvili, see Iraklii Andronikov, *Ia khochu rasskazat' vam* [*I Want to Tell You*] (Moscow, 1962), 325–27.

23. *Polnoe sobranie sochinenii,* XII (Moscow, 1929), 200.

24. *Polnoe sobranie sochinenii,* IX (Moscow, 1959), 277.

25. *Stikhotvoreniia* (Leningrad, 1956), 316.

26. *Moskovskii telegraf,* 1829, No. 21. (Emphases are mine—K. Ch.)

27. See the 1920 brochure *Principles of Artistic Translation.*

28. "Problema perevoda," *Iunost'* [Youth], 1963, No. 3.

29. *Sobranie sochinenii* (3 vols.; Budapest, 1963), II, 35.

30. *Vybrani poezii,* tr. Leonid Pervomais'kyi (Kiev, 1959), 208.

Chapter Three: Imprecise Precision

1. *Sobranie sochinenii* (4 vols.; Moscow-Leningrad, 1958), I, 91.
2. See M. Kleman, "I.S. Turgenev—perevodchik Flobera" ["I.S. Turgenev as a Translator of Flaubert"], in Gustave Flaubert, *Sobranie sochinenii,* V (Moscow-Leningrad, 1934), 148.
3. This example was reported to me by the late academician E.V. Tarle. According to him, the Kiev editor Ioganson published under the old regime a Russian translation of a German book on economic conditions in the Ukraine. The book had the excerpt from Pushkin's *Poltava* on the first page (as an epigraph). The translator (a student whom Tarle knew quite well) did not realize it was a citation from *Poltava* and translated Pushkin's lines back from German.
4. Cited from Dickens's *Oliver Twist* in his *Sobranie sochinenii* (30 vols.; Moscow, 1957–63); *The Adventures of Oliver Twist* (Chicago: Hooper, Clarke, n.d.), 339.
5. *Za spichkami. Voskresshii iz mertvykh,* tr. Mikhail Zoshchenko (Moscow, 1955).
6. *Kobzar Tarasa Shevchenko v perevode russkikh poetov* [Taras Shevchenko's Kobzar in the Translation of Russian Poets], ed. N.V. Gerbel' (St. Petersburg, 1876), 187.
7. *Kobzar' v perevode F. Sologuba* (Leningrad, 1934), 312.
8. See *Slovar' iazyka Pushkina* [The Dictionary of Pushkin's Language] (4 vols.; Moscow, 1959).
9. *Rassuzhdenie o starom i novom sloge rossiiskogo iazyka* (St. Petersburg, 1803), 36–40.
10. "Lingvisticheskie voprosy perevoda," *Inostrannye iazyki v shkole* [*Foreign Languages in the School*], 1952, No. 6, p. 13.
11. Maurice Baring, *Landmarks in Russian Literature,* 2d ed. (London: Macmillan, 1912), 29–30.
12. "Pesni Beranzhe" ["The Songs of Béranger"], in Kurochkin's *Sobranie stikhotvorenii,* new and rev. ed. (2 vols.; St. Petersburg, 1869), I.
13. *The Poetical Works of Robert Burns* (Oxford: Oxford Univ., 1960), 328.
14. *Sochineniia* (4 vols.; Moscow, 1957), III, 183. See E.S. Belashova's substantive article on Robert Burns in the translations of S. Marshak in *Uchenye zapiski Chernigovskogo gos. universiteta* [*Scholarly Notes of Chernigov St. University*], 30 (1958), p. 79.
15. *Stat'i i zametki o literature* [*Articles and Notes on Literature*] (Moscow, 1961), 75.
16. *Izbrannye stikhotvoreniia,* tr. V.D. Merkur'eva, ed. M.N. Rozanov (Leningrad, 1937), 76; *The Poetical Works of Shelley,* ed. Thomas Hutchinson (Oxford: Oxford Univ., 1952), 452.
17. For a detailed analysis of these translations, see V. Aleksandrov, "Shelli i

ego redaktory" ["Shelley and His Editors"], *Literaturnyi kritik,* 1937, No. 8.

18. Percy Bysshe Shelley, *Polnoe sobranie sochinenii,* tr. K.D. Bal'mont (3 vols.; St. Petersburg, 1903), I, 191.

19. *Avetik Isaakian i russkaia literatura* (Erevan, 1963), 129.

20. Quoted from *Literaturnoe nasledstvo* [*Literary Heritage*], VII (Moscow-Leningrad, 1933), 147.

21. "A.A. Fet kak poet, perevodchik i myslitel'," *Russkaia mysl'* [*Russian Thought*], 1894, No. 2, pp. 34–35.

22. *Satiry Iuvenala,* tr. A.A. Fet (Moscow, 1885).

23. *Zhukovskii kak perevodchik Shillera* (Riga, 1895), 171.

24. See Z.Ch. Mamytbekov, *"Evgenii Onegin* na kirgizskom iazyke" [*"Eugene Onegin* in Kirghiz"], *Russkii iazyk v kirgizskoi shkole* [*Russian Language in the Kirghiz School*], 1963, No. 2, p. 16.

25. *Iz evropeiskikh poetov XVI-XIX vekov,* tr. V. Levik (Moscow, 1956), 130.

26. *Sobranie sochinenii* (5 vols.; Moscow, 1963), IV, 214.

Chapter Four: Vocabulary—Rich and Poor

1. *Tolkovyi slovar' velikorusskogo iazyka,* 1861–68, and subsequent editions to the present time.

2. *A Tale of Two Cities* (Boston, New York, Chicago: Allyn and Bacon, 1922), 208; *Sobranie sochinenii* (30 vols.; Moscow, 1957–60), XXII, 187.

3. Unfortunately, *Pickwick Papers, Oliver Twist, Nicholas Nickleby, David Copperfield,* and *Dombey and Son*—the most prominent of Dickens's works in the edition—were translated by the literalists Evgeny Lann and A.V. Krivtsova, resulting in the depreciation and dulling of Dickens's authorial character as a whole.

4. Ernest Hemingway, *Fiesta,* tr. V. Toper (Moscow, 1935); *Proshchai, oruzhie!,* tr. E. Kalashnikova (Moscow, 1936); *Imet' i ne imet',* tr. E. Kalashnikova (Moscow, 1938). [Chukovskii probably refers to the updated versions in Hemingway's *Izbrannye proizvedeniia* (2 vols.; Moscow, 1959); also included in *Sobranie sochinenii* (4 vols.; Moscow, 1968)—LGL.]

5. W. Somerset Maugham, *Podvodia itogi,* tr. M. Lorie (Moscow, 1957). [The novel was denounced by the Central Committee of the Communist Party as "ideologically harmful" and withdrawn from bookstores. This of course made it a collector's item—LGL.]

6. [It is not clear which of Greene's novels translated by N. Volzhina in the 1960s Chukovskii refers to here—LGL.]

7. "Puteshestvie s Charli v poiskakh Ameriki," tr. N. Volzhina, *Inostran-*

naia literatura, 1963, No. 3. *Travels with Charley* (New York: Viking, 1962). [A complete text is *Puteshestvie s Charli v poiskakh Ameriki,* tr. N. Volzhina (Moscow, 1965)—LGL.]

8. John Cheever, *Angel na mostu,* tr. T. Litvinova, introd. K. Chukovskii (Moscow, 1966). The collection, from the title of the story "Angel of the Bridge," contains seventeen of Cheever's stories, including "The Bella Lingua," "Just One More Time," "A Vision of the World," and "The Ocean."

9. *Kentavr,* tr. Viktor Khinkis (Moscow, 1965). [Updike's novel is a difficult challenge to any translator, and this translation is a tour de force—LGL.]

10. *Ubit' peresmeshnika,* tr. Nora Gal' and Raisa Oblonskaia, *Inostrannia literatura,* 1963, No. 3. [The translation appeared in a large printing as *Ubit' peresmeshnika,* tr. Nora Gal and Raisa Oblonskaia (Moscow, 1963)—LGL.]

11. F. Scott Fitzgerald, *Velikii Getsbi,* tr. E. Kalashnikova (Moscow, 1965).

12. *The Life and Adventures of Martin Chuzzlewit* (London: Chapman and Hall, n.d.); *Sobranie sochinenii,* X-XI.

13. "Nad propast'iu vo rzhi," tr. Rita Rait-Kovaleva, introd. Vera Panova *Inostrannaia literatura Foreign Literature,* 1960, No. 11, pp. 28–141. I am pleased that V. Rossel's has substantiated my opinion in an authoritative article in *Translator's Notebooks* (1966). [The appearance of *The Catcher in the Rye* was one of the most sensational literary events of the 1960s in Russia—LGL.]

14. *Robert Berns* (Moscow, 1959, 1961, 1965).

15. *The Life of Oscar Wilde* (London: Methuen, 1946); *The Smith of Smiths* (London: H. Hamilton, 1934); *Doctor Darwin* (London and Toronto: J.M. Dent and Sons, 1930); *Skye High,* the record of a tour through Scotland in the wake of Samuel Johnson and James Boswell (New York: Oxford Univ., 1938); *Dickens* (London: Methuen, 1949).

16. [M. Kan's translations of Hesketh Pearson's biographies appeared in the series *Zhizn' zamechatel'nykh liudei* in the early 1960s—LGL.]

17. *Eneiida* (Kiev, 1796); *Eneida,* tr. Vera Potapova (Moscow, 1961). In all fairness it must be said that Potapova had an excellent predecessor who made her task significantly easier. This is the poet Ia. Brazhnin, whose translation of the work was published in Moscow in 1955. Brazhnin was the first to apply the method used (and perfected) by Potapova—the method of renouncing pedantic literal precision in favor of an accurate reproduction of the original's style and intonations.

18. *Sobranie sochinenii,* VIII (St. Petersburg, 1867), 306.

19. *Polnoe sobranie sochinenii,* XIII (St. Petersburg, 1903), 165.

20. *Encounter,* 1965, No. 4, p. 53.

21. *Zamechatel'nye chudaki i originaly* (St. Petersburg, 1898).

22. *Izbrannye rasskazy,* II (Moscow, 1908), 15, 270.

Chapter Five: Style

1. I have borrowed here from I. Mandel'shtam, *O kharaktere gogolevskogo stilia* [*On the Character of Gogol's Style*] (Helsinki, 1902).

2. See A.K. Tolstoi, *Sobranie sochinenii,* III (Moscow, 1964), 513.

3. *Russkaia mysl'* [*Russian Thought*], April 1913 pp. 31–32.

4. M. Lavrenskii, "Shekspir v perevode g. Feta" ["Shakespeare in the Translation of Mr. Fet"], *Sovremennik* [*The Contemporary*], 1859, No. 6. The pseudonym M. Lavrenskii belonged to the translator D.L. Mikhailovskii. Some scholars have attributed it to N.A. Dobroliubov.

5. *Polnoe sobranie stikhotvorenii* (Moscow-Leningrad, 1939), 131.

6. *Izbrannoe* (Moscow, 1958), 27.

7. See her translation of *Nicholas Nickleby* in *Sobranie sochinenii Dikkensa* (St. Petersburg, n.d.), X, 72, 76, 186, 207, 326; XI, 36, 38, 84, 243; XII, 104, 207, 316, 318, 326.

8. See her translation of *Bleak House* in *Sochineniia Dikkensa* (St. Petersburg, 1896), VI-VIII, 109, 36, as well as her translation of *Barnaby Rudge* in the same collection, IX, 38.

9. *Stikhotvoreniia* (Leningrad, 1935), 310.

10. See V.M. Zhirmunskii's study of Goethe in Russian literature in *Literaturnoe nasledstvo* [*Literary Heritage*], IV-VI (Moscow-Leningrad, 1932), 609.

11. *Sobranie sochinenii O.I. Senkovskogo (Barona Brambeusa),* VII (St. Petersburg, 1859), 331–424.

12. *Sobranie sochinenii,* VI (St. Petersburg, 1865), 63.

13. *Otechestvennye zapiski,* July 1850, pp. 21, 51.

14. *Literaturnyi kritik,* 1936, No. 10, pp. 178–79.

15. *Sovremennik,* 1851, No. 8, p. 54.

16. *Stilistika. Teoriia poeticheskoi rechi. Poetika* (Moscow, 1963), 123.

17. For similar examples see my *Zhivoi kak zhizn'* [*Alive as Life*] (Moscow, 1963), 73.

18. See Lenin's *Polnoe sobranie sochinenii,* VI (Moscow, 1959), 182.

19. "Perevod ustoichivykh obraznykh slovosochetanii i poslovits s russkogo iazyka na angliiskii," *Inostrannye iazyki v shkole* [*Foreign Languages in the School*], 1960, No. 5, p. 93.

20. *The Russian Fables of Ivan Krylov,* Verse Translations by Bernard Pares (Middlesex: Harmondsworth; New York: Penguin, 1944).

21. *Stat'i o pisateliakh* [*Essays on Writers*] (Moscow, 1957), 50.

22. *Sobranie sochinenii Dikkensa* (St. Petersburg, 1906), IX.

23. "Mova perekladiv M. P. Staryts'koho z M.Iu. Lermontova i M.O. Nekrasova," *Zbirnyk naukovykh prats' aspirantiv* [*Collection of Scholarly Works by Graduate Students*], 1961, No. 16, pp. 65–66.

24. "Mikhaylo Staryts'kyi—perekladach Pushkyna," *Pytannia khudozhn'oi maisternosti*[*Essays on the Craft of Art*] (Lvov, 1958), 64.

25. *Ezhemesiachnye literaturnye prilozheniia k zhurnalu Niva* [*Monthly Literary Addenda to the Journal Niva*], 1896, No. 1, pp. 45–48.

26. *Manas,* tr. Semen Lipkin, Lev Penkovskii, and Mark Tarlovskii (Moscow, 1941).

27. *Kozy–Korpesh i Baian–Slu,* tr. Vera Potapova, in *Kazakhskii epos* (Alma-Ata, 1958).

28. "Epos kabardinskogo naroda" ["The Epic of the Kabardinian People"], *Narty* (Moscow, 1951), 17.

29. *Sem' planet,* tr. Semen Lipkin (Tashkent, 1948).

30. *Sorok devushek,* tr. Arsenii Tarkovskii (Moscow, 1951).

31. Alexander Solzhenitsyn, *One Day in the Life of Ivan Denisovich,* tr. Ralph Parker (New York: Dutton, Signet, 1963; London: Gollancz, 1963). The Russian text cited here is A. Solzhenitsyn, *Odin den' Ivana Denisovicha* (Moscow, 1962).

32. See his monumental book (1,049 pages) *A Treasury of Russian Literature* (New York: Vanguard, n.d.), in which he popularizes Russian writers with great enthusiasm.

33. *Prikliucheniia Gekl'beri Finna,* tr. N. Daruzes (Moscow, 1963), 144.

34. See her translation in Dickens' *Sobranie sochinenii* (30 vols.; Moscow, 1957–63), XXIII, 366.

35. See Ivan Kashkin, "Mister Pikvik i drugie" ["Mr. Pickwick and Company"], *Literaturnyi kritik,* 1936, No. 5, p. 214.

36. Alexander Solzhenitsyn, *One Day in the Life of Ivan Denisovich,* tr. Bela von Block (New York: Lancer, 1963), 66.

37. Alexander Solzhenitsyn, *One Day in the Life of Ivan Denisovich,* tr. Max Hayward and Ronald Hingley (New York: Praeger, 1963), 75.

38. Alexander Solzhenitsyn, *One Day in the Life of Ivan Denisovich,* tr. Thomas P. Whitney (New York: Fawcett, 1963), 69.

39. Aleksandr Solgenitsyn, *Una giornata di Ivan Denisovic,* tr. Giorgio Kraiski (Milan: Grafiche Garzanti, 1963); tr. Raffaello Uboldi (Turin: Giulio Einaudi, 1963).

40. *Kola Briun'on,* tr. M. Lozinskii (Moscow, 1936).

41. *Zhizn' Benvenuto Chellini,* tr. M. Lozinskii (Moscow-Leningrad, 1931), 42.

42. *Sobranie sochinenii,* XI, 332–33; *The Life and Adventures of Martin Chuzzlewit,* Imperial Edition (Chicago: Hooper, Clarke, n.d.), 697.

Chapter Six: The Translator's Hearing. Rhythm. Sound Patterns

1. *Nash obshchii drug,* tr. M.A. Shishmareva, *Sobranie sochinenii Dikkensa* (St. Petersburg, 1896), 8; *Our Mutual Friend,* Imperial Edition (Chicago: Hooper, Clarke, n.d.), 14.

2. *David Copperfield* (London: Chapman and Hall, n.d.), 26.
3. *A Tale of Two Cities* (Boston, New York, Chicago: Allyn and Bacon, 1922), 1; *Povest' o dvukh gorodakh,* tr. S.P. Bobrov and M.P. Bogoslovskaia; *Sobranie sochinenii* (30 vols.; Moscow, 1957–63), XXII, 6.
4. *Teoriia stikha* (Moscow, 1939), 40.
5. *Kola Briun'on,* tr. M. Lozinskii (Moscow, 1936), 10.
6. *Kola Briun'on,* tr. M. Elagina (Leningrad, 1925), 11.
7. *The Adventures of Huckleberry Finn* (New York and Boston: Books, n.d.), 3; *Sochineniia* (Moscow-Leningrad, 1929), 6–7.
8. *Germes,* 1914, No. 5, pp. 265–66.
9. "Iskusstvo stikhotvornogo perevoda," *Druzhba narodov* [*The Peoples' Friendship*], 1955, No. 7, p. 164.
10. N. Necrassov, *Poesies populaires,* tr. E. Halperine-Kaminsky and Ch. Morice (Paris, n.d.), 188.
11. *Izbrannye proizvedeniia Shekspira,* tr. Anna Radlova (Leningrad, 1939).
12. *Polnoe sobranie sochinenii* (16 vols. and suppl. vol.; Moscow-Leningrad: Academia, 1937–59), III, 194.
13. "A Defence of Poetry," *Prose Works* (London: Chatt. and Windus, n.d.), II, 7.
14. "Na poliakh perevoda," *Literaturnaia gazeta,* 22 December 1963.
15. *The Craft and Context of Translation* (Austin, Univ. of Texas Press, 1963), 68.
16. "Zametki perevodchika" ["Remarks of a Translator"], *Znamia* [*Banner*], 1944, No. 1–2.
17. "Moral Principles in Translation," *Encounter,* 1965, No. 4, p. 55.

Chapter Seven: Syntax. Intonation. Toward a Method of Translating Shakespeare

1. "On Translating Homer," *Essays Literary and Critical* (London: Macmillan, 1911), 210–11.
2. *Polnoe sobranie sochimenii,* III, (Moscow-Leningrad, 1928), 211.
3. See "Mister Pikvik i drugie" ["Mr. Pickwick and Company"], *Literaturnyi kritik,* 1936, No. 5, p. 222.
4. *Literaturnaia gazeta,* 1933, No. 53.
5. The problem of the genitive case placed after a series of verbs, of which the first is preceded by the negative particle *ne,* was a matter of concern to Pushkin too. In notes of his younger days (1820) Pushkin asked which is better used for the direct object when the construction is, "I cannot forgive"—the accusative or the genitive case? "It seems," Pushkin wrote, "the the words depend not on the verb 'can,' but on the infinitive 'to forgive,' which demands the accusative case. But N.M. Karamzin does it the other way." (That is—Karamzin used the genitive case.) Ten years later Pushkin turned to the subject again: "Let's take, for example,

the following sentence: 'I cannot permit you to begin writing verses,' placing 'verses' in the accusative, not the genitive case, of course. Can it be that the electrical energy of the negative particle must pass through the whole chain of verbs and act on the noun? I think not." A.S. Pushkin, *Polnoe sobranie sochinenii* (16 vols. and suppl. vol.; Moscow-Leningrad: Academia, 1937–59), XI, 18, 147.

6. G. Herdan, *Language as Choice and Chance*; quoted from V.N. Kliueva in an article in *Translator's Notebooks* (1960), 3.

7. *Sobranie sochinenii,* ed. F. F. Pavlenkov, IX, (St. Petersburg, 1896), 350, 357.

8. *Izbrannye sochineniia Shekspira,* tr. Anna Radlova, 2d ed. (Leningrad, 1939).

9. *Sochineniia* (St. Petersburg, 1902).

10. See the newspaper *Sovetskoe iskusstvo* [Soviet Art], 9 Feb. 1940, *Literaturnaia gazeta,* 10 Feb. 1940, and the journal *Teatr,* 1940, No. 3.

11. *Literaturnaia entsiklopediia* (Moscow, 1935), IX, 501–2.

12. "Shakespeare and the Grand Style," in *Essays and Studies by members of the English Association* (Oxford: English Association, 1919).

13. *Literaturnyi Leningrad,* 30 Nov. 1933.

14. *Gamlet,* tr. M. Starits'kii (Kharkov, 1929). An advocate of the translator's impermissible whimsies is A. Nikovs'kyi; see Oleksandr Finkel', *Teoriia i praktika perekladu* [*Theory and Practice of Translation*] (Kharkov, 1929), 146.

15. A. V. Druzhinin's 1856 translation of *King Lear* has 2,314 lines, that is, 144 lines more than the original, besides which the translation teems with excisions.

16. *Gamlet,* tr. M. Lozinskii (Moscow, 1951).

17. A few examples of the epithets cast out of Lozinskii's translation: "beaten track" (58), "delightful bells" (71), "enticing promises" (87), "wisest friends" (58), "senseless opulence" (74), "delightful truth" (87), "soldiers' music" (130), and so forth, and so forth. These epithets would not seem to be all that important, but without them Shakespeare's lines are drained of their blood. Take only "soldiers' music." Fortinbras speaks of it upon seeing the body of the murdered Hamlet. In his capacity of military commander he gives the order to bury Hamlet as a soldier: "The soldiers' music and the rites of war / Speak loudly for him" (V, ii). The word "soldiers" characterizes both Fortinbras and Hamlet, and for all its seeming ordinariness, it bears a large artistic burden.

Chapter Eight: Today: From My Literary Notebook

1. *Vospitanie slovom* (Moscow, 1961), 219.

2. *The Complete Poetical Works of Robert Burns,* Cambridge Edition (Boston and New York: Houghton Mifflin; Cambridge: Riverside, 1897), 102; *Robert Berns v perevodakh S. Marshaka* (2 vols.; Moscow, 1963), II, 30.

3. *Pesni i stikhi v perevode Viktora Fedotova* (Moscow, 1963).

4. Of course, the translator can always say in defense of his slovenly and flabby rhymes that they are modern; but after all, Burns lived in the eighteenth century and the originals of the verses I discuss here are constructed on Pushkinian precise accordances.

5. *Nemetskie narodyne ballady v perevodakh L'va Ginzburga* (Moscow, 1960).

6. *Slovo skorbi i utesheniia,* tr. Lev Ginzburg (Moscow, 1963).

7. *Pesni bezymiannykh pevtsov. Narodnaia lirika Severnogo Kavkaza* (Makhachkala, 1960); *Pesni bylykh vremen. Lirika narodov Srednei Azii* (Tashkent, 1961).

8. *Vysokie zvezdy* (Moscow, 1962), 66, 73, 108–10, 142.

9. *V gorakh moe serdtse* [*My Heart's in the Mountains*] (Moscow, 1959), 219.

10. In addition to Rasul Gamzatov, Kozlovskii has translated two other Daghestan poets: Rashid Rashidov, *Umnyi balkharets* [*The Clever Balkhar*] (Moscow, 1961), and Nuradin Iusupov, *Solntse i tuchi* [*Sun and Clouds*] (Moscow, 1962).

11. *Polnoe sobranie stikhotvorenii* (Leningrad, 1937), 271.

12. *Sbornik svedenii o kavkazskikh gortsakh* (Tiflis, 1868).

13. *Polnoe sobranie sochinenii,* LXII (Moscow, 1953), 209.

14. *Don-Zhuan,* tr. T. Gnedich (Moscow-Leningrad, 1959), 44–47.

15. *The Poetic Works of Lord Byron* (London: Murray, 1958), 796–97.

16. See *Vechernii Leningrad* [*Evening Leningrad*], 1964, No. 12.

17. *Reginald Mainwaring Hewitt: A Selection from His Literary Remains,* ed. Vivian de Sola Pinto (Oxford: Oxford Univ., 1955).

18. *A Book of Russian Verse,* Translated into English by various hands and edited by C.M. Bowra (London: Macmillan, 1947); *A Second Book of Russian Verse* (London: Macmillan, 1948).

19. As I have already mentioned, Maurice Baring, one of the most charming persons I have ever met, was in command of a flying squadron fighting on the Belgian front during World War I. I met him there in 1916, and it was strange to listen in a Belgian village to an English officer recite one of Fet's poems with great animation in Russian.

20. It is indicative that in offering this translation, in his *Landmarks in Russian Literature,* 2d ed. (London: Macmillan, 1912), 28, Baring thought it necessary to point out in a note: "The translation is done in the meter of the original. Verbatim precision is maintained in it; and still it is hopelessly far from the original." I will note one error in the translation resulting from a misunderstanding of the Russian idiom: the second-person familiar form of the verb "to remember" in Russian refers to the first person in certain instances and means "I remember" here. Baring reproduced it literally as "you remember."

21. *The Tale of Armament of Igor,* tr. Leonard A. Magnus (London, New York: Oxford Univ., 1915).

22. His name is mentioned in a general survey of Russian literature which places him among minor men of letters like Iasinskii.

23. See Carolyn G. Heilbrun, *The Garnett Family* (London: Allen and Unwin, 1961), 189.

24. *The Oxford Companion to English Literature,* comp. and ed. Sir Paul Harvey (Oxford: Clarendon, 1960). Foreign authors are also treated in the guide—Klopstock, Paul Morand, and D'Annunzio.

25. "Konstens Garnett—perevodchik i propagandist russkoi literatury," *Russkaia literatura,* 1958, No. 4.

26. "Perevody Chekhova v Anglii i SShA," *Nauchnye doklady vysshei shkoly,* 1963, No. 1, p. 151.

27. Tove's letter is addressed to Constance Garnett's son, the well-known English man of letters David Garnett.

28. "Russian," in *The Craft and Context of Translation* (Austin: Univ. of Texas, 1961), 189–90.

29. See Miriam Morton, "Kornei Chukovsky—The Pied Piper of Peredelkino," *The Horn Book Magazine,* Oct. 5, 1962.

30. *Russian Plays,* ed., tr. and introd. F. D. Reeve (2 vols.; New York: Vintage, 1963), II.

31. *The Telephone,* tr. D. Rottenburg (Moscow, n.d.).

32. *Wash-'em-Clean* (Moscow, n.d.).

33. *Crocodile,* tr. Babette Deutsch (Philadelphia: Lippincott, 1931).

34. *Crocodile.* Verses by Richard Coe. Based on a Poem by Kornei Chukousky [sic] (London: Faber and Faber, 1964).

35. *The Cat in the Hat,* by Dr. Seuss (Boston: Random House, n.d.), 3.

36. *Poetry of Our Time* 2d ed. rev. and enl. (New York: Doubleday, 1963).

37. *An Anthology of Russian Verse: 1812–1960,* ed. Avrahm Yarmolinsky (Garden City, N.Y.: Doubleday, 1962).

38. See Vera Zviagintseva, *Moia Armeniia* (Erevan, 1964), 3.

39. "Sharl' Bodler," in *Pisateli Frantsii* [*The Writers of France*] (Moscow, 1964), 467–82.

40. *Eugene Onegin,* tr. Eugene Kayden (Yellow Springs, O.; Antioch, 1964).

41. *Eugene Onegin,* tr. Babette Deutsch (Baltimore, Md.: Penguin, 1965).

42. See *Inostrannaia literatura,* 1964, No. 10, p. 284.

43. "Moral Principles in Translation," *Encounter,* 1965, No. 4, p. 53.

Chapter Nine: Translations Past and Present

1. I here quote A. Palitsyn's translation *Slovo o polku Igoreve* (St. Petersburg, 1807). This and all subsequent quotations from the different translations of *Song* are taken from the versions of "Yaroslavna's Lament" in a remarkable article by S. Shambinago, "Khudozhestvennye perelozheniia 'Slova' " ["Artistic Renditions of *Song*"], in *Perevody "Slova o polku Igoreve," sdelannye Georgiem Shtormom i Sergeem Shervinskim* (Moscow-

Leningrad, 1934). However, I cannot agree with some of the author's assessments. For example, he labels G. Vol'skii's translation "Nadsonian" without explaining why. It is a pity, too, that in his discussion of the influence of *Song* on modern writers he does not mention E. Bagritskii's *Dumy pro Opanasa* [*Meditations on Opanas*], (Moscow: Khudozhestvennaia literatura, 1913).

2. See also the text in the Poet's Library Edition: *Slovo o polku Igoreve* (Leningrad, 1952).

3. See also the modern text *Slovo o polku Igoreve* (Moscow, 1938).

4. See *Slovo o polku Igoreve,* poetic translations and renditions ed. V. Rzhiga, V. Kuz'mina, and V. Stelletskii (Moscow, 1961), 301.

5. See note 1, above.

6. *Slovo o polku Igoreve,* tr. Ivan Novikov (Moscow, 1938).

7. *Slovo o polku Igoreve,* tr. Mark Tarlovskii, ed. N. K. Gudzii and Petr Skosyrev (Moscow, 1938).

8. *Slovo o polku Igoreve,* tr. N. Zabolotskii (Moscow, 1950).

9. See his article on nineteenth- and early-twentieth-century translations of *Song* in *Slovo o polku Igoreve. Sbornik* [*The Song of Igor's Campaign: A Collection*] (Moscow, 1961), 308–9.

10. *Poetika* (Leningrad, 1928), 142–45.

11. See Ch. Corbiére's study of Russo-French literary links in *International Links of Russian Literature,* 220.

12. See I. V. Rezanov, *Iz razyskanii o sochineniiakh V. A. Zhukovskogo* [*From Research on the Works of V. A. Zhukovskii*] (St. Petersburg, 1906), 351–53.

13. See *Don Kishot La Manskii, sochinenie Servanta* [*Don Quixote la Manche, A Work by Cervantes*], translated from the French of Florian by V. A. Zhukovskii (Moscow, 1803).

14. See *New Variorum Edition of Shakespeare,* ed. H. Furness (Philadelphia: Lippincott, 1877), IV, 143.

15. Oleksandr Finkel', *Teoriia i praktyka perekladu* [*Theory and Practice of Translation*] (Kharkov, 1929), 22.

16. *Avetik Isaakian i russkaia literatura* [*Avetik Isaakian and Russian Literature*] (Erevan, 1963), 144. See also K.N. Grigorian, *Valerii Briusov i armianskaia literatura* [*Valerii Briusov and Armenian Literature*] (Moscow, 1962), 38.

17. *Polnoe sobranie sochinenii Flobera* (Moscow-Leningrad, 1934).

18. *Puteshestviia Gullivera v stranu liliputov,* tr. M.A. Shishmareva (St. Petersburg, 1906); *Gulliver's Travels and Other Writings* (Boston and Cambridge: Houghton Mifflin and Riverside, 1960).

19. *Prints i nishchii,* tr. Lev Umants (Moscow, 1918); *The Prince and the Pauper* (New York and London: Harper, 1909).

20. *Prikliucheniia Toma Soiera* (Moscow, n.d.); *The Adventures of Tom Sawyer* (New York and London: Harper, 1903).

21. *Dombi i syn* (Moscow-Leningrad, 1928), 308; *Dombey and Son,* Imperial Edition (Chicago: Hooper, Clarke, n.d.).

22. *David Kopperfil'd* (Moscow-Leningrad, 1926); *David Copperfield,* Imperial Edition (Chicago: Hooper, Clarke, n.d.).

23. *David Kopperfil'd,* tr. Irinarkh Vvedenskii; *Sobranie sochinenii* (St. Petersburg, 1906), IX, 190.

24. See John Forster, *The Life of Charles Dickens* (2 vols.; Chapman and Hall, London: 1899), II, 46, who cites a letter Dickens received from Vvedenskii in 1848 for which the signature is deciphered as Trinarkh Wredenskii. See also M.P. Alekseev's article on Dickens's meeting with Vvedenskii in *Charl'z Dikkens. Bibliografiia russkikh perevodov i kriticheskoi literatury na russkom iazyke, 1838–1960* [*Charles Dickens: Bibliography of Russian Translations and Critical Literature in Russian, 1838–1960*] (Moscow, 1962).

25. *Kholodnyi dom,* ed. M. A. Orlov (St. Petersburg, n.d.).

26. "O perevodakh romana Tekkereia 'Vanity Fair,' " *Otechestvennye zapiski,* 1851, No. 9, pp. 61–81.

27. "Mister Pikvik i drugie" [*"Mr. Pickwick and Company"*], *Literaturnyi kritik,* 1936, No. 5, p. 213.

28. The first attempt to make a scholarly survey of the chronological stages of ideas about translation in Russia is A.V. Fedorov's *Introduction to Theory of Translation,* 355–71. An indispensable addition to this survey is supplied by Iu.D. Levin, "Ob istoricheskoi evoliutsii printsipov perevoda" ["On the Historical Evolution of Principles of Translation"], in *International Links of Russian Literature.*

Index

Kornei Chukovsky's A High Art has been composed on the Mergenthaler Variable Input Phototypesetter in eleven point Garamond with two point line spacing. Helvetica Black was selected for display. The book was designed by Muriel Underwood, set into type by Computer Composition, Inc., printed offset by Thomson-Shore, Inc., and bound by John H. Dekker & Sons. The natural finish wove paper on which the book is printed is virtually acid-free and is designed for an effective life of at least three hundred years.

THE UNIVERSITY OF TENNESSEE PRESS
KNOXVILLE